Proving Continuous Improvement with Profit Ability

Also available from ASQ Quality Press:

Mapping Work Processes, Second Edition
Bjørn Andersen, Tom Fagerhaug, Bjørnar Henriksen, and Lars E. Onsøyen

A Practical Application of Supply Chain Management Principles
Thomas Schoenfeldt

*The Executive Guide to Understanding and Implementing the Baldrige Criteria:
Improve Revenue and Create Organizational Excellence*
Denis Leonard and Mac McGuire

*The Executive Guide to Understanding Employee Engagement: Expand
Capacity, Increase Revenue, and Save Jobs*
Pat Townsend and Joan Gebhardt

*The Executive Guide to Understanding and Implementing Lean Six Sigma:
The Financial Impact*
Robert M. Meisel, Steven J. Babb, Steven F. Marsh, and James P. Schlichting

Principles of Quality Costs: Principles, Implementation, and Use,
Third Edition
Jack Campanella, editor

The Certified Manager of Quality/Organizational Excellence Handbook,
Third Edition
Russell T. Westcott, editor

The Executive Guide to Improvement and Change
G. Dennis Beecroft, Grace L. Duffy, John W. Moran

*Avoiding the Corporate Death Spiral: Recognizing and Eliminating the Signs
of Decline*
Gregg Stocker

The Path to Profitable Measures: 10 Steps to Feedback That Fuels Performance
Mark W. Morgan

Quality Essentials: A Reference Guide from A to Z
Jack B. ReVelle

Quality management—Guidelines for realizing financial and economic benefits
ANSI/ISO/ASQ Q10014-2006

To request a complimentary catalog of ASQ Quality Press publications,
call 800-248-1946, or visit our Web site at http://www.asq.org/quality-press.

Proving Continuous Improvement with Profit Ability

Russ Jones

ASQ Quality Press
Milwaukee, Wisconsin

American Society for Quality, Quality Press, Milwaukee 53203
© 2008 by ASQ
All rights reserved. Published 2008
Printed in the United States of America
14 13 12 11 10 09 08   5 4 3 2 1

Library of Congress Cataloging-in-Publication Data

Jones, Russ, 1932–
    Proving continuous improvement with profit ability / Russ Jones.
      p. cm.
    Includes bibliographical references and index.
    ISBN: 978-0-87389-742-6 (hbk. : alk. paper)
      1. Corporate profits. 2. Rate of return. 3. Capital investments. 4. Management.
    I. Title.

    HG4028.P7.J66 2008
    658.15'5—dc22   2008021018

ISBN: 978-0-87389-742-6

Publisher: William A. Tony
Acquisitions Editor: Matt T. Meinholz
Project Editor: Paul O'Mara
Production Administrator: Randall Benson

ASQ Mission: The American Society for Quality advances individual, organizational,
and community excellence worldwide through learning, quality improvement, and
knowledge exchange.

Attention Bookstores, Wholesalers, Schools, and Corporations: ASQ Quality Press
books, videotapes, audiotapes, and software are available at quantity discounts with
bulk purchases for business, educational, or instructional use. For information,
please contact ASQ Quality Press at 800-248-1946, or write to ASQ Quality Press,
P.O. Box 3005, Milwaukee, WI 53201-3005.

To place orders or to request a free copy of the ASQ Quality Press Publications
Catalog, including ASQ membership information, call 800-248-1946. Visit our
Web site at www.asq.org or http://www.asq.org/quality-press.

Printed in the United States of America

 Printed on acid-free paper

Quality Press
600 N. Plankinton Avenue
Milwaukee, Wisconsin 53203
Call toll free 800-248-1946
Fax 414-272-1734
www.asq.org
http://www.asq.org/quality-press
http://standardsgroup.asq.org
E-mail: authors@asq.org

AMERICAN SOCIETY
FOR QUALITY®

Table of Contents

Note to the Reader

It may appear at first glance that this book is primarily oriented toward manufacturing businesses. You may have gotten the same impression if you've implemented lean manufacturing, Six Sigma, or ISO 9000 quality standards. Be assured that I also focus on service businesses and distributors as well as those companies that include some elements from all three categories.

For example, in Chapter 5 I provide two different forms for gathering the financial data required to understand and apply concepts in the other chapters. One form is for a manufacturing business while the other is more suitable to a distribution or service business. Chapter 1 speaks more directly to this issue and the third section of Chapter 9 is specifically dedicated to distribution and service businesses.

All forms and charts in the book are intended to be used by you as a starting point to design your own forms that more closely resemble your current financial statements.

Throughout the text I have also tried to point out which chapters or sections of chapters have little value for a distribution or service business.

Acronym List

12MRT—12-month running total

CNC—computer numerical control

EBDA—earnings before depreciation and amortization

EBIT—earnings before interest and taxes

EBITDA—earnings before interest, taxes, depreciation, and amortization

EOQ—economic order quantity

I CARE—information understood, courtesy, attention to details, responsibility, every time

MEP—Manufacturing Extension Partnership

NIST—National Institute of Standards & Technology

P&L—profit and loss

ROA—return on assets

ROC—rate of change

SE&A—sales, engineering, and administrative (expenses)

1

Double Your Return on Assets Percent

This book presents an innovative approach to continuous improvement, entrepreneurial innovation, and business knowledge not found in any other source. The primary innovations are:

- There are only seven critical business elements in which financially sound improvements are found.

- Value analysis oriented verb/noun phrases are used to discover and name projects from each of the seven critical business elements, based on percentage return on assets.

- A project evaluation form is used to financially rank projects to define which ones will most greatly increase the profitability of the business.

- There are three groups of knowledge resources that must be managed separately, but still integrated, with their own policies, practices, and performance measures:

  - First, the operations personnel, who deliver the lowest-cost, highest-quality products and services 95 percent on time.

  - Second, continuous improvement teams, who use the seven business elements to discover, evaluate, and implement projects to double the return on assets (ROA) percent.

  - Third, the managers, who are assigned to extend the life of the business by using seven sources of entrepreneurial innovation.

Almost any manufacturing, distribution, or service business can double its return on assets percent within a three- to five-year period if it concentrates its best knowledge resources on the seven key business elements:

- Increase market coverage to increase sales dollars

- Reduce labor and nonlabor expenses per sales dollar

- Reduce lead times to minimize work-in-process inventory investment

- Minimize product and component inventory investment by reducing manufacturing and purchasing setup costs to reduce lot sizes

- Maximize capital asset utilization

- Control the customer invoice collection period to minimize accounts receivable investment

- Maximize employee asset utilization by using project teams for the seven project categories and train them to identify, evaluate, and implement projects

A manufacturing business has more opportunities to impact the ROA percent than a service or distribution business. However, all have similar financial measuring tools and similar activities performed by personnel with similar knowledge and experience.

As you read these pages you may say, "This is simple stuff that most of our personnel already know." To this I would reply, "I agree." Someone in your company probably knows most of what is included in this book. However, I've organized it in a way I wish someone had shown me when I was a young college graduate entering the business workforce.

These pages contain practical business knowledge that can be taught to employees at every level and in every function or department. I will show where employees interact within the seven key financial areas and how each decision they make has either a negative or positive impact on the size of profit, asset investment, or the percentage return on the investment in four assets: work-in-process inventory, component and product inventory, capital assets, and accounts receivable.

I focus on the financial aspects of the seven business elements because every hour, every employee, in every job, at every level, makes one or more decisions that have some impact on one or more of these seven financial measures. Therefore, why not fill their minds with the basic knowledge that leads directly to the right decision?

I've chosen to encompass each chapter within the phrase, "company-wide continuous improvement" because that's the most effective way to bring together various other improvement tools such as lean manufacturing, ISO 9000, Six Sigma, and total quality management.

SOURCES OF KNOWLEDGE
FOR THIS BOOK

The author obtained a bachelor's degree in mechanical engineering from Oklahoma State University. I am a licensed professional engineer in the state of Oklahoma. My initial business training was as a manufacturing and design engineer before spending several years as a manufacturing and quality manager. I served as a materials control manager during the design and implementation of a new material control system. In the latter half of my career I gained valuable experience as a business planner in a division of a very profitable corporation, PACCAR, Inc.

The knowledge included in this book comes from:

- Dale Morgan and Willis Allen of Gilbreath's (www.gilbreaths. com), a training and consulting firm with many years of experience in training personnel for team building, customer service, ISO 9000, and driving companywide continuous improvement to the bottom line.

- Pat Patton and John Williams of Hunt, Patton & Brazeal (www.huntpatton.com), a consulting firm with many years of focus on mergers and acquisitions, sources of funds for growth and acquisition, and searching for management and technical knowledge resources.

- Richard Kerndt and Mark May of The Richmark Group (www.richmark.com), who provide consulting related to sales growth planning, with a focus on increasing market share by increasing market coverage.

- Robert VanDeMark's books about material control principles, which provide the old-fashioned arithmetic that must be used by the simplest or most sophisticated modern material control systems.

- William Schubert, a mathematician/economist who showed me how to use rate of change arithmetic to graphically picture the business cycle for any business so that marketing and financial decisions can be made six months to one year sooner than competitors.

- The U.S. Department of Commerce, National Institute of Standards and Technology (NIST) Manufacturing Extension Partnership (MEP) (www.mep.nist.gov), the home page for lean manufacturing. For lean training you need to contact a lean trainer or lean consultant. I include an interpretation of lean principles only as a tool to discover more projects.

- Peter Drucker, a teacher and author who published 39 books between 1939 and 1999 about how the knowledge workers in a business can become more effective managers. His thinking has become a part of my business thinking process and is scattered throughout this book. In Chapter 16 I include some things I have learned about systematic innovation that can give an entrepreneurial flavor to any enterprise.

TO BUSINESS OWNERS AND MANAGERS

This book is written for businesswomen and businessmen who recognize that their knowledge and career is itself a business that they must manage effectively. It's for those who want their career to be the most rewarding, both financially and in terms of self-satisfaction. It's for people, both experienced and inexperienced, who see themselves on a mission to be a change agent and a champion of improvement projects. It is designed to harness the unique knowledge of a large group of knowledge workers to achieve really big results, such as doubling the ROA within three to five years of continuous improvement project implementation.

It's dedicated to those who yearn to achieve extraordinary financial results in a business. I use very simple everyday arithmetic and vocabulary to show how to identify the seven critical business elements within your own business that need to be managed through continuous improvement.

This book can become your training manual to educate individual employees at every level to discover and implement a vast number of financially justified projects that focus on the seven critical business elements.

I believe that this book will make employees at every level better businessmen and businesswomen.

Three of the reasons most continuous improvement, lean manufacturing, and Six Sigma programs fail to deliver good financial results are:

- They fail to invest in a few additional personnel to discover, design, and implement improvement projects.

- They fail to train personnel with knowledge about the seven sources of financially sound improvement.

- They don't have a financial tool to tell management and project teams which projects will deliver the greatest increase in profitability in the least amount of calendar time.

One goal of this book is to dramatically advance the Profit Ability of its readers.

2

The Seven Critical Business Elements

There are seven broad business and financial elements, depicted in Figure 2.1, at which continuous improvement projects must be directed to maximize profitability. I will use this graphic to prove this point.

The purpose of this chapter is to support the concept that concentrating your knowledge workers on the seven areas of improvement will result in the biggest and quickest increase in profitability of the business and Profit Ability of a broad range of your employees.

THE SEVEN AREAS

Block 1: Increase Return on Assets

I will convince you that employee teams can discover and implement projects that will double your ROA from one economic business cycle to the next. Start by asking, "*How* do we increase return on assets?"

First, I will often mention the economic business cycle, in which every business experiences a high and a low in sales dollars every three to five years. During a complete business cycle, businesses record bigger profits and a higher ROA percent when annual sales are at a peak. That's because fixed costs and capital assets are being utilized more efficiently.

On the other hand, the year when annual sales are deep in the valley, we expect the ROA to be lower because fixed costs and capital assets are being underutilized.

When I mention ROA, I mean the average ROA over an entire business cycle. Since business cycles range from three to five years in length, I encourage that your overall financial improvement goal cover three to

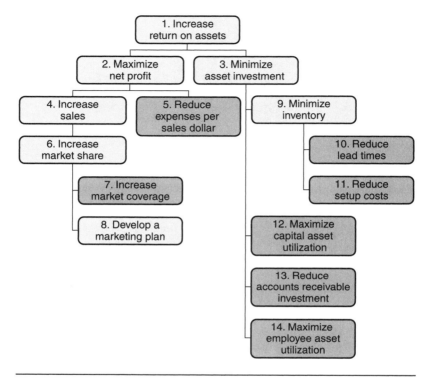

Figure 2.1 The seven broad business and financial elements at which continuous improvement projects must be directed to maximize profitability.

five years. In Chapter 14, I show you how to calculate the historical business cycle of your own company.

Second, let me show you the formula for ROA percent used in this book in case you've forgotten it or have never learned it:

$$\text{Return on assets percent} = \frac{\text{Net profit dollars}}{\text{Total of four assets dollars}}$$

The four assets are *work-in-process inventory, component and product inventory, capital assets,* and *accounts receivable* (shipments to customers for which you haven't been paid).

This formula joins together net profit and asset investment. I use the ROA percent to measure continuous improvement results because it helps you determine whether the net profit and asset investments are in balance.

Block 2: Maximize Net Profit

I place blocks 2 and 3 side by side to get across the point that both the net profit (recorded in the profit and loss statement) and asset investment (recorded in the balance sheet) are dependent on each other, both by formula and as a practical fact. This is important since every employee, in every function, at every level, and every hour, makes decisions that affect one or both of these measures, whether or not they or management realize it.

For example, every capital investment creates an expense for depreciation on one hand but, on the other hand, hopefully reduces an offsetting labor expense. The codependence of net profit and asset investment is the reason why I use the verb/noun combinations *maximize net profit* and *minimize asset investment*. Throughout the following chapters, over and over, I will make statements that illustrate the codependence of these two measures.

Let us briefly examine the formulas that relate to net profit so that we have a common language. All employees who participate in continuous improvement projects need to keep in the back of their minds that net profit is the result of sales (or shipments) minus all expenses:

$$\text{Net profit} = \text{Sales dollars} - \text{Total expense dollars}$$

$$\text{Net profit percent} = \frac{\text{Total expense dollars}}{\text{Sales dollars}}$$

That leaves only *increase sales* and *reduce expenses* as possible verb/noun combinations to identify and evaluate continuous improvement projects to increase net profit.

Blocks 4, 6, and 7

I've asked the question, "*How* do we maximize net profit?" It's natural to say "increase sales" and "reduce expenses" as shown in blocks 4 and 5. However, we will see that the key to increased sales is increased market share and that increased market share comes from increased market coverage.

These facts are illustrated by the following Richmark Group graphic (Figure 2.2). The five market coverage areas are:

- Product coverage

- Price coverage

- Distribution channel coverage

- Promotion coverage

- Brand coverage

I will go into greater detail about market coverage in Chapter 13. For now, all I want to do is plant the seed that market coverage is the key to increasing sales by increasing market share. To see this picture more clearly I must again bring up the subject of the economic business cycle, which occurs every three to five years in almost every business. The reason I must plant the two seeds of market coverage and the economic business cycle in your mind is that the only sales increases that are permanent from year to year are those that occur every year from annual market share increases in every phase of the business cycle.

Perhaps a picture of the business cycle, which we describe in greater detail in Chapter 14, will give you a handle on it, since we mention it so frequently (see Figure 2.3).

Analytical Assessment of Market Share

- When selling through indirect channels (who carry competing brands), there are five coverage measurements

- When selling through indirect channels (who are exclusive), there are four coverage aspects (that is, brand coverage becomes 100 percent)

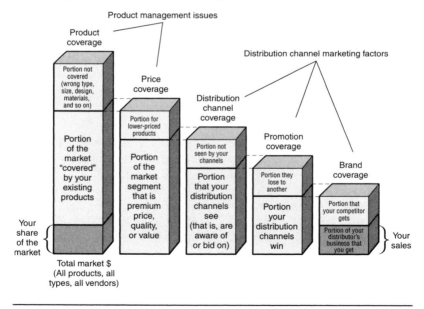

Figure 2.2   The five market coverage areas.

Source: The Richmark Group (www.richmark.com). Used with permission.

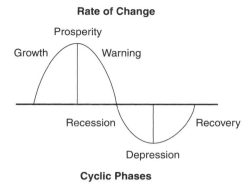

Figure 2.3 The economic business cycle.

I make a big deal out of market share increasing during every phase of the business cycle because if you aren't confidently investing in greater market coverage each year, you won't maximize or double your company's net profit and ROA within three to five years.

It's critical that you get the message that you must be implementing continuous improvements during every phase of your company's business cycle. This is because the average ROA improvement from business cycle to business cycle will become a source of investment funds for long-term improvement projects within the seven key business elements.

In a 2007 issue of *PACCAR World,* Mark Pigott, the fourth-generation chairman and chief executive officer of PACCAR, unveiled plans for a $400 million truck engine manufacturing and assembly plant in the southeast United States. He said, "PACCAR's outstanding profits, excellent balance sheet, and intense focus on quality, technology, and productivity enhancements have enabled the company to consistently invest in products, services, and processes during all phases of the business cycle."

In a nutshell, this quote by Mark Pigott delineates the success we hope you will incorporate into your business by implementing the concepts presented in this book.

Block 5: Reduce Expenses per Sales Dollar

This is the second critical business element on which you must concentrate. Teams of knowledge workers can continuously lower this ratio from month to month when sales are both high and low during a business cycle. You must reduce expenses for both labor and nonlabor costs per sales dollar, primarily because your customers expect you to raise prices at a rate lower than inflation.

The ratio or percent "Expense dollars ÷ Sales dollars" is used to show project teams that if this percent doesn't become smaller from year to year, for both labor and nonlabor expenses, there can't be an increase in net profit.

Sales and expenses are codependent on each other. This is because each business has both fixed costs and variable costs. In the peak phase of the business cycle, net profit shows a dramatic improvement because there are fewer fixed costs per sales dollar. In the valley phase of the business cycle, net profit is dramatically lower because fixed costs are a greater percentage of total expenses. A review of the line items in your annual budget will tell you whether fixed or variable expenses offer the greatest opportunity to reduce total expenses.

The main point I would make to you and your employees is that you need a measurement that shows the percentage relationship between sales and expenses from month to month. You could use many different measurements as a way to discover new improvement projects or as a way to measure improvement from year to year:

- Labor expenses ÷ Sales
- Variable labor expenses ÷ Sales
- Fixed labor expenses ÷ Sales
- Nonlabor expenses ÷ Sales
- Variable nonlabor expenses ÷ Sales
- Fixed nonlabor expenses ÷ Sales
- Total expenses ÷ Sales
- Total variable expenses ÷ Sales
- Total fixed expenses ÷ Sales
- Manufacturing direct labor ÷ Sales
- Setup direct labor ÷ Sales
- Overhead labor ÷ Sales
- Administrative salaries ÷ Sales

In Chapter 8, I show ways to segregate the expenses in your profit and loss statement, and in your operating budget, to discover projects that find the most fruitful places to focus your knowledge workers on ways to improve these ratios. Even if your customers don't come out and say it, your best and most loyal customers expect you to reduce your expenses fast enough so that your prices increase at a rate lower than inflation. You owe this to them just as your suppliers owe it to you.

The section in Chapter 8 about lean waste discovery, and Chapter 3, which lists many verb/noun combinations to name projects, will help you identify waste.

By now you have noticed the mention of verb/noun or verb/phrase combinations. This is an easy way to name projects as you keep asking the question, "*How* do we . . . ?"

Block 3: Minimize Asset Investment

Now let's look at the company's asset investment side of the ROA formula by asking, "How do we minimize asset investment?" The investments to minimize, if they exist in your particular business in any significant dollar amounts, are:

- Work-in-process inventory
- Component and assembled product inventory
- Capital assets—land, buildings, and equipment
- Accounts receivable—what your customers owe you for products or services you have delivered

Remember, in blocks 2 and 3 we are looking for the best financial balance between net profit and asset investment. I will show that there are only a few things on which you must focus improvement projects to effectively minimize these investments.

You will see that most investments in capital assets, which bring advanced technology into your manufacturing processes to lower setup costs and lead times, can be expected to lower your investment in inventory more than they increase your capital investment.

Block 10: Reduce Lead Times

We could say "reduce work-in-process inventory." However, that doesn't directly identify the kinds of projects required.

Many knowledge workers have never been told that work-in-process inventory is controlled by manufacturing lead time. They may even think that order quantity may help determine the size of this investment. The same thing is true with your suppliers' and customers' employees. In Chapter 10,

I show you a simple formula to prove my point. I will show you and your employees many places between the receiving dock and the shipping dock where lead times can be eliminated.

In Chapter 11, I will show you how to evaluate a material control system to identify problems that keep you from reducing lead times. This is an aspect that isn't normally included in most lean manufacturing or Six Sigma programs.

One simple measure will tell you if you have serious lead time or material control problems. If your percent of customer orders shipped on the original date accepted by your customer is very much less than 95 percent, I would ask you to look at Chapters 9 and 11 about lead time and material control. I particularly encourage you to use start dates of manufacturing operations for production control scheduling rather than a due date for completing each part or each processing operation.

See the section in Chapter 9 about lean value stream mapping to determine if you have a considerable amount of paperwork processing that needs a shorter clock or calendar processing lead time. Go to the lean Web site (www.mep.nist.gov) to learn more.

Block 11: Reduce Setup Costs

For ROA increases, you must reduce setup costs for both component and assembled product, and for both manufactured and purchased components, so that your inventory investment for these items will be minimized.

For block 11, we could use *reduce component inventory* or *reduce assembled product inventory,* but that wouldn't directly identify the right kinds of projects. What is specifically required is reduction of setup costs.

If you've implemented a lean manufacturing program you may have already done considerable setup cost or setup time reduction.

If your business is one that has a promised customer order delivery lead time that is shorter than your purchased material lead time plus manufacturing and assembly lead times, you are forced to carry an inventory on some components or assembled products to meet your customers' on-time delivery demands.

Chapter 9 details how to eliminate much of this mismatch between your customer order delivery lead time and the current lead times required to buy material, process it into components, and assemble these components into a finished product.

Until you solve this lead time mismatch, you must invest in a certain amount of inventory of both components and/or assembled products. In Chapter 9 I show how your material control personnel can make a cycle time chart for each major assembled product so they can quickly identify which component lead times are forcing the necessity of inventory, which is equal to a certain amount of investment measured in days or weeks.

Another reason to focus your personnel on setup cost reduction is because this will show them that lot size, or order quantity, controls the size of component inventory and assembled product inventory:

- The size of your inventory investment for each component is one-half the lot size you authorize for that component multiplied by its unit cost. After you total this value for all components, you have a very good idea about your total inventory investment for all components.

- Lot sizing is a financial decision and not a manufacturing decision only.

- Design a lot sizing formula that balances the component inventory investment with the setup cost that employees are currently required to live with.

- Relate existing programs for lean manufacturing with the realities of being forced to maintain an inventory to meet on-time customer delivery requirements.

- Identify the costs in your operating budget that relate to setup costs so a financially sound lot sizing formula can be designed.

- Evaluate your material control and purchasing systems to help employees make financially sound decisions from hour to hour.

- Use your financial data to evaluate investments in tooling, manufacturing cells, or capital equipment to reduce setup costs.

Block 12: Maximize Capital Asset Utilization

You must minimize the investment in capital assets by maximizing the utilization of equipment and facilities. Maximizing the utilization of equipment and facilities is what happens at the peak of your economic business cycle. At the peak of your business cycle, you have your highest percent of capital asset utilization, your highest level of sales, and the maximum level of net profit, which results in the ROA percent being at its highest during the business cycle.

When sales are at their peak during a business cycle, the most highly utilized pieces of equipment may be what limit the company in making on-time delivery of products. This is when well managed production control systems, reduction of lead times, and reduction of setup times may be the most urgent project implementation activities.

At the peak of your business cycle, use the material control system described in Chapter 11 to identify and monitor the most highly utilized equipment and be prepared to shift manufacturing hours to alternate processing methods, add additional shifts, or move work orders to suppliers who have appropriate, capable equipment and quality controls.

In Chapter 11, I will show you how to get the most out of existing capital assets and, using the plotting of your own business cycle, when to invest in new capacity and when to eliminate excess capacity.

I will also show you how to measure utilization percentages in total and for individual pieces of equipment.

Block 13: Reduce Accounts Receivable Investment

Do this by controlling the period of time between invoicing for product or services and the receipt of payment (accounts receivable collection period). In other words, if your contract with a customer requires them to pay within a certain time period, you should expect them to pay by that date, just as they expect you to deliver on time and just as your suppliers expect you to pay them on time.

Some customers may habitually pay late, thereby increasing your accounts receivable investment. This may be their way of forcing you to invest in their business. Your financial systems should easily identify these customers so you can control them.

Block 14: Maximize Employee Asset Utilization

You must increase sales without increasing total personnel expenses at the same rate, as we suggest in block 5. This doesn't mean you pay lower wages. It means you pay higher individual wages to retain personnel that you train and empower to utilize themselves effectively and creatively.

To double your ROA, you must continuously train and empower the broadest possible range of employees to discover, design, and implement continuous improvement projects. With this book you can provide your knowledge workers with enough information about finances and basic business principles to help them concentrate their minds on one or more of the seven critical business elements.

If I've convinced you to approach companywide continuous improvement by concentrating on these seven very broad areas, this should encourage you to invest in and assign the appropriate knowledge resources to one or more projects for each of the seven critical elements.

I must impress upon you that these teams must be allowed "quality time" during every phase of the business cycle if you expect to double your ROA within three to five years. There's little difference between capital investment and knowledge investment when it comes to investing to get a big financial return from continuous improvement.

3

Seven Project Groups for Project Teams

Hopefully I've shown you a new way to see continuous improvement, in financial terms, as a companywide effort. I've also introduced you to the concept of verb/noun or verb/phrase combinations to discover and name broad groups of projects. Now we will move on to the next logical step by showing you how to explode these seven broad project categories into a great number of less broad groups and then into specific projects.

The seven broad project categories previously listed are:

- Increase market coverage to increase sales dollars

- Reduce labor and nonlabor expenses per sales dollar

- Reduce lead times to minimize work-in-process inventory investment

- Minimize product and component inventory investment by reducing manufacturing and purchasing setup costs to reduce lot sizes

- Maximize capital asset utilization

- Control the customer invoice collection period to minimize accounts receivable investment

- Maximize employee asset utilization by using project teams for the seven project categories and train them to identify, evaluate, and implement projects

I will expand the above list slightly before exploding each of the seven project groups into more specific team projects. But first, a brief review.

OVERVIEW

How Do We Name Broad and Specific Projects with Verb/Noun and Verb/Phrase Combinations?

We ask the question, "How do we . . . ?" as in Figure 2.1.

How Do We Increase Return on Assets (ROA)?

Blocks 2 and 3: We maximize net profit and minimize asset investment.

How Do We Maximize Net Profit Dollars by Increasing Sales Dollars?

Blocks 4, 6, 7, and 8: We increase market share percent by increasing market coverage, as defined in Chapter 13. Focus on the 20 percent of the models, product lines, and market segments that make up 80 percent of the sales dollars.

How Do We Maximize Net Profit by Reducing Expenses per Sales Dollar?

Block 5: Reduce labor and salary dollars per sales dollar.

Block 5: Reduce nonlabor overhead dollars per sales dollar. Segregate and focus on the 20 percent of the budget line items that make up 80 percent of the expense dollars.

How Do We Minimize Asset Investment by Minimizing Inventory Investment (Block 9)?

Block 10: Reduce lead times to reduce work-in-process inventory investment.

Block 11: Reduce setup cost to reduce lot sizes and reduce average component inventory quantity levels. Focus on the 20 percent of components that make up 80 percent of the inventory investment dollars and focus on the lead time mismatch between customer order lead time and product processing lead time. I explain this lead time mismatch in detail in Chapter 9.

How Do We Minimize Capital Asset and Accounts Receivable Investment?

Block 12: Maximize capital asset utilization percent for the 20 percent of the individual assets that make up 80 percent of the investment dollars.

Block 13: Control the customer invoice collection time period stated in the contracted agreement. Focus on the 20 percent of your customers who force you to invest in their business by paying later than agreed.

How Do We Maximize Employee Utilization (Block 14)?

The chances of doubling average ROA over a three- to five-year business cycle is very slim if you don't invest in and empower your companywide knowledge resources in a team in one of the seven project categories.

How Do We Explode These Seven Project Groups into More Specific Projects?

Gather a group of employees together in a room with bare walls, with a package of sticky notes large enough to write down a verb/phrase combination. Then, looking at any one of the seven project groups, have the group start writing down verb/phrase or verb/noun combinations by asking the question, "How do we . . . ?" for that particular project group. Stick that sticky note on the wall. Then, for each of the verb/noun combinations you record on a sticky note, keep asking the question "How" and place it by its appropriate sticky note until you get to a more detailed project name, such as a part number, to which you can assign a project team.

For each new verb/noun combination, ask the question "Why?" to see if you've selected the best words for the preceding verb/noun. If not, try a different verb/noun combination that more precisely answers both the *how* and *why* questions. Apply team brainstorming to get closest to the core verb/noun combination.

At some point the only right answer to the *how* question is, "We don't know how." This is a signal to schedule training. The chances are that there is a place in this book where I have the answer to that question.

The remainder of this chapter is a list of verb/phrase and verb/noun combinations for each of the seven project groups. Use them to prompt combinations that more precisely fit your business, or that fit improvements you are already planning or implementing.

If you have enough personnel, you can assign a team to make a list of verb/phrase combinations for each project group. If you are a smaller company, you may have to work on only one or two project groups at a time.

How Do We, Inside and Outside of Sales and Marketing, Increase Market Share?

One important point about this list of verb/phrase combinations is that company functions not directly connected with the sales and marketing function have a big impact on increasing market share. Any department that assists on-time delivery, consistent quality, and cost control, so that prices aren't increased as fast as inflation, can add to or defend market share every year and in each phase of your company's business cycle.

To Increase Product Coverage

- Design new products
- Acquire another company/competitor
- Acquire another product line

To Increase Price Coverage

- Redesign the existing product line to reduce cost
- Acquire an accepted low-cost product line
- Create a new line that is private-labeled

To Increase Channel Coverage

- Change channels
- Add more distributors
- Pull more through existing distributors

To Increase Promotion Coverage

- Improve delivery and advertise it
- Telemarket products and services
- Change advertising to emphasize customer financial benefits
- Increase advertising
- Target specific industries

- Improve distributor training
- Provide the sales force with better targeted selling tools

To Increase Brand Coverage

- Increase sales force contact
- Change the discount structure

To Estimate Market Share

- Assess market coverage position
- Assess competitors' market coverage
- Analyze the market
- Segment markets
- Enter new market segments
- Segregate distribution channels

To Compose a Marketing Plan

- Include key customers in planning
- Plot the company's business cycle
- Document customer order processing time
- Shorten customer order processing time
- Measure customer satisfaction
- Improve customer satisfaction
- Improve after-sale service

To Include Other Functions in Marketing Planning

- Approve credit in advance
- Consider advance payment for slow-paying customers
- Drop slow-paying customers
- Implement material control improvement
- Improve delivery performance
- Deliver customer orders on time

- Document on-time delivery percent

- Design product components for shorter lead time

- Evaluate order driven pull systems

- Evaluate forecasting use

- Document customer order/manufacturing lead time mismatch

- Improve quality consistency

- Implement ISO 9000

- Control costs/prices so they increase at a rate lower than inflation

- Divest part of business (for example, abandon some products)

How Do We Reduce Expenses per Sales Dollar?

This includes both labor and nonlabor expense reduction that can be found in the line items of the annual budget.

To Segregate Budget Expenses

- Segregate using the 80/20 rule

- Track labor dollars per sales dollar

- Track nonlabor dollars per sales dollar

- Track overhead dollars per sales dollar

- Evaluate projects by ROA

- Prioritize projects by ROA

- Segregate material costs using the 80/20 rule

- Segregate inventory-carrying line items in the budget

- Segregate setup line items in the budget

- Identify major paperwork costs

- Document product standard cost

- Segregate overhead expenses

- Minimize tax expense

- Rationalize interest expense

- Segregate depreciation expenses using the 80/20 rule
- Segregate insurance expenses using the 80/20 rule
- Segregate material handling expenses
- Segregate personnel expenses
- Segregate sales, engineering, and administration (SE&A) expenses
- Segregate direct labor costs
- Segregate indirect labor costs
- Analyze scrap costs
- Analyze rework costs
- Identify quality costs
- Track quality costs
- Rationalize use of purchasing quantity price breaks
- Document cost of the annual physical inventory
- Use cycle counting to keep accurate inventory records
- Document setup cost ÷ direct labor cost percent

To Implement Six Sigma and Lean Concepts and Eliminate Waste

- Eliminate waiting waste
- Eliminate transportation waste
- Eliminate processing waste
- Eliminate inventory waste
- Eliminate defect waste
- Eliminate motion waste
- Eliminate people waste
- Document non-value-added waste
- Improve workplace organization
- Utilize cleaning as inspection
- Inspect at the source

- Implement, schedule, and perform preventive maintenance

- Improve processing scheduling

How Do We Reduce Lead Times?

Remember, the reason you need to reduce processing lead time is to reduce work-in-process inventory investment. This includes reducing the mismatch between customer order processing lead time and manufacturing lead time to reduce component inventory investment.

To Document Current Lead Times

- Calculate customer order processing lead times

- Calculate current component processing lead times

- Document processing queue times

- Calculate assembly lead times

- Document purchasing lead times

- Document paperwork lead times

- Plot product cycle times

- Shorten purchasing and raw material lead times

- Shorten component processing and assembly lead times

- Shorten packaging and shipping lead times

To Improve the Material Control System

- Improve inventory and production control

- Improve process scheduling

- Calculate manufacturing capacity

- Classify equipment utilization percent

- Calculate safety allowance

- Expedite purchased items by safety allowance

- Maintain processing routers

- Schedule shop orders by start date

- Expedite shop orders by start date

- Decide on a component reorder calculation
- Schedule setup/changeover preparation
- Prepare setups in advance
- Improve cycle time/lead time mismatch
- Implement receiving and receiving inspection cell
- Include suppliers on project teams

To Define the Lean Value Stream

- Perform process mapping
- Document process flow
- Implement visual displays and controls
- Identify product families
- Implement product family cells
- Implement paperwork cells
- Document the current process in a flowchart
- Design the future/ideal flowchart
- Implement the future flowchart
- Solve upstream quality problems
- Coordinate product and process design

How Do We Reduce Setup Costs?

Remember, the reason to reduce or eliminate setup cost is to reduce lot sizes so component inventory investment will be minimized.

To Design a Lot Sizing Formula

- Calculate lot sizes
- Balance setup costs with inventory carrying cost
- Minimize component inventory investment
- Minimize lot sizes
- Reduce setup cost

- Calculate the inventory carrying cost
- Calculate manufacturing setup cost
- Calculate the purchasing setup cost
- Document the item-by-item setup cost
- Document most recent usage history and lot sizes
- Document component unit cost
- Calculate lot sizes for purchased item quantity price breaks
- Identify families of parts
- Calculate lot sizes for part families processed together
- Implement cellular component processing
- Invest in tooling for setup reduction
- Design setup cost and time out of components
- Design for fewest number of parts in each assembly
- Design for fewest number of operations
- Separate external and internal setup
- Complete external setup ahead of the next setup

How Do We Maximize Capital Asset Utilization?

There is a linkage between capital processing equipment utilization and a good material control system. This is reflected in some of the verb/phrase combinations:

- Calculate machine utilization percent
- Classify equipment by utilization percent
- Document plant capacity
- Identify processing equipment bottlenecks
- Identify overloaded processing equipment
- Schedule/perform preventive maintenance
- Improve processing accuracy with preventive maintenance
- Match machine capability/accuracy to design requirement

- Relate plant capacity to the business cycle
- Provide special schedule control for high utilization percentages
- Farm out processing for low utilization percentages
- Sell off underutilized, expensive equipment
- Sell off/rent underutilized space

How Do We Control the Accounts Receivable Collection Period?

For every day a customer pays later than agreed, operating or investment cash is reduced and is limited for other continuous improvement investments you need to be making, particularly in extra personnel who can be assigned to teams for improvement projects.

To Improve the Collection Period

- Approve credit in advance
- Compare terms with actual results
- Consider advance payment from slow-paying customers
- Provide financial advice to slow-paying customers
- Provide special higher pricing to slow-paying customers
- Provide high-interest loans to slow-paying customers
- Consider dropping slow-paying customers
- Build control into the marketing plan
- Build improvement projects/action into marketing plans

How Do We Maximize Employee Asset Utilization?

Remember, your employees are individual businesses. To earn the highest wages they must lower their cost and increase their knowledge. To make them most Profit Able, you must invest in their Profit Ability training.

To Accomplish This

- Decrease percent salary and wage dollars ÷ sales dollars
- Take inventory of employee knowledge that your business needs

- Identify knowledge gaps

- Hire people based on new or specific knowledge needed

- Schedule training for specific knowledge needed

- Train employees to be businessmen and businesswomen

- Promote from within your trained knowledge resources

- Train for promotion

- Empower employee assets

- Manage change

- Identify and encourage change agents and champions

- Organize project teams for each of the seven business elements

- Assign the best knowledge resources to the most profitable project

- Train employee teams

- Build employee teams

- Invest in time for teams to implement improvement projects

- Invest in time for teams to increase the ROA annually

- Improve company information on financial performance

- Encourage individual creativity

- Encourage team creativity

- Recognize high contributors

- Allow peers to recognize and encourage high contributors

- Implement financial incentives

- Consider proven gain-sharing plans

- Retain your knowledge resources with competitive wages

In this chapter I've demonstrated the vast number of verb/phrase combinations that can be generated by asking the questions "How?" and "Why?" The goal is to save you time as you look for both broad and specific projects in each of the seven critical business elements. As you read the rest of this book, keep a note pad handy to compose a verb/noun or verb/phrase combination that fits improvements you want to make in your company or in your individual life or career. Then take action to invest the necessary time to implement some improvement every day.

Life, and your job, will be much more enjoyable if you don't put it off and if you don't stop fighting for changes and improvements your gut tells you to make.

4

Seven Project Groups You Can Start Today

A few key planners, decision makers, or project teams may have already identified and implemented several obviously good projects that happen to fall within each of the seven project groups. More than likely, some knowledge resources may already be assigned to each of these seven improvement project groups.

In fact, you and your personnel may be saying, "We don't have a problem discovering enough projects. Our problem is having enough human resources with spare time to design and implement projects we are relatively sure will increase profit." If this is your response, it shows that you don't yet understand that to double ROA will require you to systematically invest in enough people resources to specifically do continuous improvement work.

In the next chapter I ask you to prove financially how much profit, investment reduction, or ROA increase the potential projects will yield. Then I will provide you with a form that will help you financially evaluate and rank each project you discover. For now, I want to provide you with some additional thoughts about discovering and naming projects within the seven critical business elements.

Your personnel already know most of what I will reveal to you in this book. About all I do for you is to organize what you know and what I know so you can get started today. Time is slipping away and so is your increased profit.

Even before team training starts, there's no reason why you shouldn't assign a change agent or champion to get continuous improvement started in a big way. The longer you wait to add the necessary knowledge resources to get started, the more of your future net worth you are allowing to waste away. You're also allowing competitors to get a jump on you with their own continuous improvement.

Continuous improvement will be hard work, but it won't be as hard as you are working now. And even if you invest in a few additional employees up front to get started on a more broadly focused continuous improvement process, you will eventually require fewer employees per sales dollar than you do now. Having various projects that involve a high percentage of your personnel will turn their going to work each day into a game for which they will now have a measurable way to keep score.

Now let's just casually walk through your facility to see how easily we can discover projects in each of the seven project groups that are crying out to be improved.

PROJECT GROUP: MAXIMIZE EMPLOYEE ASSET UTILIZATION

Set a goal to reduce personnel salary and wage costs per sales dollar by 10 percent over three to five years' time.

A logical starting place is to invest in training projects that increase the utilization of the creative talents of your human assets. If you don't have a formal training schedule that links with one or more of the seven project groups, you have found one logical starting place.

Even if you are already using project teams, they can be continuously improved. If you don't have at least one team, with the right knowledge resources, working on each of seven improvement areas, you have discovered one of your most important projects.

Next, ask if the improvement process requires that each team has a step-by-step schedule. Just as you schedule customer products and services to deliver them on time, you need a schedule to be sure that human resources are available and scheduled to complete improvement projects on time to meet ROA improvement goals.

This is logical since every project will be evaluated to prove that it will yield a measurable ROA increase. To fail to deliver profitability improvement on time is just as bad as not delivering products and services on time. Just as with products and services, failure to provide adequate capital investment and personnel will put you behind schedule. Failure to invest money and knowledge resources in improvement projects will delay ROA improvement.

This project group might be given the responsibility to schedule employee training and monitor project completions for each of the project groups.

Measure the companywide ratio of salary and wage costs divided by sales for the past three or four years. Ask if there is a current goal to improve it. If you aren't currently using this measure, what better project can you quickly implement to communicate the trend?

PROJECT GROUP: INCREASE MARKET COVERAGE AND SALES DOLLARS

Set an initial goal to increase sales at least 10 percent by increasing market share and coverage over the next three- to five-year business cycle.

More than likely, your business plan or marketing plan has a goal to increase sales dollars. I don't want to mince words about increasing sales or increasing market share; if you have a specific plan to increase market coverage, the chances are favorable that you will increase both sales and market share. The key is, do you know for sure that each part of your marketing plan will increase the ROA? If you don't have a marketing plan that invests in more coverage, better on-time delivery, improved quality, and expense reduction, you don't have a complete marketing plan.

In the next chapter I will show you how to determine whether the investment to increase market share will increase ROA. In Chapter 13, I show you how to estimate your market share and the share of each competitor by estimating the market coverage of each business. Also in Chapter 13, I will show you what I think a marketing plan should look like.

You already have a supply of knowledge resources doing certain things to increase sales. This group probably has a formal marketing plan to get the required results by a certain time. I can suggest some specific things this team can do to build a team that might expand the scope of the marketing plan and improve the chances of success. Three examples will explain the things I suggest.

First, I will attempt to convince you that your marketing team needs to include members and projects from other company functions such as design engineering, quality, product cost reduction, processing cost reduction, on-time delivery, and customer satisfaction. If customers are considering increasing your market share from them, they expect new products and services to be available when promised. They expect your company to reduce costs so prices to them increase at a rate less than the rate of inflation. They want consistency and predictability in products and services to improve so they will know that your quality program is really working for them. They expect you to reduce lead time for customer order delivery.

I believe that your marketing plan should schedule improvement in these company performance areas and should involve personnel in these functions. This is an improvement that will support greater market share.

Second, I will attempt to convince you that you won't have sales increases throughout each economic business cycle if you don't plan to increase market share by naming projects to increase your coverage for products, price, marketing channels, promotion, and your brand label. In Chapter 13, I will show you numerically how each percent of increased coverage will result in a predictable percent increase in market share.

Third, also in Chapter 13, I will show your marketing team a sample marketing plan that they can use to generate ideas for additional marketing projects that can be evaluated for their ROA contribution.

Ask the marketing team for the current specific sales increase goals and what specific plans and actions are being implemented. Ask where you are in your business cycle. Ask about the level of customer satisfaction and the most important things your customers are asking them to improve. Ask to see the marketing plan and check it to see if it includes projects to increase market coverage so that market share will be increased. Check to see if appropriate projects are included for non-sales personnel to reduce lead times and improve on-time delivery, and whether goals are set to raise prices at a rate lower than inflation.

PROJECT GROUP: REDUCE EXPENSES PER SALES DOLLAR

Set a goal to decrease nonlabor material and overhead costs per sales dollar by 10 percent over the next three to five years.

Your annual budget plan is a good starting place for projects to reduce labor, material, and overhead costs, even if you haven't implemented team training. All of these expenses, listed as budget line items, are the detailed expenses you will subtract from annual sales to determine your annual profit. As expenses go down, profit goes up.

Your employee teams can start by looking at the 20 percent of budget line items that account for 80 percent of the total expenses. In one day (like *today*), you can discover enough projects to evaluate and implement very soon. The point is, there will never be a shortage of improvement projects. Your task is to invest in personnel to evaluate and implement them.

In every chapter of this book I will show you other fertile places to discover a massive number of profitable projects.

As an experiment for the team assigned to this project group, take the word/phrase list in Chapter 3 for "How do we reduce expenses per sales dollar?" and see how many match with improvements you already have in the back of your mind but just haven't made the decision to invest in the time for your best knowledge resources to work on them.

PROJECT GROUP: REDUCE LEAD TIMES

Set a goal to cut work-in-process inventory in half by reducing various lead times.

The primary goals of lead time reduction are to reduce inventory of work-in-process items and to shorten your customer order lead time so you can give customers better service than your competitors. You do this to help increase sales, particularly during the peak of your business cycle.

Lead time projects should require an evaluation of your customer order processing and material control systems. The time spent processing new customer orders and the lead time control provided by your material control system will give you some of the easiest projects to implement. In Chapter 11, I will show you a step-by-step process that can guide you through the evaluation of your current material control system. A simple test to determine whether this evaluation will increase your sales and ROA is to just make a quick estimate of the percentage of times you ship on the date promised to each customer. Anything less than 95 percent tells you that this is a project screaming to be given some attention.

As an experiment for this project team, use the appropriate list of noun/phrase combinations in Chapter 3 and take a casual walk through your facilities.

To shorten customer order processing lead time, count how many different people and departments the paperwork passes through before a purchase order or shop order can be released. Determine how many days are consumed to do this paperwork and information processing. Less than one day should be a normal expectation.

To minimize work-in-process inventory, ask if shop orders are scheduled by start dates or due dates for each operation. Ask how many shop orders have been started before or after their specified start date. Count how many shop orders are in queue and not being processed. Ask how queue times and processing lead times are determined and whether these lead times are realistic or predictable. Count the number of shop orders that have due dates older than the current date. Determine whether behind-schedule shop orders are expedited by counting the number of processing hours, by machine, that are behind schedule or whether current orders are just shuffled to solve the most urgent customer delivery problem. Find out who in the company understands that in-process inventory is controlled by in-process lead time. Ask how many people do some expediting of customer orders. Find out who understands that all expediters can be eliminated and that their activities are a symptom you need to evaluate to improve the material control system and reduce lead times.

PROJECT GROUP: REDUCE SETUP COSTS

Set a goal to cut setup costs in half.

One easy test to discover how important setup cost reduction will be for manufacturers is to estimate what percent of direct labor hours are used for setup of direct labor operations. This is particularly critical for component manufactures in both your shop and your suppliers' shops. If the percent is as much as 10 percent, setup cost reduction projects can make big reductions in your inventory investment. The reason for this inventory reduction is that lower setup cost results in smaller lot sizes, which means fewer dollars invested in inventory.

The reason I encourage you to include your suppliers in setup reduction projects is that their setup costs affect the size of your inventory investment. The way to know that this is true is to see how many of the components you buy from a supplier have quantity price breaks. The reason they give you price breaks is because they have setup costs for which they require you to pay.

Until you and your suppliers implement projects to reduce setup costs, you will never maximize your ROA. In Chapter 10, I show you how to determine the price break (or lot size) that is most financially sound.

This brings up another project I encourage you to implement as quickly as possible. You need a financially sound formula to calculate lot sizes in your own shop. Lean manufacturing courses encourage you to reduce changeover costs so you can manufacture components in lot sizes of one. This isn't practical for businesses that don't have mass production lines. Most small manufacturers are forced to produce in reasonable lot sizes because they haven't been able to cut setup costs on all components.

In Chapter 10, I will show you the requirements for a formula to calculate lot sizes that will minimize your inventory investment and maximize your ROA.

For this project group, a casual talk with your personnel who perform setups and a casual talk with your personnel who set lot sizes will reveal the best starting point for this project team.

Find out what is being done now to minimize raw material inventory. For manufacturing businesses, raw material can be moved directly from receiving to where it will be processed. Determine how soon the raw material will be consumed. Ask whether raw material delivery appears on process routers with a start date the same as the start date of the first processing operation.

Ask what is being done to minimize component inventory, both purchased and manufactured. For manufacturing, get a feel for what percentage of direct labor hours are used to perform setups. For manufacturing, distribution, and service businesses, get a feel for the amount of component inventory on hand. Ask how purchased and manufactured lot sizes are determined. Ask how much it costs to process each purchase order and shop order. Find out who knows that component inventory is controlled by manufacturing and purchasing setup costs. Find out who knows that there is a purchasing setup cost and how to calculate it. Find out how much knowledge and money is being invested to reduce setup times. Ask personnel in product and process design how they systematically design setup time and cost out of new or existing parts. Determine the level of knowledge about lean manufacturing and cellular processing for both product and paperwork. Get a feel for how many weeks' supply is carried on the 20 percent of components that make up 80 percent of the inventory investment.

PROJECT GROUP: MAXIMIZE CAPITAL ASSET UTILIZATION

Set a goal to increase capital asset utilization five percent.

Every percent you increase the utilization of capital assets is the same as getting that amount of production capacity at zero cost.

You may also have expensive pieces of equipment that you only use on one shift. Most stockholders would consider that to be underutilization of their investment. This kind of underutilization may be justifiable for short periods of time when you are expecting increased sales soon.

However, there are other projects that will be implemented within the preceding project groups that will increase the utilization of existing capital investment and delay the time when new investment will be required.

These other projects will also be like getting new equipment or space for free. Here are only a few examples:

- If over the next three to five years you implement enough projects to absorb 15 percent to 25 percent more sales dollars, it will be like getting 15 percent to 25 percent more capital equipment for free. I believe this is an improvement you should expect. I know that this book will show your employees more than enough projects so they can make it happen.

- If over the next three to five years you implement projects to significantly shorten lead times so that your customer order delivery time is reduced, you can expect them to yield increased market share, which will occupy some of the underutilized capital assets.

- If you implement projects to shorten lead times for manufacturing or assembly operations, every day that you eliminate from the current utilization of that asset will be equal to one day of production from that asset at no new investment.

- If you implement projects to shorten paperwork or information lead time in office or data processing operations, you can expect to delay the buying of new capital equipment.

- Every time you implement a financially justified project to reduce setup cost by one hour, you have gained an hour's worth of production capacity for that piece of equipment.

This project team can discover projects they won't find in any other way by going into the shop or office and talking to the people who operate and schedule the use of each major capital asset, including office, warehouse, assembly, and manufacturing floor space.

Determine what procedures are currently used to increase equipment utilization. Identify the most highly utilized equipment. If data isn't currently available, make a guess about utilization rates. Ask how preventive maintenance is used to maintain the statistical capability of precision machines in comparison to their capability when new. Ask if utilization rates are used to load and schedule processing steps. Ask if there is equipment and floor space that is seldom used and how much it costs to maintain it, to heat and cool it, and how much it costs in terms of insurance and taxes.

PROJECT GROUP:
CONTROL THE CUSTOMER INVOICE
COLLECTION PERIOD

Set a goal to get all customers to pay within one or two days of the date you and they agreed on when you accepted their order.

The marketplace usually determines the contracted length of time between the day you issue an invoice for goods or services delivered and the day you receive payment. The reason customers are tempted to take too much time to pay is because they want to force you to invest in their inventory so they will have a higher ROA. If you want to recover this investment from them so you can increase your ROA, or use the cash to implement improvement projects, you must find a way to get them to live within the contracted collection period to which they agreed when they placed their order with you.

There may be some competitive reasons why you tolerate late payment from some customers but there is never a good financial reason. Sometimes you find that even without the sales you get from them, you will have a higher ROA if you allow your competitor to take their business. This is the reason why I will provide you with a project evaluation form to help you make these thorny financial and customer relations decisions.

WHAT COMES NEXT?

Now that we've looked at the seven critical business elements and the seven project groups from several different perspectives, we need to move on to the next basic step.

In the next chapter I will present a form to evaluate and rank each project you have named with a verb/noun combination. Completing this form will help you to know which projects in each of the seven project groups will increase your ROA the most and the quickest.

I will also provide you with a similar form that can be used to set annual ROA percent improvement goals or longer-term goals for a three- to five-year business cycle.

5

Project Evaluation and Project Goal Setting

Now it's time for me to prove my claim that you can double your
ROA in three to five years if you organize your best knowledge
resources into project teams and make time and money available to
them in every phase of the business cycle.

There are three purposes of this chapter:

- First, I provide a sample form for gathering financial data that
  will be used in the following chapters.

- Second, I will show you a simple way to evaluate each large and
  small project to determine whether the project will cause the
  ROA to go up or down.

- Third, I show you how to do the calculations to set your own
  improvement goal for each of the seven project groups, and for
  overall improvement.

This chapter includes seven forms that you can customize to fit your
own business:

- Worksheet for gathering financial data for a manufacturing
  business.

- Worksheet for gathering financial data for a service or
  distribution business.

- Project Evaluation Form to determine how much an individual
  project will increase the ROA.

- The first of four worksheets used to set a goal for each of the
  seven project groups. In each worksheet there is a column for each
  of the seven project groups. These individual columns will also

serve as a guide to completing the Project Evaluation Form for a project in that particular project group. The first worksheet is for Increase Sales and Reduce Salary and Labor Cost.

- The other three worksheets are for Reduce Overhead Costs and Reduce Lead Times, Reduce Setup Cost and Increase Capital Asset Utilization, and Reduce Invoice Collection Period. The last column is the accumulated total for all seven groups.

The first two worksheets are to help you gather your own company data to compare with our sample company.

Completing the sample project evaluation form for each of your projects will make sense after we've gone through the next four worksheets.

Notice that all seven worksheets have 24 lines and that the line descriptions are the same except for the second worksheet for gathering financial data for a service or distribution business. We will focus our explanation of these forms on a manufacturing business because we need to cover manufacturing setup costs and lead time issues. Even some service businesses may have some manufacturing elements, for example, a rain gutter business that makes its own guttering components.

If you decide to evaluate and prioritize projects, you will want to make your own forms that conform to your own financial statements. You may also need to segregate some costs into additional budget line items. For example, if you don't separate setup costs from other direct labor costs, you will limit the information that your reduce setup cost team needs to make their contribution.

WORKSHEETS FOR GATHERING FINANCIAL DATA

We encourage you to use one of these two forms (see Figures 5.1 and 5.2) to see how your business compares to our sample company. We suggest that you complete one when sales are at their peak during a business cycle and another when sales are at their lowest during the same business cycle. This won't take much time and it will tell you two things:

- First, you will quickly get an idea about the length of your normal business cycle.

- Second, you will see the difference in your ROA for high and low sales years. This will give you a feel for how much different these years would be if you increase your market share for future business cycles.

**Worksheet for Gathering Financial Data
Manufacturing**

Line	Data description	% of sales	Sample data	Your data
1	**Total sales**	100%	10,000,000	
2	Purchased materials and parts	30%	3,000,000	
3	Setup—direct labor	1%	100,000	
4	Run—direct labor	6%	600,000	
5	Indirect labor	6%	600,000	
6	Manufacturing salaries	6%	600,000	
7	Manuacturing non-wage overhead	21%	2,100,000	
8	**Less total manufacturing expenses**	**70%**	**7,000,000**	
9	SE&A salaries	13%	1,300,000	
10	SE&A overhead	7%	700,000	
11	**Less SE&A expenses**	**20%**	**2,000,000**	
12	Net profit before tax	10%	1,000,000	
13	**Asset investment:**			
14	In-process inventory	7%	700,000	
15	All other inventory	23%	2,300,000	
16	Capital assets	56%	5,600,000	
17	Accounts receivable	14%	1,400,000	
18	**Total assets**	**100%**	**10,000,000**	
19	**ROA percent**	**10%**		
20	Number of employees		70	
21	Investment per employee		143,000	
22	Sales per employee		143,000	
23	Total salaries and labor		3,200,000	
24	**Wage expenses ÷ sales**		**32%**	

Figure 5.1   Worksheet for gathering manufacturing financial data.

All of these forms combine elements from your profit and loss statement and four of the investments from your balance sheet.

You will notice that the form for a service or distribution business includes a line called *gross profit*. You will find it helpful to add this

Worksheet for Gathering Financial Data
Service and Distribution

Line	Data description	% of sales	Sample data	Your data
1	Total sales	100%	10,000,000	
2	Purchased product	50%	5,000,000	
3	Gross profit	50%	5,000,000	
4	Payroll expense	9%	900,000	
5	Payroll tax and fringes	3%	300,000	
6	Auto and travel expense	6%	600,000	
7	Promotion expense	5%	500,000	
8	Contract expense	3%	300,000	
9	Purchase order setup costs	3%	300,000	
10	Administration and operations expense	8%	800,000	
11	Depreciation expense	3%	300,000	
12	Total operations expenses	40%	4,000,000	
13	Net profit before tax	10%	1,000,000	
14	Asset investment:			
15	Inventory	60%	6,000,000	
16	Capital assets	26%	2,600,000	
17	Accounts receivable	14%	1,400,000	
18	Total assets	100%	10,000,000	
19	ROA percent	10%		
20	Number of employees		70	
21	Investment per employee		143,000	
22	Sales per employee		143,000	
23	Total salaries and labor		3,200,000	
24	Wage expenses ÷ sales		32%	

Figure 5.2   Worksheet for gathering service and distribution financial data.

same line to the other forms so you can evaluate various product lines or market segments by their gross profit contribution. This will help you to decide if your ROA would increase if you abandoned a product line or market segment.

PROJECT EVALUATION FORM

Figure 5.3 shows an example of the form you should use to determine how much each individual improvement project will increase the ROA. Each year, based on the past year's actual budget numbers or your current year's budget plan, you will enter the correct values in the *sample data* column and calculate the appropriate percent of sales for each line. These two columns become your current base for evaluating proposed projects.

Then, for each proposed project, you would enter the appropriate higher or lower value for any of the lines that represent what this financial statement would look like after the project is implemented. The line you are most interested in is line 19, ROA percent.

If the new ROA percent is smaller than the base ROA percent, you will reject the project. If the new ROA is larger than the base ROA percent, compare the ROA for this project with the ROA for all other proposed projects to see which will have the greatest or quickest positive impact on the ROA.

For example, let's assume that your base ROA percent is 10.000 percent, the same as in our sample. If you have five projects with new ROA percents of 10.015 percent, 10.522 percent, 10.120 percent, 10.03 percent, and 10.501 percent, you will be able to rank them from the highest to lowest percent. After ranking them, you can then make a commonsense judgment as to which of those with almost the same ROA percent would be the one you want to approve first. Sometimes a decision might be made on the availability of the right knowledge workers within a given project group.

To evaluate projects in each of the seven project groups, you can follow the instructions for the remaining four worksheets about ROA goals.

ROA IMPROVEMENT GOALS

For Increase Sales Column

In our sample business, we decided to implement projects to increase market share/coverage enough to increase sales 10 percent. I will show which of the lines will require some adjustment for any project evaluations that are designed to increase sales (see Figure 5.4). The calculations are the same for project group goal setting:

Line 1. The 10 percent sales increase is entered on line 1 for this column.

Lines 2, 3, and 4. For a 10 percent sales increase, it's reasonable to estimate that product and component raw materials, direct labor for setting up and running components, and purchased components will increase

Project Evaluation Form

Line	Data description	% of sales	Sample data	Project data
1	**Total sales**	100%	10,000,000	
2	Purchased materials and parts	30%	3,000,000	
3	Setup—direct labor	1%	100,000	
4	Run—direct labor	6%	600,000	
5	Indirect labor	6%	600,000	
6	Manufacturing salaries	6%	600,000	
7	Manuacturing non-wage overhead	21%	2,100,000	
8	**Less total manufacturing expenses**	**70%**	**7,000,000**	
9	SE&A salaries	13%	1,300,000	
10	SE&A overhead	7%	700,000	
11	**Less SE&A expenses**	**20%**	**2,000,000**	
12	**Net profit before tax**	**10%**	**1,000,000**	
13	**Asset investment:**			
14	In-process inventory	7%	700,000	
15	All other inventory	23%	2,300,000	
16	Capital assets	56%	5,600,000	
17	Accounts receivable	14%	1,400,000	
18	**Total assets**	**100%**	**10,000,000**	
19	**ROA percent**	**10%**		
20	Number of employees		70	
21	Investment per employee		143,000	
22	Sales per employee		143,000	
23	Total salaries and labor		3,200,000	
24	**Wage expenses ÷ sales**		**32%**	

Figure 5.3   Project evaluation form.

10 percent. Therefore, a 10 percent expense increase is added to each of these lines.

Lines 5 and 7. For this example, I have assumed that indirect labor and non-wage overhead will increase two percent. For your calculations for your company, you might want to use a larger percent if you have a logical

ROA Goals for Increase Sales and Reduce Salary and Labor Cost

Line	Data description	Base data × 1000	Plus 10% sales	Minus 10% salaries
1	Total sales	10,000	1,000	
2	Purchased materials and parts	3,000	300	
3	Setup—direct labor	100	10	−10
4	Run—direct labor	600	60	−60
5	Indirect labor	600	12	−60
6	Manufacturing salaries	600		−60
7	Manuacturing non-wage overhead	2,100	42	
8	Less total manufacturing expenses	7,000	424	−190
9	SE&A salaries	1,300	150	−130
10	SE&A overhead	700		
11	Less SE&A expenses	2,000	150	−130
12	Net profit before tax	−1,000	426	320
13	Asset investment:			
14	In-process inventory	700	70	
15	All other inventory	2,300	230	
16	Capital assets	5,600	112	−280
17	Accounts receivable	1,400	140	
18	Total assets	10,000	552	−280
19	ROA percent	10%	13.5%	13.6%
20	Number of employees	70	75	63
21	Investment per employee	143	143	154
22	Sales per employee	143	141	159
23	Total salaries and labor	3,200	3,450	2,880
24	Wage expenses ÷ sales	32%	31.3	28.1

Figure 5.4 ROA goals—Increase Sales and Reduce Salary and Labor Cost.

reason to believe it is more accurate. Or you could use a larger percent just to be more conservative in your estimate.

Line 6. I assumed that for a 10 percent increase in sales, there is no need for increased salaries for manufacturing managers, supervisors, and technical/support personnel.

Line 8. This is the total of lines 2 through 7. Though a line isn't on this form for gross profit, for the base data column the gross profit would be

$10,000 Total sales – $7,000 Total manufacturing expense =
$3,000 Gross profit ÷ $10,000 Sales = 30% Gross profit

For the 10 percent sales increase the gross profit would be 32.5 percent because indirect labor and non-wage overhead were only increased two percent.

Line 9. Sales, engineering, and administrative salaries will not normally be increased for a 10 percent sales increase. For this line I've entered 150 ($150,000) as the investment required to increase market share. I've placed the investment on this line to make the point that you can treat an investment as an expense or as an increase in asset investment (line 13). For project evaluation or goal setting, treating it as an expense is a more conservative approach because it will result in a lower ROA percent increase than if it is treated as an investment.

Line 10. I assumed no increase in SE&A overhead. If you have reason to believe that your project for a market share or sales increase will increase overhead in any of these functions, not covered by the above $150,000, you will want to add an estimate so you won't be disappointed if you don't reach your goal. There's an old adage that almost always fits when you are making estimates about any activity that involves time or money. It says, "It always costs more and takes longer than you plan." Try to add an extra room to your house and you'll never forget this little truth.

Lines 11 and 12. These lines are similar to line 8. You subtract lines 8 and 11 from line 1, total sales, to get an idea about how much profit will increase as a result of a given project or as a result of the goal you have set for each project team. In the example for this column, the numbers say a $1,000 ($1,000,000) increase in sales could result in a $426 ($426,000) increase in net profit. The new net profit percent for this one column would be

$1,000 + $426 = $1,426 ÷ $10,000 Base sales 14.6 percent

Line 13. This line for a manufacturer is the same as line 14 on the worksheet for gathering financial data for a service or distribution business.

Lines 14, 15, and 17. A 10 percent increase in sales will, at most, require a 10 percent increase in investment for work-in-process inventory, component inventory, product inventory, and accounts receivable for the additional dollars in invoices shipped to customers.

Line 16. Capital assets won't need to increase 10 percent for a 10 percent sales increase. I've estimated a two percent increase for more manufacturing capacity. For various projects you may know the exact dollars required. For setting an ROA percent goal you will have to make an educated guess based on your equipment or floor space that is most highly utilized. Our two percent estimate kept line 21, investment per employee, at the same level so I felt comfortable with that guess.

Line 18. A 10 percent ($1,000,000) increase in sales resulted in a 5.5 percent ($552,000) increase in total asset investment. The value of using this form, to see the impact of increased sales on the affected financial lines, should be revealing to you if you haven't done this sort of analysis before. For line 18, if you don't maintain a healthy cash reserve, you may be required to borrow money to achieve each higher level of sales. This demand for up-front cash for project investment is one of the biggest reasons why you need to increase your average ROA percent over a business cycle. Using all seven project groups to increase your ROA will generate extra cash for you to grow your market share and drive your expenses down. The extra cash can also be used to increase your capital assets for equipment and tooling to reduce your inventory investment. You can almost always expect a capital investment to reduce setup and lead time to be much less than the inventory it eliminates.

Line 19. This is the project evaluation and ROA percent goal you are looking for. The base ROA percent for our sample is 10 percent. In the increase sales column, when you divide line 12, net profit ($1,000 base + $426 increase = $1,426), by line 18, total assets ($10,000 + $552 = $10,552), you get a new ROA of 13.5 percent or an increase of 3.5 percentage points. In other words, for our sample company, a 10 percent increase in sales results in a 35 percent increase in ROA. Think about this. With only the goal set for one of the seven project groups, we're already one-third of the way toward doubling the ROA percent.

Lines 20 through 24. These are just other ratios to give your project teams a feel for other ways to measure continuous improvement company-wide. Before we're finished with the analysis for all seven columns, we're going to see the potential for a 16 percent reduction in line 24, wage (salaries and labor) expenses per sales dollar. This is on the low side of what you should expect after three to five years of continuous improvement.

For Reduce Salaries Column

In the sample company I decided to set a goal to reduce total employee compensation expenses 10 percent (see Figure 5.4). Our goal isn't to arbitrarily cut every employee's take-home pay. In fact, since we have invested in their training and business knowledge, our goal is to increase their individual take-home pay. You may even plan to reward them with some type of incentive bonus to assure that the improvements will be continuous. Your true goal is to implement projects that will maintain a constant number of current employees as you increase sales from one business cycle to the next.

Lines 3, 4, 5, 6, and 9. Total salaries and labor for our sample company is $3,200 ($3,200,000). A 10 percent improvement would equate to a profit increase of $320 ($320,000). This could be the result of absorbing 10 percent more sales without adding salary and labor costs. It could also be from a reduction of labor and salary expenses at the current level of sales. Or it could be a combination of the two.

Line 12. The new profit would be $1,000 + $320 = $1,320 ÷ $10,000 base sales = 13.2%.

Line 16. For practical purposes, this improvement, without increased sales, would eventually allow disposing of something less than 10 percent of capital assets. Or, if there was an increase in sales without adding additional personnel, it would be like the company being given more capital assets for free. For the sample company, and for this calculation, I have estimated that we would gain a five percent advantage for the future capital assets. This reduction is equivalent to a new capital asset total of $5,600 − $280 ($280,000) = $5,320 ($5,320,000).

Line 18. The new total assets would be $10,000 − $280 = $9,720 ($9,720,000).

Line 19. The new ROA percent for this one column only would be $1,320 net profit ÷ $9,720 total assets = 13.6% or an ROA increase of 3.6 percentage points.

Line 24. Obviously we would expect this ratio to improve. That's why I encourage you to use the ratio of wages ÷ sales to measure the performance of your personnel on a companywide basis. This 10 percent improvement, even if part of it were to be paid out as an incentive bonus, would still be a net financial improvement for the company because of the free capital assets it would receive. Couple this with reduced scrap and rework resulting from an incentive bonus system and the urgency of employees to more quickly implement continuous improvement projects, and a companywide incentive bonus makes good sense. In Chapter 6, I will explain how to install a gain sharing bonus plan.

For Reduce Overhead Costs Column

For the sample company, the logic for this column is the same as for the previous column. I decided to set a goal to reduce nonlabor related overhead expenses 10 percent (see Figure 5.5). This is the project group that will rely heavily on segregating out similar or related line items in your annual budget. This is a good place to apply lean waste reduction concepts and the verb/phrase combinations you will find in Chapter 8. Some of these expense reductions will come as a result of specific projects. Some of them will come from successfully implementing projects from the next three columns, in which the expenses just seem to magically evaporate. For example, when you reduce setup costs for manufactured components, you experience a reduction in lot sizes. Smaller lot sizes means a smaller inventory investment. When you successfully reduce your inventory investment and the space required to warehouse it, you end up with lower taxes, lower insurance premiums, less scrap from obsolescence, lower material handling costs, plus many other costs you will think of. By the time you've gone through all seven project group goals, you will have a better appreciation of how these seven key business elements are interlinked.

Lines 7, 8, 10, 11, and 12. These lines will result in a $280 ($280,000) cost reduction and a $280,000 net profit increase. The new profit for this column would be $1,000 base profit + $280 = $1,280 ÷ $10,000 = 12.8%.

Line 19. Since there is no change in the base asset investment of $10,000 ($10,000,000), the new ROA percent for this column is $1,000 + $280 = $1,280 ÷ $10,000 = 12.8%, or an increase of 2.8 percentage points. The new accumulated ROA percent for these three columns is $1,000 base net profit + $426 + $320 + $280 = $2,026 ($2,026,000) ÷ base total assets $10,000 + $552 − $280 = $10,272 or $2,026 ÷ $10,272 = 19.7%. As you can see, we have set goals for only three of the seven project groups and already we see the probability of doubling the ROA percent of the sample company.

For Reduce Lead Times Column

It's not unreasonable for most manufacturing businesses that are currently carrying inventory to meet customer order lead time requirements to cut their lead times in half. This column shows only a token amount of possible

ROA Goals for Reduce Overhead Costs and Reduce Lead Times

Line	Data description	Base data × 1000	Minus 10% overhead	Minus 50% lead time
1	Total sales	10,000		
2	Purchased materials and parts	3,000		
3	Setup—direct labor	100		
4	Run—direct labor	600		
5	Indirect labor	600		
6	Manufacturing salaries	600		
7	Manuacturing non-wage overhead	2,100	−210	
8	**Less total manufacturing expenses**	**7,000**	**−210**	
9	SE&A salaries	1,300		
10	SE&A overhead	700	−70	
11	**Less SE&A expenses**	**2,000**	**−70**	
12	**Net profit before tax**	**1,000**	**280**	
13	**Asset investment:**			
14	In-process inventory	700		−350
15	All other inventory	2,300		−354
16	Capital assets	5,600		
17	Accounts receivable	1,400		
18	**Total assets**	**10,000**		**−704**
19	**ROA percent**	**10%**	12.8%	10.8%
20	Number of employees	70	70	70
21	Investment per employee	143	143	133
22	Sales per employee	143	143	143
23	Total salaries and labor	3,200	3,200	3,200
24	**Wage expenses ÷ sales**	**32%**	32	32

Figure 5.5   ROA goals—Reduce Overhead Costs and Reduce Lead Times.

improvement (see Figure 5.5). I haven't included any increased sales as a result of a higher percent of on-time delivery of customer orders. I also haven't included any expense reductions as a result of shorter lead times for many material handling activities between the receiving dock and the shipping dock. No waste elimination has been claimed for such things as inspection of purchased components at the source. The main purpose for this column is to get you to set a goal for reduction of work-in-process inventory as a result of reducing specific lead times.

Lines 14 and 15. For this column there will be no change in base expenses or base net profit. Only the investments will be reduced by improving three lead time issues.

First, there is often a mismatch between customer order lead time and manufacturing lead time. Customer order lead time is the number of days a customer allows between the day you receive the customer's purchase order and the day you ship their order. The manufacturing lead time is the time required for you to purchase material, process components, and assemble the product. The number of days the manufacturing lead time exceeds the customer order lead time is an indication of how many component items you must carry in inventory to meet customer delivery promises. The ideal is to reduce your manufacturing lead time to fewer days than your customer order lead time, so you can wait until you receive the customer order to start the manufacturing process. Until this project team can resolve this mismatch, you must carry inventory on the components whose processing lead time is more than what the customer will allow. For the sample company, I assumed that the average component manufacturing lead time is four weeks longer than the customer order lead time. This requires line 15 to be 4 weeks ÷ 52 weeks = 7.7% of the component inventory. The current line 15 investment is $2,300 ($2,300,000). The investment reduction would be $2,300 × 7.7% = $177 ($177,000).

Second, when lead times are very erratic for manufactured and purchased components, it's necessary to carry some inventory components in the form of a safety allowance to assure that customer delivery dates will be met. For our sample company I decided it was necessary to maintain a permanent component inventory equal to four weeks' usage to assure that customer orders are shipped on time. The investment would be the same as in the preceding example, $177 ($177,000). In Chapter 11, I show you how to calculate a safety allowance on each component you must carry in inventory.

Third, in-process inventory investment is totally controlled by manufacturing processing lead time from the day a shop order is started until the component is placed in stock, transferred to assembly, or shipped. If processing lead times could be cut in half, the in-process inventory investment would be cut in half. For the sample company, line 14 investment would be reduced $350 or $350,000. The total investment reduction for this column is $177 + $177 = $354 + $350 = $704 ($704,000). The new total investment = $10,000 – $704 = $9,296. ROA percent for this column would be $1,000 net profit ÷ $9,296 = 10.8%. As you can see, all three of these lead time reductions only yield a total new ROA of 10.8 percent. However, the real payoff from reduced lead times is the high probability that they will increase market share if your competitors can't match your improvement. Therefore, assume that the above three lead time improvements result in a sales increase of one percent. Based on the results of the increase sales column, each one percent sales increase would increase the ROA .35 percentage points from 10 percent base to 10.35 percent. When you test this column in your own company to establish an improvement goal or to evaluate an individual project, consider adding some ROA increase for a sales increase.

For Reduce Setup Cost Column

For the sample company, total expenses for lines 3 and 4 are $700 ($700,000) (see Figure 5.6). Setup expense ($100) is 16.7 percent of total direct labor expense. This is probably a high percentage for most manufacturing businesses. If the percent for your company is much less, you may expect a smaller ROA increase. In Chapter 10, I show you ways to cut setup cost at least in half. These calculations for setting an ROA goal are the same as for evaluating individual projects.

The most powerful way to minimize component inventory investment is to reduce setup cost. This fact presumes that you use a financially sound formula to calculate lot sizes. In Chapter 10, I demonstrate that a financially sound lot sizing formula must be based on setup cost.

You can make a reasonable estimate about how much the ROA would increase by reducing lot sizes. You need to consider the 80/20 rule. Statistically, 80 percent of your setup costs come from 20 percent of your components. Also, for that reason, 80 percent of your inventory dollars are made up from 20 percent of your components. Therefore, for the sample company, we can estimate that if something less than 80 percent of the setup costs is eliminated, something less than 80 percent of the inventory investment would be eliminated. For the sample company I assume that a 50 percent reduction is an achievable goal. Note: purchased components also have a setup cost or purchase order cost per purchase order line item. In Chapter 10, I will show you how to calculate the purchase order setup cost.

Line 3. A 50 percent reduction in manufactured component inventory investment will require a 50 percent cut in setup cost expenses on line 3. Therefore we show −$50 ($50,000) in this column for line 3. For this example we will let the $50,000 expense reduction also include the cost reduction for purchase order costs, which would actually come out of the expenses on lines 5, 6, and 7.

ROA Goals for Reduce Setup Cost and Increase Capital Asset Utilization

Line	Data description	Base data × 1000	Minus 50% setup cost	Plus 5% capital asset utilization
1	Total sales	10,000		
2	Purchased materials and parts	3,000		
3	Setup—direct labor	100	−50	
4	Run—direct labor	600		
5	Indirect labor	600		
6	Manufacturing salaries	600		
7	Manuacturing non-wage overhead	2,100	−172.5	
8	**Less total manufacturing expenses**	**7,000**	−222.5	
9	SE&A salaries	1,300		
10	SE&A overhead	700		
11	**Less SE&A expenses**	**2,000**		
12	**Net profit before tax**	**1,000**	222.5	
13	**Asset investment:**			
14	In-process inventory	700		
15	All other inventory	2,300	−1,150	
16	Capital assets	5,600	575	−280
17	Accounts receivable	1,400		
18	**Total assets**	**10,000**	−575	−280
19	**ROA percent**	**10%**	13%	10.3%
20	Number of employees	70	69	70
21	Investment per employee	143	137	139
22	Sales per employee	143	145	143
23	Total salaries and labor	3,200	3,150	3,200
24	**Wage expenses ÷ sales**	**32%**	31.5	32

Figure 5.6   ROA goals—Reduce Setup Cost and Increase Capital Asset Utilization.

Line 15. Cutting the setup costs in half will reduce the investment on this line by 50 percent. Therefore, 50 percent of the line 15 base value of $2,300 ($2,300,000) will be shown as a negative $1,150 for this column.

Line 16. You need to recognize that setup cost reductions, to permanently reduce inventory investment, require a one-time investment in capital equipment and/or tooling. We can conservatively estimate that as much as 50 percent of the −$1,150 ($1,150,000) reduction in inventory investment would be invested in capital equipment to get the $1,150,000 reduction in inventory investment. Therefore, 50 percent of the −$1,150 reduction (+$575) is added to line 16 to increase the investment in capital assets.

Line 7. Two adjustments need to be made to line 7:

- To be financially precise, the capital asset increase would increase annual depreciation expenses. I have assumed a depreciation expense of 10 percent to represent that this $575 ($575,000) investment would be transferred from an investment to an expense over the next 10 years. Therefore, line 7 must be increased by $57.5 ($57,500).

- However, there is an additional expense reduction that occurs when you implement projects to cut setup cost. In Chapter 10, I provide a list of expenses for inventory carrying costs, which will automatically disappear every time you reduce the setup hours, or costs, on a given component. These expenses disappear simply because you have a smaller inventory as a result of smaller lot sizes. These expenses include cost reductions for obsolescence, material handling, and taxes and insurance for the dollars invested in component inventory. For most manufacturing businesses the total annual carrying cost averages about 20 cents annual expense for each one dollar of inventory investment. We can express this as 20 percent of the annual inventory value. Therefore, if there is a $1,150 reduction on line 15 for the inventory investment reduction for the sample company, there would be an annual expense reduction of 20% × $1,150 = $230 ($230,000). Therefore, on line 7 we show + $57.5 depreciation expense −$230 cost reduction = −$172.5 expense reduction.

Line 12. New net profit will be $1,000 base net profit + $50 setup cost reduction − $57.5 annual depreciation expense + $230 inventory carrying cost reduction = $1,222.5.

Line 18. New total assets = $10,000 base − $1,150 line 15 inventory reduction + line 16 capital assets increase = $9,425 total assets.

Line 19. New ROA percent = $1,222.5 net profit ÷ $9,425 total assets = 13.0% or a 3.0 point increase in the ROA.

For Increase Capital Asset Utilization Column

In the preceding two columns, I didn't claim any ROA increase for the extra hours that equipment will be available due to shorter lead times, fewer hours consumed by setup hours, fewer rework hours from improved quality, better material control scheduling to eliminate cutting approved lot sizes to meet delivery dates, improved equipment uptime due to preventive maintenance performed at prescribed intervals to prevent breakdowns, increasing the number of shifts for the most productive equipment, shortening setup times by having tooling preset prior to completing the preceding work order, and many other improvements your personnel will discover through the verb/phrase process.

To show you the ROA goal setting calculations and how to evaluate individual projects to increase the utilization percent, I have assumed that this project team, or other teams, will discover enough projects to reduce capital assets an equivalent of five percent. In other words, project teams will implement enough projects to absorb five percent more sales without investing in additional capital asset capacity (see Figure 5.6).

Line 16. Five percent of the $5,600 base capital assets is $280 ($280,000).

Line 18. The adjusted total assets will be $10,000 − $280 = $9,720 ($9,720,000)

Line 12. There will be no change in the $1,000 base net profit.

Line 19. The new ROA percent for this column only will be $1,000 ÷ $9,720 = 10.3% or an increase of .3 ROA percentage points.

For Reduce Invoice Collection Period Column

The size of the accounts receivable investment depends on how closely the actual invoice collection period matches with the collection period the customer accepts when the order is acknowledged by your company. For the sample company, to show how the calculation is made, I have assumed that if it meets the collection period goal, the accounts receivable investment will be reduced $200,000 (see Figure 5.7).

Line 17. The accounts receivable will be reduced $200 ($200,000).

Line 18. The adjusted total assets will be $10,000 − $200 = $9,800 ($9,800,000)

Line 12. There will be no change in the $1,000 base net profit.

ROA Goals for Reduce Invoice Collection Period and Total of All Goals

Line	Data description	Base data × 1000	Invoice collection period	New base
1	Total sales	10,000		11,000
2	Purchased materials and parts	3,000		3,300
3	Setup—direct labor	100		50
4	Run—direct labor	600		600
5	Indirect labor	600		552
6	Manufacturing salaries	600		540
7	Manuacturing non-wage overhead	2,100		1,759.5
8	**Less total manufacturing expenses**	**7,000**		6,801.5
9	SE&A salaries	1,300		1,320
10	SE&A overhead	700		630
11	**Less SE&A expenses**	**2,000**		1,950
12	**Net profit before tax**	**1,000**		2,248.5
13	**Asset investment:**			
14	In-process inventory	700		420
15	All other inventory	2,300		1,026
16	Capital assets	5,600		5,727
17	Accounts receivable	1,400	−200	1,340
18	**Total assets**	**10,000**	−200	8,513
19	**ROA percent**	**10%**	10.2%	26.4%
20	Number of employees	70	70	67
21	Investment per employee	143	140	127
22	Sales per employee	143	143	164
23	Total salaries and labor	3,200	3,200	3,062
24	**Wage expenses ÷ sales**	**32%**	32	27.8

Figure 5.7   ROA goals—Reduce Invoice Collection Period and Total of All Goals.

Line 19. The new ROA percent for this column only will be $1,000 ÷ $9,800 = 10.2% or an increase of .2 ROA percentage points.

For the Accumulated New Base

To show the ROA total improvement results for the seven project groups, we add the results of each line and show the sum in the last column (see Figure 5.7).

Line 19. The ROA goal we have set for the sample company is line 12 net profit $1,248.5 increase + $1,000 base net profit = $2,248.5 ÷ line 18 total assets $8,513 = 26.4 ROA % or a 16.4 percentage point increase in the ROA.

The implication of the preceding paragraph is that total assets are $1,487,000 less than the original base of $10,000,000. This implies that the sample company, in only three to five years, has generated $1,487,000 in cash that it can use to acquire competitors or to invest in market coverage to increase market share to grow the business.

However, before spending all that cash and the new annual base net profit of $2,248,500 per year, we must recognize that the sample company wouldn't have made these improvements if it hadn't invested in the knowledge resources to discover, design, and implement projects in all seven project groups.

Therefore, let's look at the worksheet that has the two columns, base data plus 10 percent sales and minus 10 percent salaries (Figure 5.4). On line 20 we have assumed that the number of employees in these respective columns is 70 for the base and 63 for greater productivity. For greater employee productivity, we assumed it would take seven fewer employees than the base of 70 after personnel implemented labor cost reducing projects.

So that we can staff continuous improvement project teams, let's assume that we retained all existing 70 employees and assigned seven of them to work on project teams full time from now on. Based on the minus 10 percent salaries column, the annual expense (or annual investment) would be $320,000, the increased net profit we were expecting from this project. Therefore, if we treat the $320,000 as an annual expense, the adjusted net profit in the adjusted base column would be $2,248.5 − $320 = $1,928.5. Then the revised ROA percent would more realistically become $1,928.5 ÷ $8,513 = 22.7 ROA %, still more than double the original base of 10 percent.

What is the logical conclusion to draw from these first five chapters? The sample company can, by investing in continuous improvement projects, generate enough cash to buy competitors to increase market share or invest in coverage to increase market share.

The remaining chapters of this book are provided to give you more detail about things you can build into your company culture to develop the very best businessmen and businesswomen to staff a rapidly growing company.

6

Empowering
Employee Teams

SEVEN REALITIES TO INTERNALIZE

To support my claim that your company's personnel can double your ROA over the next three to five years, I will lay out some concepts as if I were presenting a training program to some employees. I would start by helping them improve their "Profit Ability" the first day they start making the smallest decisions in your company. As you read through this basic new-employee indoctrination, you may realize that many of your managers and key decision makers also need to be reminded and convinced of the truth of these seven conceptual facts.

Your employee training manual and training course might look something like the contents of this book.

Reality #1: Every Employee at Every Level Makes Decisions Every Hour That Increase or Decrease the Financial Value of One of the Seven Business Financial Elements

My mission is to transfer from my mind to the minds of your employees what I have learned through practical application of these financial realities. What I have documented in this book is what I wish someone had taught myself and my coworkers about the few things on which to concentrate our creativity very early in our business careers when our Profit Ability was very limited. We could have made the business to which we had committed ourselves much more profitable if our employer had handed us this book to read and follow as a condition of employment.

Reality #2: Employees Must Commit Themselves to Four Different Sets of Bosses for Their On-the-Job Education

These four sets are:

- *The person who hired you and your peers.* They can teach you everything they have learned in the business world. There's nothing like on-the-job training from your boss and peers to bring theory into practice.

- *The stockholders of the business,* who have invested a lot of money to provide you with a job. In the sample company example in Chapter 5, line 21 it states that the sample company invested about $140,000 to provide a job for each of its 70 employees. They've invested in your future before you even arrived. Why shouldn't you invest yourself in *their* future?

- *Customers* are really important too. Without them you wouldn't have any company income. It seems logical that your customers will expect you to improve your quality, customer service, and on-time delivery, shorten lead times, and keep price increases at a rate slower than inflation. You also have internal customers who expect the same things from you, their internal supplier.

- Another "boss" is *yourself and your career.* For practical purposes, you are a business. You should have your own set of verb/phrase combinations for your future. Don't waste your career at a place that doesn't value you enough to train and empower you. Your salary and benefits represent the sales of your personal business. Hopefully, you are controlling your personal expenses so you end up with money you can invest in stocks of other businesses.

Reality #3: Most of the Knowledge Found in This Book Is Already in the Minds of Your Personnel and Procedure Manuals

What is probably missing is that your accumulated knowledge isn't organized into a logical process. You may not have a process to focus procedures and knowledge resources on how to discover and evaluate continuous improvement projects found in the seven partitions of your continuous improvement treasure chest. Start with this book and fit the puzzle pieces into a picture that looks the way you want your specific company to be organized.

Reality #4: Few Companies Can Expect to Maximize Profitability without Harnessing the Creative Profit Ability of Employees at Every Level

This reality implies that a process needs to be designed and employees need to be trained to implement profitable continuous improvement. This concept also implies that team training may be one the first training investments necessary to accelerate implementation of improvement projects.

Reality #5: Many Company Personnel, Including Owners, Managers, and Supervisors, Don't Pursue Change

For many, change is a scary, unwelcome practice. This book should convince your personnel that the right kind of purposeful change is much more fun than the status quo. Sometimes top-level managers may not want to see the current culture change. Your mission, for the good of your business, is to convince your personnel and managers that applying this book to your business will result in much less work, much more fun, and much greater financial rewards than you and they could previously imagine.

Reality #6: Every Companywide Continuous Improvement Project Requires an Assigned Change Agent

This individual doesn't have to be a high-level member of management if top management is actively committed to the continuous improvement process. What you need is at least one individual who is equipped by experience and leadership to clarify why management and other personnel should be dissatisfied with the profit results of the current business (even if performance is the best it's ever been) and excite them about the certainty of continuous profitability improvement if the change process is implemented. For practical purposes, this book functions as a change agent by attempting to make you dissatisfied with the current situation and excite you about how much better the changed situation will be.

Reality #7: Money and Key Knowledge Resources Must Be Invested in Every Phase of the Economic Business Cycle or You Won't Get Maximum Results for Continuous Sales and Profitability Improvement

You've already read about how all businesses experience an economic business cycle every three to five years. High ROA and net profit are relatively easy to achieve at the peak of the business cycle when capital equipment and facilities are heavily utilized. In the valley of the business cycle the opposite is true. The ROA and net profit will be lower because capital investments aren't highly utilized.

Therefore, to maximize ROA increases throughout the business cycle, money and knowledge resource investment must be made throughout each year of the business cycle to permanently increase market share every year and to improve the other seven financial areas every year. In other words, every month of every year continuous improvement projects must be implemented on a planned schedule and must be completed on time.

It may be a big cultural change for your investors to give the same commitment to continuous improvement when sales are at their peak and you are tempted to transfer key knowledge resources to get products or services to customers on time. That's why you need to invest in dedicated people you keep assigned to improvement teams in all phases of the business cycle.

GET THE MOST OUT OF EMPLOYEE ASSETS

Note to top management and stockholders: one of the goals of our verb/noun continuous improvement process is to train and empower employees to become better businessmen and businesswomen so that as your business generates enough excess cash to expand your products, market segments, and distribution channels, or to acquire new businesses, you will have managers and knowledge resources ready to meet the demands of both the current and new business.

Measure Employee Value

It may seem to you that this book wants to put a dollar value on almost everything. That's the truth. It's easy to show employees as a dollar expense in your budget or on your profit and loss statement. It's not possible to put a dollar value for your employee assets on your balance sheet, although sometimes you may say your employees are your most valuable asset.

You can certainly claim you are making an investment in your employees when you provide training for them, even though you may not currently have a way to prove that you actually got a good return on your training investment.

However, as I have said before in this book, employee value can be measured when, as a whole, the percentage for total salary and wage expenses per sales dollar gets smaller from year to year and from business cycle to business cycle. This doesn't mean you arbitrarily cut everyone's pay. It means you will individually pay each of them higher wages to retain your investment in their knowledge inventory. You can use this same measure to motivate them with financial incentives based on decreased salary and wage costs and/or on increased ROA. (See Employee Gain Sharing Incentives later in this chapter.)

Therefore, the measure we propose is the companywide percent of total annual salaries and wages divided by your annual sales.

If for each of the last several years you calculate the percent of total salaries and wages divided by sales, you may see a similar percent for each year or you may see a trend that is getting larger or smaller. You may see the percentage rise and fall as you go through each business cycle. Using this percent, every employee will be able to put a dollar value on their overall total performance and determine whether there is a good reason for the stability or trend. It will also give them an improvement target as a companywide team. You should publish it monthly.

Every competitive sports team has a way to measure its team performance. This published performance measure will make employment more of a game by giving your company teams one way to document their part in the continuous improvement effort.

To cut the percent of total annual salaries and wages divided by annual sales by one-third its current value isn't an unreasonable target.

Bring out the Best in People Through Empowerment

Once you've decided to discover projects, and have decided to identify and name them with verb/noun combinations, it becomes obvious that an investment in many employee teams will be required to implement projects as quickly as possible. Chapter 5 shows a simple way to evaluate and prioritize projects to increase your company's ROA the most and the quickest. In each section of this chapter, I want to provide you with some basics required to unleash the knowledge and creativity of your employees to get the most out of each of them and each project.

As a result of applying this book, each employee will become an excellent businessman and businesswoman. You will also discover some excellent leaders as you empower them by delegating more and more financial responsibility through project teams and their Profit Ability.

TEAM BUILDING

I have used training material from www.gilbreaths.com for this section of the book.

Use Project Teams to Manage Change

If you implement the concepts and principles included in this book, you will need to empower teams. Your company and your employees will experience significant cultural change.

Natural change agents, or project champions, intuitively know how to bring about change. They start by making people dissatisfied with how things are currently. Then they get people excited about the way things can become. That's what I've attempted to do in this book. I'm trying to make you dissatisfied with your ROA over the past several years and excite you about the probability that your current level can be more than doubled.

Ronald Reagan was an effective change agent. In his campaign for president, he created dissatisfaction by saying our nation was in an "economic quagmire." He wanted to make us dissatisfied with the current situation. He then held out hope that economic change would give the economy a "firm footing." The emphasis was on the positive changes, with just the right blend of dissatisfaction to keep us moving forward. He used the same change agent tools to make people in the Soviet Union our allies by making "tear down the Berlin wall" a symbol of the change the two nations must make.

This section provides tools for employees to bring about change more smoothly. Whether your company is small, medium, or large, you will need multiple change agents and champions to inspire others to get on and stay on the road to measurable improvement and excellence.

Use Project Teams to Excite Employees About Going to Work

There are few things better than having fun at your job and having a measurable sense of accomplishment each day. This comes from knowing that when you discover things that can be done more profitably, you have a chance to contribute the idea and champion it as your own, or pass it on to a more appropriate team. And from getting personal recognition from your peers and internal customers for discovering an idea that makes their job more effective or more enjoyable.

There's something special and valuable about receiving recognition from your peers when you can make their job easier and more productive. That's one of my definitions of empowerment. However, your company must customize a definition of empowerment that fits your company culture and your combination of personalities.

If employees haven't experienced empowerment before, they need an idea about how it feels, what to do differently, and how it will be defined within your company. They need to know about the responsibilities of delegation and what the limits may be. Empowerment and delegation are two things employees must customize for themselves. I simply remind you to discuss it among yourselves or contact a consultant for help if you're not certain about your conclusions.

Since employee training from each chapter of this book results in interaction among employees, the training itself and the implementation of projects can serve as the change agent and give employees a feel for what it's like to function in a team.

Build a Coaching Staff from your Best Knowledge Resources

Use the verb/noun combinations in Chapter 3 to take an inventory of your knowledge resources. You will be pleasantly surprised at how much knowledge you have at your disposal that is underutilized. Every professional team has a coaching staff. It isn't unusual that one of the players also acts as a coach. With a coaching leadership style, like a professional sports team, you also create an atmosphere of excellence by trying to beat past records.

For employee empowerment and delegation, using project teams to yield the greatest financial results, managers and supervisors will need to give up some of their power and control. This will be a big change for some. At the very beginning of the change process, it will be wise for managers and supervisors to evaluate themselves to decide if this change will be so dramatic or traumatic they will no longer enjoy their job. The same applies to employees who feel intimidated by this kind of change. There will be some few people who just won't fit into the new culture, though some of these employees may have been very loyal in the past. We encourage you to consider these possibilities in advance.

Treat Team Building As Continuing Education

If most of your employees haven't participated in project teams before, you need to consider, as a minimum, investing in training about the basic mechanics required for teams to be most effective. You may want to incorporate one of your small verb/noun projects into each basic training session. This allows team members to get some hands-on training and, at the same time, pay for the training investment with an implemented project.

Also, consider making team training part of the indoctrination of all new employees. Your interviewing process for new employees, at every level, should discover whether potential new employees will contribute to the team effort and whether they will actually fill gaps in knowledge found in your knowledge inventory.

Interviewing is particularly critical if you decide to hire a new manager or supervisor rather than promote from within. After you have taken the patterns from this book and have customized them to fit your own current and future company culture, you won't want a new manager to arbitrarily make changes without financially evaluating the change. And, if you truly believe in your ability to double or triple your ROA, or have proven by experience that it is working, you might want to require potential new managers to commit to the current pattern until they can use the project evaluation process in Chapter 5 to prove that their ideas will increase the ROA percent faster than existing ranked projects.

After you start implementing the suggestions in this book, and as you go into team-building training of current employees, you need to include training from some of the chapters in this book. One goal of this book is to provide project teams with a reference to help continuously identify new projects and to maintain basic principles and concepts so that projects will be kept in the best sequence.

Hopefully, you will take the many patterns included in the book and rewrite them to include the vocabulary of your own company. After all, I learned them from some other teacher or from the scar tissue of experience. Each chapter includes knowledge I wish someone had taught me when I was first hired into a business. Henry Ford once said, "Working in a business is the best school for business people. The only problem is that its graduates are too old to practice." Don't let that happen to you no matter what your age.

A Pattern for Your Team-Building Training

In this section I won't attempt to go into great detail about team building. I will only give you a brief summary of things included in a course conducted by one training consultant.

There are certain dynamics that take place in a team environment, particularly in team meetings. Personality traits are displayed that might seldom be seen in normal day-to-day discussions. Normal day-to-day discussions and problem solving between two or three people are often extemporaneous and don't require a lot of preparation or formal presentation of facts. These types of discussions aren't usually designed to cause significant change or to implement significant improvements in ROA.

In general, a training pattern for team building should include a few basic considerations:

- You will want to know enough about various types of teams so that you can customize the training to focus on projects that will be generated by your inventory of prioritized projects.

- Your training needs to allow room for short training courses about specific knowledge that is new to most team members. This happens when you have a project generated by the verb/noun process and you answer, "I don't know *how*."

- Team participants will want to make meetings as short as practical by following a pattern about how to conduct an effective meeting. Planning by using an agenda is the best time-saver to practice. Another time-saver is preparation. Have team members gather and organize facts in advance of team meetings. Having the appropriate facts on the table always speeds up team consensus. Meeting planning also contributes to the most effective participation by team members.

- Document the meetings with minutes to make it much easier to draw conclusions for follow-up, such as assignments to be completed before the next meeting.

Investing in Team Projects and Scheduling Project Completions

Controlling a great number of projects and getting them implemented on time isn't much different than scheduling customer orders and shop orders. All required operations need a start date and the investment in adequate human and equipment resources to complete each project step by its due date.

Unfortunately, almost every business that decides to implement improvement projects fails to invest in enough additional human and knowledge resources to get enough of the vast number of projects implemented week in and week out. Managers somehow imagine that the current key knowledge resources can just implement the projects in their spare time.

However, as production control is used to schedule and ship customer orders on time, project control is required to complete projects on time. Every project is like a customer order your customer wants delivered on a specific date. Therefore, project team leaders should insist that the project be started on time and that each project design and implementation step be started on a specified date. Then, as with material control for expediting product schedules, extra hours, or paralleling and overlapping of project steps, can be triggered when projects fall behind schedule. Paralleling for project teams could include breaking the team into parts so several steps can be performed during the same time period.

EMPLOYEE GAIN SHARING INCENTIVES

Earlier in this chapter, I encouraged you to measure employee utilization using the percent ratio of total salaries and wages divided by sales. I also stated that a 33 percent improvement in the ratio is a reasonable expectation. This is an excellent measure currently used by many profitable companies to compensate employees for their extra effort and creativity to make the company more profitable more quickly. In the industry it is commonly known as *gain sharing* or *the Scanlon plan*.

This chapter wouldn't be complete if I didn't share this powerful tool with you. It's the incentive pay plan I would use if I were going to implement the culture presented in this book.

You aren't likely to double or triple ROA if employees don't put forth extra effort and creativity to discover projects that will allow you to increase sales without adding a proportional number of new people. It is less likely that employees will risk their jobs if they don't stand a chance of sharing in the rewards.

The reason I suggest the measurement of total salaries and wages divided by sales is because, as a group, total salaries and wages is one of the few things over which employees have complete control. It gives them incentive to implement projects that contribute to sales growth, because greater sales help absorb current employees as they perform more efficiently. Initiation of an incentive pay system works best when sales are increasing from one business cycle to the next as a result of increased market share.

Incentive systems should be designed to get employees to do what management and stockholders want them to do. Therefore it's logical that you would also want to include an increase of average ROA percent over an entire business cycle as a part of the performance measurement.

The Incentive Calculation

Incentive bonuses are most effective when paid as frequently as practical, such as monthly. In a nutshell, the monthly incentive pay should be established by setting as the base a business cycle historic percent of annual salaries and wages divided by sales. An incentive bonus should be paid each month, based on a percent of the amount total salaries and wages are less than the monthly sales multiplied by the historical base percent. A portion of the employee bonus is reserved each month in case there are months when a bonus isn't earned. At the end of each year, the bonus for the year is calculated and the reserve is used to compensate the company for months in which the bonus is negative. If the reserve is a positive number, a year-end bonus is paid. There are a variety of alternatives and refinements your company can incorporate into this incentive plan to make it do what you want done.

A company can't lose money on this plan because if there are no savings there is no bonus payment. The primary reasons it fits so well with the concepts promoted in this book are:

- It accelerates the implementation of profit-improving projects, increasing the number of projects implemented.

- It reduces scrap and rework because, as soon as the incentive system is initiated, employees realize that they provide the labor cost to replace or rework defective parts.

- Inventory will come down more rapidly because employees will be directly compensated for reducing setup or changeover labor costs (both direct and indirect).

- Since labor costs will be reduced more than 25 percent, it can be anticipated that 25 percent more sales can be absorbed without making additional capital investment to provide the needed capacity. In other words, 25 percent more capital assets are made available to stockholders at no cost.

- As projects to reduce lead times are implemented, the reduced lead time almost always reduces people time and increases sales due to better on-time delivery.

- As inventory is reduced by reduced setup costs and shorter, more consistent lead times, less labor and space are required to store the required inventory.

- As employees are empowered and trained to make better financial decisions, fewer supervisors and managers are required and can be reassigned to provide the knowledge resources for more project teams.

- As projects are implemented to improve the material control or scheduling control system, fewer people will be needed for expediting.

- Employee conversations on and off the job will be about creative ways to eliminate costs and increase sales.

7

More About Project Evaluation and Ranking

In Chapter 5 I provided a sample form to determine if and how much a given project will increase the base ROA percent. In this chapter I make a few more statements that I believe will be helpful in ranking projects.

USING PROFITABILITY TO PRIORITIZE PROJECTS

As you realize the large number of projects you will discover, and how many teams will be working at any given time, you will realize that you need a simple approach to decide which projects will increase your ROA the most and the quickest.

By documenting the ROA percent increase, management can prioritize the inventory of projects to determine which ones have the resources available for implementation.

You don't need accounting precision for the dollar values you enter into this form. You are just using it as a guide to compare one project with another and to verify whether a project will increase rather than reduce the current ROA.

Each year your accountant will update the form by entering new numbers in each of the lines that include the word "base." The base values for each line can be an average of the last three to five years of your most recent business cycle. These numbers will stay the same all year because they will be the basis upon which project teams evaluate their proposed projects and submit them for approval by a designated company leader or committee. This leader or committee should maintain an inventory of projects by project group, in priority order, and should compare each new project with those waiting to be assigned to see where each new project should be placed in priority sequence.

USE OF ACTUAL CONFIDENTIAL FINANCIAL NUMBERS

Most company stockholders treat financial numbers as confidential information and want to minimize the number of employees who know actual sales and profitability. However, for project teams to be most effectively empowered, some financial information needs to be revealed in some form and in some detail.

Enough financial information needs to be made available to project teams so that they can financially compare one project with another or to make a project proposal. One way is to provide appropriate proportionally understated or overstated financial numbers for project teams to use and inform the teams that the information is for project evaluation only.

Information for the form needs to be accurate enough to make correct prioritization decisions. This is a communications issue that will be more transparent as you implement more projects.

If management is totally opposed to revealing financial data to teams, designate a person who has the financial facts and have them use the Project Evaluation Form to rank projects.

USING YOUR COMPANY'S BUSINESS CYCLE TO TIME PROJECT IMPLEMENTATION

I believe that projects should be prioritized by ROA and payout period measurements so that projects can be implemented every year, even in the valley of a business cycle. That's why you should use your own business cycle as a decision-making tool.

For example, a project might require no new investment because the team members are already on the payroll and can do the implementation as a normal part of their workweek. These projects can be implemented immediately or can be saved to be implemented during the recession phase of the business cycle.

Another similar example might require the time and knowledge of a direct worker. In this case, part of the investment would be the cost of another direct worker to do this team member's job. Or, in the case of a design engineer, the investment could be the profit lost because of the delay in the design or testing of a new product. These are additional reasons for you to purposefully budget specific numbers of personnel to concentrate long periods of time on implementing the highest-ranked projects.

Another project might require capital investment for new production equipment. If this project is discovered as the business is going into a recession cycle, it can be delayed until capital money is more freely available just ahead of the growth phase. Over the long haul, your projects should be generating enough cash that the timing of capital investments will be less critical.

MAKE USE OF THE 80/20 RULE

You will find that 80 percent of the ROA increase will come from 20 percent of the projects. Usually, this 20 percent of projects will require three to four years to pay back the investment and will be the projects you should try to implement just ahead of the growth phase of your business cycle. The other projects, the 80 percent that will produce 20 percent of the ROA increase, will usually have payback periods of less than one year.

8

Projects to Reduce Total Expense per Sales Dollar

Financial facts from your accounting function are some of the most important tools your continuous improvement teams will use. It's like the facts shown in your personal checkbook, which is essentially a combination profit and loss statement to list expenses and a balance sheet to show your cash asset balance.

A FEW ACCOUNTING TRUTHS

I will provide your employees with a simplified version of typical formulas and principles they need to discover and evaluate improvement projects. Some of these accounting truths will be a repeat or expansion of what has already been said in previous pages.

Truth #1: Discovery of Continuous Improvement Projects, and Their Analysis and Evaluation, Don't Require Normal Accounting Precision

Accounting is a precise activity which, for legal reasons, requires great accuracy. Most improvement projects won't require that precision. Most projects will require estimates of future events and a variety of accounting information drawn from accounting budget line items. Once a project idea is defined, these estimates can be refined as more facts are gathered.

We encourage accountants to participate on teams to improve the integrity of these estimates. The project itself will raise a flag as more and more facts are required. As the project is being designed and as its implementation is being planned, you will know whether more accurate numbers are needed.

Truth #2: Seven Financial Formulas Are Used to Understand the Evaluation Process for Projects, Their Actual Profitability Results, and to Measure Year-to-Year Overall Performance

Net Profit. In its most simple format, the annual profit and loss (P&L) statement can be broken into three main parts: sales, expenses, and profit.

#1   Sales dollars – Expense dollars = Net profit dollars
#2   Net profit dollars ÷ Sales dollars = Net profit percent

This arithmetic shows that to improve profitability, sales must be increased and expenses must be reduced.

Net profit can be expressed as before taxes or after taxes. Most businesses pay over 40 percent of their profit in taxes. For project team purposes, it is preferable for you to include some or all taxes as an expense in the P&L because some of the taxes will decrease as you reduce inventory investment and because there may be a misconception by employees about how much profit the stockholders are receiving if all tax expenses aren't included.

Gross Profit. Three major expenses for manufacturers are *MLO expenses* (material, direct labor, and manufacturing overhead). MLO expenses are often called the *cost of sales* or the *cost of goods sold.*

#3   Gross profit dollars = Sales dollars – MLO dollars
#4   Gross profit percent = Gross profit dollars ÷ Sales dollars

Gross profit is an important tool for manufacturing project teams. It shows which product lines or product models contribute the most to the net profit of the business. It may tell you which products are designed best so you can apply those design and processing techniques to products with a low gross profit. Or, it may tell you which products should be improved or removed from the product line because their gross profit percent is too low.

The gross profit percent is usually a fairly large percent because most of a company's manufacturing overhead costs are included. As you can see, if you increase your selling prices, gross profit increases. Or, if you reduce MLO costs, gross profit also increases.

Gross profit percent is important to know if teams decide to create a project to find any current products or market segments that, if eliminated, would result in an increased ROA. One project might be to segregate products and market segments into appropriate groups and compare the gross profit for each group. This analysis might prompt you to raise the price of some product lines before you arbitrarily decide to eliminate the product line. The analysis might also tell you which critical product lines need cost reduction or redesign investment. By using the 80/20 rule, it might also tell you from which of the market segments you might get the greatest return on an investment by investing in greater market coverage.

Return on Assets (ROA). This profitability formula is critical as a project ranking tool. It forces project teams to consider the impact that any project will have on the increase or decrease in the ROA percent. Obviously, you won't have a profitable project if it increases the net profit percent but causes a reduction in the ROA percent. For this book's purposes, only assets for inventory, capital assets, and accounts receivable are considered.

#5   ROA percent = Net profit dollars ÷ Asset investment

Continuous ROA improvement is the best performance measurement for the overall continuous improvement program, as well as a measure of how well the companywide program has minimized asset investment.

Profit and Loss Statement Performance Measurement. You're relatively sure that cost reduction has done its part if the net profit percent is continuously increasing over each consecutive economic business cycle. Two other broad measures are needed to assure that the two main groups of P&L expenses are both showing improvement.

#6   Total salaries and wages ÷ Sales = Percent performance
                                    and
#7   Non-salary and wage expenses ÷ Sales = Percent performance

If one of these performance measures is outpacing the other, there's a good chance improvements are being missed within the lower-performing measure.

Truth #3: The Annual Budget Plan Is Primarily a Profit and Loss Statement in Its Most Detailed Format

Expenses for overhead are usually minutely detailed for each function or department. This is where project teams go to get cost reduction details to increase profitability.

The key is to discover projects that decrease total wages, salaries, and all other expenses per sales dollar.

In between the simple net profit formula and a very detailed annual budget, your project teams will need the accounting function to provide them with a profit and loss statement that will directly relate to the seven critical business elements I've been emphasizing. This can serve as your first cut at segregating expenses into a format that will facilitate project discovery in the seven areas and assure profitable projects. See the worksheets in Chapter 5 for gathering financial data.

Notice that the sample P&L statement in Figure 8.1 is designed to be an example for a manufacturing, distribution, or service business. The reason for using one example is to impress upon you that all businesses use similar financial information.

Each line will be expanded upon in the section following truth #5 in this chapter. For now, we want to tie the seven critical business elements in with the appropriate lines on this sample statement.

Line	Combination manufacturing/distribution/service profit and loss
1	Sales
2	Material or purchased product, including freight
3	Setup direct labor and/or purchase order setup costs
4	Direct labor applied to raw material or purchased parts
5	Manufacturing overhead or receiving/inspection overhead
6	Gross profit (Consider ranking by product lines or models)
7	Manufacturing indirect labor or distribution/service departmental payroll
8	Other manufacturing salaries or distribution/service payroll tax and fringes
9	Manufacturing non-salary expenses or distribution/service auto and travel
10	Total manufacturing expense or distribution/service sales non-salary expense
11	Sales and marketing salaries
12	Manufacturing product design expenses or distribution/service operating expenses
13	Appropriate sales, engineering, and administrative expenses
14	All SE&A overhead (excluding interest, taxes, depreciation, and amortization)
15	EBITDA/net profit or earnings before interest, taxes, depreciation, and amortization
16	Interest
17	Taxes
18	Depreciation
19	Amortization
20	Net profit after taxes

Figure 8.1 Sample profit and loss statement with expense categories.

- Obviously, we want line 1 (Sales) to be increasing from one business cycle to the next so that line 6 (Gross profit), line 15 (Net profit before taxes), and line 20 (Net profit after taxes), will continuously increase as you implement profitable projects.

- Lines 2 through 5 are categories of expenses that relate to purchased and manufactured products. You want to implement projects and practices that create reductions in these expenses so you can prove that gross profit is continuously increasing.

- Lines 7 through 10 are manufacturing-related expense categories for a manufacturer, distributor, or service business.

- Lines 11 through 14 are the unique expense categories for sales, engineering, and administrative expenses.

- Lines 16 through 19 are expenses that normally appear within other categories in the P&L. The reason I've structured the P&L this way is so I can show you later in Chapter 13 how the EBITDA (earnings before interest, taxes, depreciation, and amortization) can be used to set a market value for your business or a competitor's business that you might buy. You also want to separate out expenses for interest, taxes, and depreciation. I will show you how interest and taxes will drop as the inventory investment goes down. I will also show you how depreciation expenses may go up as you add new equipment to reduce setup costs that drive inventory investment down, and how depreciation expense goes down as you more effectively utilize capital investment.

Truth #4: For a Continuous Improvement Program, Only Four Asset Investments Need to Be Used in the ROA Formula

The four asset investments project teams need to focus on to improve the ROA percent are:

- *Work-in-process inventory investment,* which is cut by reducing manufacturing and paperwork lead time.

- *Product and component inventory investment,* which is cut by reducing setup costs.

- *Capital investment,* which is minimized by increasing the utilization rate of equipment and facilities.

- *Accounts receivable investment,* which is minimized by controlling the number of days a customer takes to pay an invoice after the customer order is shipped.

Truth #5: The 80/20 Rule Is a Good Tool to Use to Analyze the Facts Related to Projects and to Decide on Which to Concentrate

Some examples will explain how to use this tool:

- 80 percent of sales come from 20 percent of products or models.
- 80 percent of sales come from 20 percent of market segments.
- 80 percent of setup costs come from 20 percent of components.
- 80 percent of a manufacturer's component inventory is made up of 20 percent of the inventory items.

SEGREGATING BUDGET LINE ITEMS

Segregating sales and budget expenses into logical categories is a good tool for getting at facts needed by project teams. This process is an expansion of truths #3 and #5. In this section I will dramatize what a great source the annual budget plan is for discovering numerical values for a massive number of projects that won't be discovered by more traditional analysis tools.

Many projects will be concentrated on cost reductions that may also result in investment reduction. That's why, in truth #3, we structured a P&L statement as a pattern to help you identify groups of expenses that will help you discover projects or understand calculations I will show you in other places in this book.

Identifying the 20 percent of production machines that account for 80 percent of depreciation cost will help you determine if the most expensive equipment is being heavily utilized to maximize the ROA.

Segregate material and supplies costs to determine if a slight increase in material or supplies costs, to utilize material with less variation, might result in lower labor and reject costs.

Taxes and insurance for real estate, capital equipment, and inventory need to be investigated and/or included in the cost analysis of some projects.

These segregated groups are where the 80/20 rule should be used aggressively to provide employee teams with facts that will take the guesswork out of which projects are the best.

The cost that is usually most dominant is the total cost of employee salaries and wages. It is so important that I have suggested in truth #2 that a performance measurement be tracked to compare the year-to-year trend of total annual salary and wage costs divided by annual sales.

The segregation of salary and wage costs is also a powerful revealer of project opportunities. Salary and wage expenses should be segregated by departments or business functions, including use of the 80/20 rule, to analyze specific functions to discover projects.

Since at this point in the book I am leading you into improvement project discovery that impacts the seven key financial areas, we will go through the P&L statement in Figure 8.1 line by line to clarify the expense segregation process.

Line 1. Segregate product lines or models to find the 20 percent of models that make up 80 percent of your sales. This analysis coupled with line 6 will likely trigger some ideas about which products you might consider eliminating or which products you will take through a redesign project.

The marketing function might want to segregate sales by market segment or distribution channel to discover things to discontinue or places to expand to increase sales by increasing the market coverage elements covered in Chapter 13.

These facts will cause you to see things you never saw before about your business. Your goal is to determine the quickest and easiest way to increase sales in one or more of the segregated groups and then estimate the increase in ROA percent as a way to compare these potential projects with others that may be focused on cost reduction or inventory reduction.

Line 2. A manufacturer can segregate raw materials to identify the 20 percent of raw material categories that account for 80 percent of the total raw material requirements. You might consider doing this analysis within different categories. For example, you might analyze castings as one category and bar stock as another category. You might look for opportunities to standardize on fewer materials or find ways to reduce your raw material inventory by negotiating shorter lead times on your most frequently used materials.

For distributors, the purchased products are the raw material and may or may not require some labor or material to make them usable for individual customers. To counteract the additional freight expense and erratic lead times resulting from offshore sourcing, you may want to segregate freight from purchased product cost.

Line 3. Verify whether setup labor is treated as direct or indirect labor. Manufacturers need to track what percent of total direct labor is setup labor because reducing this overall percent is one of the primary reasons for setup reduction and lean cell design.

Setup cost for each component can be an average of the setup cost from several most recent shop orders.

Distributors should segregate costs related to purchase orders because reducing these costs financially justifies smaller lot sizes and a lower inventory investment.

Line 4. This is direct labor that manufacturers call "run time." For distributors it is usually the cost for components or products sold. This part of the cost is normally treated as a constant no matter what the lot size. In practice, the average unit run time or purchased item cost usually becomes less as lot sizes are increased. The total cost of each manufactured component is the average setup cost divided by the lot size plus the run cost.

Line 5. For manufacturers, this is usually the overhead that is only related to the direct labor departments, depending on how your annual budget is formatted. If direct labor departments have their own budgets, this budget will likely include salaries and wages for personnel who directly support the processing of material, supplies used within the department, plus depreciation on the capital assets used to manufacture the components. Many of these costs will decrease as you define projects to reduce setup time and lead time.

For distribution and service businesses, this could include the overhead expense for receiving incoming shipments and receiving inspection functions.

Line 6. Gross profit may not normally appear on your P&L. It's included in this pattern because I suggest that you rank the product line and models you segregate in line 1 so you can discover the products or models you might consider eliminating. Alternatively, you might consider raising their prices, even if that would make them less competitive for some customers.

Line 7. For manufacturers, indirect labor should be significantly reduced as you define projects to shorten lead time, move toward arranging for purchased components to be inspected at the source, minimize in-process inspection, reduce the number of components for which you need to maintain inventory, eliminate expediting, and many other improvements discovered in the verb/noun project discovery process.

Distribution and service businesses can use this line to segregate department-by-department payroll.

Line 8. You should segregate all other manufacturing salaries. As you empower employees and minimize expediting, you will need fewer supervisors and support personnel. These supervisory and support employees can be much more valuable by investing their time in project discovery and implementation.

For distribution and service business, this line can be used to segregate payroll costs in line 7 from payroll taxes and fringes.

Line 9. For manufacturers this line is similar to line 5. It includes everything left over from the manufacturing budget that isn't included above. As you check through these leftovers, consider whether something is left over that should have been included in one of the previous lines. You might add lines to your customized P&L pattern if it will aid project discovery or project evaluation.

Distribution and service businesses can use this line for other major cost categories such as auto and travel expenses. Even these expenses can be broken down and grouped into other categories such as foreign travel by sales and purchasing personnel.

Line 10. This is the total of lines 2 through 9 for a manufacturing business. For a distribution or service business, it can serve as another category that might be significant in an individual business.

Line 11. You may want to expand this line to separate field or branch sales personnel from those who process sales orders in the home or branch office. If you maintain a customer service, product repair, or spare parts service, you will also likely want to segregate it out. If you have field sales offices, you may want to show their salaries and overhead on separate lines.

Line 12. Manufacturers can segregate engineering salaries by new product design, processing engineering changes, customer service, or product testing. As project teams in these functions segregate their expenses, they will discover many ways to do the routine things with less time and expense so they can focus more time on projects that will reduce product processing costs, setup costs, and lead time. Shortening paperwork and information processing lead time in these areas should be a major contributor to increased sales and reduced inventory investment.

A distribution or service business may have functions that don't fit any of the preceding categories.

Line 13. Break out these salaries into additional lines, depending on how your annual budget is broken down. Be sure personnel in these departments are generating projects that will increase the ROA and provide shorter lead times for internal customers.

Line 14. Study these budget line items to identify the 20 percent of expenses that make up 80 percent of the total expense so you can discover ways to reduce them. For example, one of the reasons you lower your inventory carrying costs and lower your purchase order setup costs is to have smaller lot sizes so that you can lower local or state taxes on your inventory assets.

Line 15. This line applies if your stockholders want to place a value on your business or another business they want to buy.

Line 16. You will generate considerable cash as you increase your ROA. Interest costs will just disappear as your need to borrow money becomes less.

Line 17. Tax included on this line is the tax your accountant will include to establish after-tax net profit.

Line 18. The only time project teams are going to have a chance to impact depreciation expense is when a project recommends disposing of underutilized equipment and facilities or when a project can justify the investment in additional capital assets.

Line 19. Amortization expense will be of minimal interest to most project teams. It is an annual expense shown on the P&L statement and balance sheet for such things as setting aside funds in advance to pay off a debt before maturity or writing off obsolete inventory over a period of more than one year. It will have minimal impact on the average ROA over a three- to five-year business cycle.

Line 20. This line represents the annual cash generated after all expenses, including all taxes.

Note: The primary mission of the accounting function is to provide accurate information for the company employees, knowledge workers, and managers, so that they can keep the profit and loss statement and the balance sheet in financial balance.

LEAN WASTE DISCOVERY

Lean manufacturing is part of lean enterprise, a product of the Manufacturing Extension Partnership (MEP). MEP is part of the National Institute of Standards and Technology, an agency of the U.S. Commerce Department. If you go to its Web site, www.mep.nist.gov, you will find that MEP promotes strategic business planning, quality systems, marketing, and human resources to increase profitability.

The verb/noun process to discover projects in the seven key business areas was not designed to match what MEP does as a government agency.

The mission of this book is to look at every function of a business through a financial lens. Where appropriate, I encourage you to focus on the lean concepts that aren't traditionally incorporated into the culture of your business.

Advice from some Authors of Lean Thinking

The authors of MEP's value stream mapping resources warn against plunging into waste reduction projects without first converting your manufacturing process from mass production to continuous flow. They say, "To reduce the lead time from raw material to finished goods, you need to do more than try to eliminate obvious waste. Too many lean implementation efforts have been waste scavenger hunts. While it is good to be aware of waste, future continuous flow process designs need to eliminate the sources or causes of waste in the old value stream. Once the problem of mass production can be seen in a way that reveals these root causes, your company can work at finding original solutions."

Wastes and Their Root Causes

This step helps identify the various categories of non-value-added wastes that are present in your company. It will give you checklists of potential causes from which you can create verb/noun combinations to name projects. Every observed cause of waste in your company should signal the need to name and define a project.

General Causes of Waste

Overproduction is to produce more of something earlier than is required by the next process. It applies to the purchase or manufacture of components you are forced to make ahead of the receipt of a customer order because of lead times and setup cost issues.

That's why a material control system similar to the one described in Chapter 11 is critical to maximize ROA. Material control, coupled with lead time and setup cost reduction, can control causes of overproduction.

There should be no overproduction in the component manufacturing area if you do everything you can to reduce setup costs, have a formula to calculate financially sound lot sizes, and reorder components no earlier than required.

Even though the causes of overproduction described in lean courses are primarily discussed in terms of mass production and continuous-flow operations, you should look at them for potential projects and in instances when you may be forced to use one of them in your job shop operations.

Just-in-case logic implies that your system doesn't provide acceptable controls. When this logic is used frequently, you've identified an important project. There may be occasions, such as a potential strike at a supplier's plant or the installation of equipment in your plant, when temporary early production of the related components might be a sound business decision.

Misuse of automation refers to overproduction waste that occurs when large setup costs force large lot sizes.

Long process setup implies large lot sizes. The resulting inventory will cause financial wastes.

Un-level scheduling implies that, over the whole mass production process flow, more is made sooner than required at one of the process islands. This cause of waste will disappear when a well balanced continuous-flow process is implemented. It also hints at poor utilization of capital assets.

Unbalanced workload is a cause that can exist in a mass production island that causes un-level scheduling. It can exist in a continuous-flow process if each process that makes one and passes one to the next step isn't properly designed.

Overengineering can exist in the product design and process design phases, depending on your definition of overengineering and whether it causes overproduction.

Redundant inspections may cause overproduction because this activity must have its own wasteful inventory in order for the work to be done. If you eliminate unnecessary non-value-added inspections, a probable waste in itself, you also eliminate the wasted inventory investment and the costs resulting from carrying the inventory. How many other redundant activities might you discover that are adding non-value-added cost and investment?

Waiting Waste

Waiting waste is relatively easy to discover and quantify. At various times you just take a mental photo of your assembly area, paperwork flow, or inactive shop and office people. Another example is customers standing in queue at a service counter. You count the number of people who aren't doing productive, value-adding work. It's easy to detect when an assembly line isn't flowing smoothly due to the following root causes. These same causes for waiting waste can occur in your component manufacturing area but have a different impact and need a different kind of project to eliminate them. When you look at the causes, compose a verb/noun combination to name a project. Then, when you evaluate the project for its ROA impact, you will be more likely to assign knowledgeable team members to it for implementation. Look for both people and equipment waiting.

Unbalanced workload, anywhere in the business, is an indication of poor planning on the part of all people in the company, at every level, particularly the people who are doing the waiting. If you empower your employees to recommend project ideas to eliminate the causes of waiting waste, it will be like discovering a new vein of ore in a gold mine. If you pay them an incentive bonus, as described in Chapter 6, much of the waiting waste will disappear without projects being formalized. Remember, planning is the least expensive form of control.

Unplanned maintenance is a financial crime committed against your stockholders, customers, and product quality. Your stockholders are robbed because preventive maintenance is the lowest-cost method to maintain equipment. Customers lose because unplanned maintenance results in missed delivery dates. Product and process quality lose because dimensional variation isn't held to a minimum, as you use preventive maintenance to control process capability.

Long process setup times are a cause of waiting waste. Expensive capital equipment must wait longer than necessary to get back into production. Long setup times also force people to wait, and force you to have more funds invested in capital equipment than will be necessary when you reduce your setup times.

Upstream quality problems result in waiting in both production and paperwork processes. This can result in unnecessary waiting by a customer needing service. In the component manufacturing area, it may cause missed delivery dates.

Un-level and unplanned scheduling can be a cause of waiting in a production or paperwork process. It is less likely when processes are designed around continuous-flow concepts. In the manufacturing area, look for poor schedule planning or poor management of a good scheduling system.

Failure to provide instructions should never be a cause for waiting. Think about the many times a supervisor, manager, or other decision maker has been tied up in a meeting, or is traveling, and you are waiting for a decision. This cause disappears as your employees are empowered to make more decisions at the lowest level. Let them make a few mistakes and learn from them. That's how each of us learned to make decisions more confidently.

Large staging areas are obvious clues that too much waiting has been designed into the process. Look for these staging areas and formalize a project to eliminate them. Think about how impressed you would be to go to a very busy doctor's office where there was very little waiting time after signing in. This also applies to unnecessary inventory, patiently waiting to be consumed, or material waiting in queue to be processed.

Transportation Waste

Transportation waste applies to production and office paperwork processes or a service business where customers are the product in the process. This waste and its causes relate to material handling activities as you move product and information within the lead time stream. Value stream mapping is described in Chapter 9. Product transportation is limited by speed limits to physically move materials, particularly by human operated wheeled equipment. Some of these limits can be overcome with automated equipment and conveyors and by reducing the total distance people and transport equipment travel each day. Fortunately, much of your information can travel by computer, at the speed of light, making distance a nonissue.

Poor plant and office layout and *poor understanding of continuous process flow* are causes of transportation waste. You have many crisscrossing travel lines and distances that are excessive. In office and paperwork layouts, a continuous-flow design will be an excellent tool to minimize this waste. Using the flowchart depicted in Figures 9.2 through 9.5, pages 106–16, you might want to look at your product flow from receiving dock to shipping dock and paperwork process flow from customer order receipt to invoice as areas in which to design two continuous-flow projects to see how transportation waste can be eliminated. Apply what you learn from the value stream mapping in Chapter 9.

Staging and holding areas and large lot sizes are a part of your product and paperwork transportation value stream. They require handling when material is moved in, plus handling as it is moved out. To eliminate transportation wastes, drastically reduce lot sizes and lead times so fewer and fewer components are required to be manufactured or purchased prior to the receipt of a customer order. This is an even more serious issue in your assembly area. Any time you see material being staged in your assembly area for long periods of time, it's a project crying out to be noticed. You will probably find it is an upstream material control problem caused by an inadequate material control system or a good control system being poorly executed.

Processing Wastes

Processing wastes are those activities that add no value to the product or service from the customer's point of view. These wastes occur in both manufacturing and office processes.

Failure to define true customer requirements is a cause of process and material waste. Defining exactly what the customer wants is the starting place in eliminating this waste and its causes. Be aware that you have both external and internal customers. Each group has high expectations so you must learn what it takes to satisfy each. Your external customers think it's a waste for you to provide product features they aren't willing to pay for, even if your engineers and sales people feel they need them. Your external customers want the lowest price, the required quality and dependability, and on-time delivery. That's also pretty much what your internal customers want, and have a right to expect. Anything less makes their job more difficult and less enjoyable.

Failure to coordinate product and process design is a waste you can eliminate at the product design stage. Coordinate the design of components with the appropriate manufacturing equipment that is capable of consistently holding the design tolerance. One major potential waste is then controlled. Six Sigma processes are good tools to use here.

Product changes without process changes is like the preceding cause of process waste. Obviously, a design change that doesn't get implemented by the appropriate process change isn't really a change.

Lack of communication or excessive communication are causes for processing waste as well as many other wastes such as waiting, excess inventory, defects, and underutilized people. If you distribute too many copies of a communication, someone has to read them and often get unnecessarily involved.

Redundant approvals are less likely to exist when your employees are empowered and adequately trained. Approval at the lowest level is the least expensive policy.

Redundant databases and related reentering of data are usually a result of a poorly designed data processing system, incomplete networking, or procedures that are poorly composed.

Inventory Waste

Inventory waste is defined in lean as, "Any quantity in excess of a one piece flow through your manufacturing process." This is a good definition if you implement lean to replace mass production with continuous flow. It is also a reasonable definition if all your processes, including component purchasing, require almost zero setup cost. The lean definition is very confusing to small or medium-sized manufacturers who are forced to release purchase orders and shop orders for components because their product cycle time (see Chapter 9) is longer than the lead time promised for new customer orders. Inventory can't correctly be termed a waste when it is required, under current lead time and lot size restrictions, to meet customer order delivery requirements. It would be more precise to identify setup costs as a primary waste that needs to be minimized so that less inventory investment will be required to meet customer delivery promises.

The misconception that inventory protects the company from inefficiencies and unexpected problems is a result of your personnel having inadequate knowledge about the reasons why you are forced to make an inventory investment and the kind of material control system you must use until you have dramatically reduced your lead times and setup costs.

Product complexity must be tempered by how accurately you define and design the products your customer wants. If the customer wants and is willing to pay for a complex product, and this forces you to maintain inventory to provide it, you're doing what is expected. You might be able to relieve product complexity issues by reconfiguring product bills of material to shorten the product's cycle time, as described in Chapter 9.

Un-leveled scheduling and unbalanced workload in mass production operations can be cured by converting to a continuous process flow. In component manufacturing operations, the best control is manufacturing capacity planning, described in Chapter 11 (blocks 7 and 12, page 169) about your material control system.

Poor market forecasting is a cause of excess inventory if you rely on forecasting as your method to determine future demand. I don't recommend that you place too much reliance on sales forecasts to forecast future product demand. If you have an aggressive sales force, you should expect their forecast plan to be greater than actual customer orders. Instead, you will be most accurate in your estimating of future demand if you rely on your usage rate from the most recent past (see Chapter 11).

Unreliable supplier shipments cause excess inventory. Unreliable on-time delivery is a symptom that a material control system isn't taking steps to control supplier lead time, including replacing suppliers who don't have short, predictable lead times.

Defect Waste

Defect waste can have many definitions. In a service business, it could be any service provided that doesn't meet customers' requirements. For components, it would be any design feature that falls outside the dimensional or specification tolerances. For paperwork and information processes, it is incorrect information or instructions, or incorrectly following documented procedures. The causes for defects are as varied as the places within a business where they occur too frequently.

Customer needs not matching product and process design is the birthplace for most defects and other wastes. It takes a project team made up of customers, product designers, process designers, suppliers, and sales personnel to implement a proper design process. When this cause for defects is eliminated, many of the other causes will disappear along with it.

Inadequate equipment and poor preventive maintenance are causes of defects related to product dimensions and specifications. Not only must customer requirements match with product and process design, but product design must match with the tolerance-holding capability of your equipment. In addition to minimizing downtime, the most important purpose of preventive maintenance is to maintain the dimension-holding capability of your equipment.

Eliminating poor quality, such as through implementing ISO 9000 specifications, is an activity that eliminates many other causes for defects, such as inadequate work instructions.

Inadequate education and training is a cause that can be eliminated by following my suggestions in Chapter 6 about getting the most out of your employee assets.

Motion Waste

Motion waste is any movement of people, product, paperwork, or machines that doesn't add value to your product or service. It can relate to the distance traveled by a person's hands, feet, or mind. This waste is related to waiting waste and transportation waste. Visually observe the layout of the entire facility, manufacturing and paperwork processing areas, or individual workstations in the shop or offices. Look for poor housekeeping or poor workplace organization in individual employees or groups of employees. It's very likely you will discover activities that, when eliminated, will reduce hidden setup costs or lead time. Motion, transportation, or waiting wastes, and their causes, such as the following, are things you might not think about if lean didn't suggest them:

- Poor people/machine interfaces

- Inconsistent work methods or inconsistently followed procedures

- Unfavorable facility or cell layout

- Poor workplace organization and housekeeping

- Extra "busy" movements while waiting

People Waste

People waste, particularly of their minds, is a big sin managers and stockholders commit. When corrected, it will provide a greater and faster ROA increase than increased sales, reduced inventory, or reduced lead time. Fortunately, there are ways to be forgiven for this sin. Just eliminate the causes.

Failure to empower employees is a mind-set that may exist within many of your company's key decision makers. It is safe to say that without empowered project teams you won't get the maximum results from your efforts to implement lean or continuous improvement. Put another way, without empowered project teams, the odds that you will double or triple your ROA aren't in your favor. Without empowered teams, you will never discover nor implement the massive gold mine of projects contained in these chapters. See employee empowerment in Chapter 6.

Poor hiring practices need to be replaced by good hiring practices. I suggest that you focus on hiring the best knowledge resources available that match your business plan. One major part of a business plan should include project priorities rated by the project evaluation process found in Chapters 5 and 7. Don't just hire the very best people available. Hire the specific knowledge resources you need to implement future projects. Perform a knowledge inventory, using the verb/phrase combinations found in Chapter 3, to discover and fill knowledge gaps. It's a waste to hire knowledge you now possess in ample supply. Look at these verb/noun combinations and at your highest-priority future projects. You then have a precise target for your knowledge search. If you don't have a change agent who can act as the champion to guide the project teams to implement the many projects discovered in each chapter, that person may be your most critical initial investment. Sometimes it might be more economical to hire temporary consultants to fill knowledge gaps that aren't needed long-term.

Low investment in training is a cause for the wasting of employee knowledge and creativity. The important point here is to invest only in the most urgent knowledge and training needed to complete high-priority projects. Adults learn best when they learn something today that they can apply tomorrow. Match training with simple projects so that each training session completes a project.

High turnover resulting from low pay is a cause that can be easy to resolve when you realize that it's less expensive to pay above-average wages than to continuously be searching to replace key knowledge resources. Just think about a statistical normal distribution bell curve. There aren't many really poor employees on one end of the bell curve, just as there aren't many stars at the other end of the bell curve. You will have more than your share of stars if you train them well, coach them well, and pay them well. There's another point to consider. Most employees will put a monetary value on empowerment when they decide to seek their fortunes elsewhere. If they decide to leave, many of them will want to come back very soon. Be sure to let them know they are welcome to return. Job enjoyment from job empowerment and recognition is a priceless fringe benefit employees seldom are willing to give up. It buys a lot of loyalty.

Failure to provide financial incentives is why most businesses never maximize their ROA. Properly designed and executed financial incentives increase ROA more quickly because employees have a bigger incentive to lower the costs in the profit and loss statement and minimize the investment in the balance sheet. It's a financial decision that no knowledgeable stockholder will pass up. It lowers wage and salary expenses per sales dollar more quickly because one measure of the incentive should be the improvement in the percent of total salary and wage dollars divided by sales dollars. The net profit increases because the new total for wages plus incentive pay is less than the old total wages. The investment is lower because capital buildings and equipment are utilized much more effectively, essentially giving the stockholder more equipment at no additional investment. Higher net profit divided by a lower investment results in a higher ROA. There are few, if any, projects to increase sales, lower costs, lower inventory investment, or reduce lead times that can compete with a project to implement a companywide incentive system as described in Chapter 6.

LEAN IMPROVEMENT BUILDING BLOCKS

This section summarizes the building blocks used to implement lean manufacturing concepts. This is not a lean course. But these lean features will help you to discover more verb/noun projects.

Standardized work eliminates waste caused by various personnel having their own individual procedures and methods for manufacturing or paperwork. When you have empowered teams, these knowledge resources will put their heads together and document the process that produces the most value with the least waste. The standardization goal should be to document each process or operation with all the operations or steps performed in the best sequence with the best combination of people, raw materials, methods, tools, and equipment.

An *organized workplace* is another way to reduce waste. We are impressed when we see an office, desk, or workplace that is clean and orderly. You're probably thinking, "This sounds like something my parents said to me over and over to get me to clean and straighten up my room." Most of us wish we had the discipline to keep our workplace neat and orderly. Wouldn't it be satisfying if you never again needed to do special cleanup when some big-wheel manager or customer comes to visit your facility? Lean has developed a system, called the *5S* program, to help eliminate waste that results from being disorganized:

- *Sort* through workplace items and move seldom used items to a temporary holding area. If after a period of time you don't need any of these items, dispose of them in the most economical way.

- *Set in order* all remaining items, identify the best location for them, and devise a visual indicator so you and your coworkers will know where each item is to be returned after being used.

- *Shine* every item by inspecting it each time it is cleaned and returned to its prescribed place.

- *Standardize* the rules and visual controls to make the first three S's work for you as you discover other items you decide to use in place of existing items.

- *Sustain* the 5S program through good communications with coworkers who utilize the same items. Train new coworkers to stick with the standard until consensus is reached about a change. Practice self-discipline by inviting your parents to come and inspect your workplace.

Visual controls are signals to visually communicate some action for those mutually involved in a process. The signal can be a card, flag, light, or lines on the floor to identify storage areas, walkways, or work areas. It's what you do at a family dinner when, during the conversational noise, you motion to someone that you want some more of something. At all-you-can-eat restaurants, you might be provided with a little flag to signal a waiter that you want more of a food item. The value of visual signals is that they are inexpensive, self-regulating, and are managed by value-adding workers:

- Lean suggests *kanban* cards, a signal a coworker displays at their workstation when their current supply of parts needs to be replenished.

- In Chapter 11, I suggest bin reserve cards for your branch inventory control or to control the reorder of some of the 80 percent of your components that make up less than 20 percent of your inventory investment.

- Also in Chapter 11 (block 55, page 184), I suggest using shop routers to signal materials personnel to deliver raw materials for shop orders and to signal supervisors when a shop order start date has been missed so that overtime, paralleling, or overlapping can be used as expediting methods.

- Similar signals are color coded fixtures, tools, pallets, paperwork forms, and paperwork folders.

Point-of-use storage is defined as locating materials and information resources as close to the user as possible as a way to eliminate waste:

- For some pieces of equipment, it may be possible to arrange for raw material to be delivered directly from receiving and stored near the machine.

- For some purchased components, such as nuts, bolts, screws, and fittings, it can be arranged for vendors to bypass receiving and deliver items directly to assembly stations, eliminating inventory tracking, storage, and handling.

- Supplies used by a limited number of users can be delivered directly to their workstation.

Quality at the source can be applied to purchased components, manufactured parts with several operations, assembly line operations, or paperwork operations. The idea is to eliminate inspection waste and the inventory and lead time required for it. The concept is to make the person responsible for the work also responsible for the inspection approval before moving the work on to the next operation:

- For outside sources of supply, critical dimensions, or specifications, you can document the criteria required by your inspector. Surely you can provide the same documentation to your supplier and require certification that they have done the inspections. Random sampling by your inspector should be the maximum amount of duplicated inspection you should require.

- For your own manufacturing operations, one of the best ways to be able to eliminate inspection of critical features and dimensions is to utilize preventive maintenance to document process capability as you periodically perform planned and scheduled preventive maintenance.

9

Projects to Reduce Lead Time and Inventory

This chapter provides added detail to help you reduce both work-in-process inventory and component inventory by reducing paperwork and processing lead times.

DOCUMENT CUSTOMER AND MANUFACTURING LEAD TIME MISMATCHES

An ideal goal is to shorten manufacturing lead time so it's less than the lead time you promise for shipment of customer orders. The goal is to do your material control scheduling from customer orders rather than from forecasts. For most businesses there is usually a measurable mismatch between how quickly a customer wants their order filled and the lead time you require to process components and assemble a product. In these cases you carry an inventory on certain manufactured or purchased components to fill the gap in the mismatch. A pattern chart is provided in this section so that you can learn how to document your own mismatches and initiate appropriate projects to minimize the mismatch problem.

Document your company's product cycle time so everyone in the company can see why you must maintain inventory on some components. This condition will exist until you reduce your manufacturing lead times to less than the lead time customers give you to deliver their purchases, and until you reduce your setup costs so that you can economically produce in quantities as small as those shown on customers' purchase orders.

How to Graphically Illustrate the Lead Time Mismatch

We will use the chart in Figure 9.1 to show you the mechanics of using material lists (indented exploded bills of material) to make cycle time charts for your various product lines. This pattern will help personnel visualize the problem. Study this pattern and customize it to make your own cycle time chart for each unique product line.

Cycle time chart				Each column equals one week					
Part no.	Item name				Spec. eng. dwg.	Info lead time	Cust. order rec.		
1	End-item assembly	■							
2	Subassembly		■						
3	Purchased part			■					
4	Manufactured component			■					
5	Bar stock material					■			
6	Manufactured component			■					
7	Casting material						■		
8	Special subassembly		■						
9	Special manufactured part			■					
10	Tubing material						■		
11	Purchased part			■					
12	Customer part			■					
13	Manufactured component					■			
14	Bar stock material					■			
15	Purchased part			■	■				
16	Purchased part			■					
17	Manufactured component			■					
18	Casting material			■					
19	Grinding operation			■					
20	Heat treat operation				■				
21	Machining operation					■	■		
22	Bar stock material							■	
23	All hardware		■						

Figure 9.1   Cycle time chart.

We suggest making a separate cycle time chart for each product line that requires significantly different processing operations and equipment. For example, you might have different product lines because you use two different types of mechanisms or different mountings for different market segments.

The chart in Figure 9.1 is a pattern you can customize to show your own product cycle time charts. It represents a company product whose customers are happy with a delivery lead time of six weeks (the calendar time between the day their purchase order is received by the company's sales staff and the day their order is shipped and invoiced). This is an indented material list for this product line, showing the average lead time for end-item assembly, subassemblies, components, and raw materials.

Information Lead Time. This is the column to the left of the customer order receipt column. This sample company takes a week to process the customer's order in the sales office, obtain credit approval, and get the paperwork processed through inventory control so purchase orders and shop orders can be released to suppliers and the shop. This week is no longer available for purchasing to use as supplier lead time or for the shop to use as manufacturing lead time. This week to process the customer order also forces the company's stockholders to invest in another week of inventory for each component whose lead time extends to the right of the customer order receipt column.

For this sample company, if the customer order requires a special component or a customer-supplied component, another week of lead time is required to coordinate with the customer for design specifications, drawings, and process routers (assuming no special tooling will be required). In these cases, another week is consumed from what could have been allowed for supplier and shop lead time. A third column, special engineering drawing, must be added to the cycle time chart so you can visualize the impact of these requirements. Only the lead times for the special subassembly and its special components are actually impacted by this extra one week information delay.

The Analysis to Recognize Which Components Must Be Carried in Inventory in Advance of the Customer Order

Now you can look at the cycle time pattern to see how you, if you worked for this company, would decide which components must be kept in stock to assure that you can meet the six-week customer lead time you normally promise. You might also recognize why this sample company may consistently miss delivery dates for this product line, even though the company may do a considerable amount of expediting. Study the cycle time chart, one line at a time, and see if you draw the same conclusions I do. Any lead time to the right of the heavier vertical line must be stocked ahead of customer orders.

Line 1. One week is required for the assembly operation. All subassemblies and components that go directly into the end item will start their lead time at the beginning of the second week of the time cycle. Obviously, you will initiate a project to reduce the assembly lead time.

Line 2. This component is a subassembly that is common to this product line. With only one week lead time required, it doesn't need to be stocked. Its assembly shop order can be issued after the customer order is received. If this lead time can be reduced, you will reduce your assembly in-process inventory investment by a few days.

Line 3. This purchased component goes into the common subassembly. Its three-week lead time falls into the information lead time column. It might be wise for you to control this component with a reorder quantity, including a safety allowance, until you implement a project to reduce the order processing time to one day or get the supplier to reduce its average lead time. Then you wouldn't need to issue a purchase order until the customer order is received. These are places to discover projects to reduce supplier lead times, such as through just-in-time delivery, as a way to eliminate the need to carry component inventory on some items in your stock.

Line 4. You can wait until the customer order is received before you issue a shop order for this manufactured component, since its lead time lies within the safe area.

Line 5. However, the raw material for line 4 butts up next to the customer order receipt column and you probably should have material on hand before the customer order is received. However, that wouldn't be necessary if the manufacturing lead time were reduced for line 4. This is an example of how inventory investment and its related costs magically disappear as you reduce manufacturing, supplier, and paperwork lead times.

Lines 6 and 7. This is a manufactured component made from a casting. A shop order won't need to be issued until a customer order is received if the casting is kept in stock in quantities that match line 6 lot sizes.

Lines 8, 9, and 10. Only four weeks lead time is allowed for this special subassembly, its special component, and raw material. Its assembly shop order must be completed by the start date for the end-item assembly. Its raw material can't be ordered until engineering drawings are released. This company has a material control problem here that will surely result in a late customer order delivery. There is no problem with the subassembly or component manufacturing lead time after receipt of the customer order. The problem is with the raw material lead time. You must initiate a project to resolve this problem, with your customer being one of your project team participants. It may be a simple solution if the material is a common material for which the quantity required for the customer special component is insignificant. The customer may be required to keep the special part in stock if there isn't any way to anticipate its future need. Perhaps a design change for an alternative material is called for. Either the lead time problem needs to be solved or the customer needs to agree to a longer lead time when they need this product.

Line 11. Even if the lead time issue for the line 9 component can be resolved, you still have a control issue with this purchased component. These examples of the lead time mismatch between your customer order lead time and your cycle time lead time are included in this chapter not only to reinforce the goal to reduce lead times, but also to reinforce the reality that you must have a reliable and rational tool like a cycle time chart to identify the items that must be reordered in anticipation of the receipt of a customer order.

Line 12. If you use customer-supplied components, the chances are that your customer may have some of the same cycle time mismatch problems you have. You can't expect their material control system to be so organized that they will check the lead time of the component they are to supply before they ask you how much lead time you actually need. And if you haven't made your cycle time chart, you may make some promises you can't keep. In this specific example, the customer must do the expediting and reschedule their shipping date to one week after you receive their material or they must maintain an inventory of their part.

Lines 13 and 14. This is another example of a component that won't require inventory or a safety allowance if the raw material is kept on hand. However, you should learn to look at these situations as one because if you reduce the average processing lead time by one week, you won't need to stock the raw material.

Lines 15 and 16. These purchased component examples should be looked on as opportunities. As they stand now, you must reorder with a safety allowance in lot sizes appropriate to their setup costs. Line 15 might be improved by putting your suppliers on your project teams and getting them to commit to a shorter maximum lead time or a shorter average lead time. Line 15 lead time might be cut to one week by buying from a distributor rather than directly from a manufacturer and by deciding to tolerate an increased unit cost for that part. If your purchasing function is given performance goals that focus only on unit cost, rather than also considering lead times, ask them to read this chapter and estimate how much they might be able to reduce the company's investment in purchased component inventory if they were to focus attention on both unit cost and lead time reduction that will get more purchased items under the customer order lead time wire.

Line 17. Here is another component that is ordered after the customer order is received. However, don't jump to the conclusion that you can order enough only for this one customer order. You can order only the quantity the customer order requires if setup cost for the component is very low in comparison to its unit cost. If your calculated method for setting lot sizes requires it, you may have to order more than a given customer order requires.

Line 18. Castings will almost always have a lead time that exceeds the lead time you promise to customers. You will likely have to order castings ahead of receiving customer orders. A given casting may be used as material for only one machined component or one casting may be used to make several similar-looking components. Since this casting is used to make the line 17 component, your material control system must also be tuned with the lot sizes for the one or more components the casting is used to make. Your casting quantity on hand will need to be equal to or greater than the specific component that will be reordered next. Remember, if your casting supplier agrees to maintain an inventory of castings for you, they must add enough cost to pay themselves for their increased investment in your inventory.

Lines 19 through 22. This component's lead time problem might be improved by maintaining stock on a semi-finished part that could go through the heat treat and grinding processes after the customer order is received.

Line 23. Most hardware items have a short lead time. They can be kept in inventory because of the low inventory investment they create.

Summary

This sample company is allowed a customer order lead time of six weeks. If its customers only allowed one week lead time, you can see why it would be forced to carry inventory for most of the components or end items.

REDUCE MANUFACTURING LEAD TIME

As a manufacturer, you must drastically reduce total lead time if you are going to eliminate the mismatch between customer order lead time and processing lead time. Any manufacturing, purchasing, or paperwork lead time reduction will reduce your in-process inventory and, most importantly, will increase sales because of on-time delivery. Any reduction in customer order processing lead time will also reduce component inventory investment.

Most companywide process flowcharts begin with a customer order and end with the invoicing of customer shipments. Ideally, the lead time requested by the customer is equal to or more than the time required to process a given customer order between these two points.

Imagine what your increased sales and ROA would be if you could take sales away from your competitors and if you could, year to year, shorten your customer order lead time. Or imagine your ROA increase if, because of shorter component and paperwork processing lead times, you reduce your inventory investment. The financial rewards for reduced office, warehouse, or shop lead times will greatly contribute to the probability that you can double or triple your ROA.

To discover projects to implement shorter lead times, you can customize the flowcharts in Figures 9.2 and 9.3 to define the variety of office and shop processes you currently have that directly apply to processing customer orders between customer order receipt and customer order invoicing.

Figures 9.2 and 9.3 relate to manufacturing businesses. They could also relate to distribution businesses or service businesses that manufacture or assemble some of their products. They are longer than Figures 9.4 and 9.5 (pages 115–116) because they include the extra lead time elements required to manufacture and assemble products sold to customers.

The first block in Figure 9.2 is titled "Customer order receipt." It needs no explanation.

Lead Times from A to Z for Manufacturers

Block A—Product Line Cycle Times Charts. Figure 9.1 shows a cycle time chart for one product line. Make one for each product line if there is a significant difference in the equipment, materials, or processes used.

Block B—Master Plan and Forecast Schedule. Chapter 11, blocks 12 through 16 (pages 170–71) show how to match customer demand with current shop capacity plans so that the components requiring reordering before customer orders are received can be reordered early enough to avoid missing customer order delivery dates. As projects are implemented to shorten lead times, fewer components will need to be ordered in advance of receiving customer orders.

Block C—Customer Order Processing Lead Time. This is a place to apply lean value stream mapping. If only one person processes these orders,

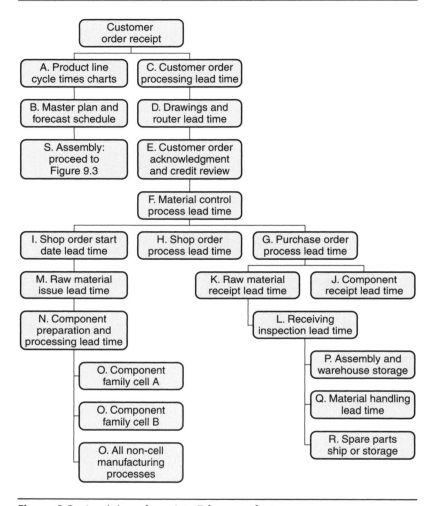

Figure 9.2 Lead times from A to Z for manufacturers.

eliminate or shorten the steps in order processing to free that person up for other duties.

You might eliminate this whole block, and block E, if you allow major customers who order most frequently to have computer access to your master plan. One of their personnel could be trained to acknowledge their own orders.

If you have several employees doing this function, you should consider implementing an order processing cell and other elements from the lean value stream method.

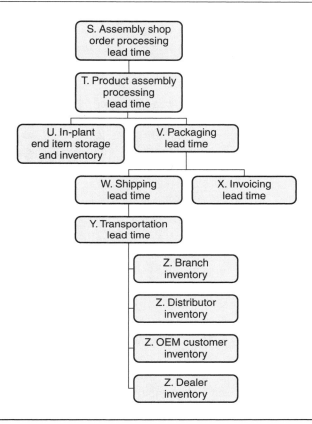

Figure 9.3   Lead times from A to Z for manufacturers.

Also consider the differences in flow for spare-parts-only components, standard products, or special products that require special drawings or special processing operations and tooling.

For every day you shorten the customer order processing time, you remove one day of component inventory investment.

Block D—Drawings and Router Lead Time. Any time new drawings or new material lists are required, you need dedicated personnel, and cells if possible, to process the work quickly. You can consider immediately releasing the standard part of the material list. Special components, as a subgroup, can be released later after drawings and routings have been completed. The special components must have a lead time short enough to not delay the customer order before the customer order and its delivery date are acknowledged. Be sure you have a special short lead time process to release drawings for special components. Be sure your engineering personnel are trained to understand that a short lead time for their part of the paperwork process can result in a lower inventory investment for many other components on the cycle time material list.

Block E—Customer Order Acknowledgment and Credit Review. Consider combining the process for blocks C and E into one person if you are a small company or into your block C cell if several people process sales orders. If you require a credit review, do it in advance of customer acknowledgment so it doesn't add to processing lead time. Your alternative is to require a longer customer order lead time for customer orders that don't have documented credit arrangements agreed to in advance.

Block F—Material Control Process Lead Time. This is another logical place to apply lean value stream mapping. If you think in terms of work cells rather than departments, normal paperwork and data entry might include block F in the blocks C and E cell. For manufacturers, any shop orders with a start date of the current date or sooner (see block H) should be immediately given to production control to start shop order processing.

Block G—Purchase Order Process Lead Time. What you do in this area to shorten lead time depends on your company's size. If you have several people involved in blocks F, G, and H, you have an opportunity to look at work cells that combine blocks F and G, blocks F and H, or blocks F, G, and H. Some purchasing functions are organized around various commodities or suppliers rather than using a cell approach. It could be that block G release of purchase orders can be automatically triggered by block F if all quotes and negotiations are completed in advance of the next reorder. It wouldn't be impossible to find a way for blocks C through H to require only one day or one hour lead time.

Block H—Shop Order Process Lead Time. If you are using start dates on your shop orders, as I suggest in Chapter 11, blocks 54, 55, and 56 (pages 185–87), they will provide you with lead time control. All production control needs to do with a new shop order, or a batch of shop orders, is place them in start date sequence with other shop orders. This applies to both component and assembly shop orders. Any shop orders with a start date of the current date or sooner should be delivered immediately as the paperwork is being processed so that shop orders can be issued within an hour.

Block I—Shop Order Start Date Lead Time. This is the lead time that determines in-process inventory investment for components and assembled end items. This is when a shop supervisor and production control personnel concentrate on shortening lead time to reduce the company's in-process inventory investment.

The first requirement is, don't start shop orders early. That puts inventory dollars into work-in-process too early.

The second requirement is, once a shop order is started, move the shop order from operation to operation with a minimum of queue time between operations. This is what happens when you have a cell for a family of similar components.

To make your noncellular operations act like a cell, you can parallel and overlap operations (Chapter 11, blocks 59 and 60 [page 189]) particularly for components that have a high unit cost (material, labor, and overhead, Chapter 11, block 26 [page 174]) or a high usage value (Chapter 11, block 31 [page 175]). In-process inventory investment is most greatly reduced by moving these high-dollar-value components through your shop in the fewest days possible. However, don't arbitrarily cut lot sizes to do this. Let your lot size calculation method, Chapter 11, block 30 (page 175), do this for you if you want your ROA to reach its highest level.

Blocks J, K, and L—Receiving and Receiving Inspection Lead Times.

If you perform a receiving inspection process, perhaps you might creatively consider a cell that combines receiving, receiving inspection, purchasing, and material handling. Your goal is to have the shortest lead time possible from the time the components or raw materials arrive at the receiving dock until the purchase order is closed. This is another place where your personnel must be taught to think like businesspeople or investors. The group of people in this cell can, by closing purchase orders more quickly, shorten the purchasing lead times and cause more components to have lead times shorter than the customer order lead time. If purchase order setup costs are reduced, as a result of block G improvements, purchases can be made in smaller lot sizes. The combined actions of blocks G, J, K, and L will result in lower inventory investment.

Some companies only receive shipments during certain hours of the day. This forces batching. The cell would rather have receipts flow more smoothly. Even if deliveries can be made at any hour, there will be some batching.

Receipts should be grouped by the due date, with the oldest due date entering the cell first.

For manufacturers, if the due date is older than the current date, the process waiting for this material needs to be informed about the receipt so that plans can be made to start the process because its start date is already behind schedule and expediting per Chapter 11, blocks 57 through 60 (pages 188–89) must be initiated.

The next step in the cell might be to count to verify the quantity. Consider performing receiving inspection first. If the components or material can't be accepted, why count them? Better yet, initiate projects to eliminate counting and receiving inspection. Eliminate counting by having a record and sampling process by component or by supplier. Counting is a waste of time if your suppliers can prove they do an accurate job. Receiving inspection is a waste of time if you tell your supplier which features on a component you are most concerned about and ask them to provide documentation that they have made these inspections.

By using a cell approach and eliminating the counting and receiving inspection, you can reduce your receiving lead time from days to minutes and significantly lower your component inventory investment. Both will result in a higher ROA.

Block M—Raw Material Issue Lead Time. Be sure that an operation to issue raw material appears on routers with its own start date. If you issue material too soon, it may trigger a reorder too soon. By material issue having its own start date, there's no need for its delivery to delay the completion date of the shop order or to allow the shop order to be started sooner than it should.

Blocks N and O—Component Preparation and Processing Lead Time. This chapter and Chapter 10 describe the preparation activities that will reduce setup time and lead time. As with raw material issue, give preparation activities their own operation on a router. You should give these operations zero lead time because they should be performed in parallel with the current processing operation.

These kinds of operations are where you should consider setting up cells for families of similar components. There are some CNC machines, with multiple pallets and permanently positioned cutting tools, that function as a cell within themselves. The setup time is normally so short that deliveries to assembly might be based on hourly or daily batches. In most cases, because of small lot sizes, your investment in this type of CNC machine will be less than the inventory investment you eliminate. In Chapter 11, blocks 59 and 60 (page 189), I show how to parallel and overlap to experiment with how a cell might function. Chapter 10 covers cellular manufacturing and component families in detail.

Block P—Assembly and Warehouse Storage. Ignore this block if you don't have assembly operations. Warehouse lead time is eliminated when setup cost for components is so low that any small lot size can be delivered directly to assembly.

However, even with a lead time on the cycle time chart that allows the shop order to be scheduled after receipt of customer orders, calculated lot sizes (Chapter 11, block 30 [page 175]) may force you to issue shop order quantities that are larger than required by a customer order. In these circumstances some of the quantity can be delivered directly to assembly, with the remainder being delivered to the warehouse.

Block Q—Material Handling Lead Time. Material handling contains lead time. As seen in Figure 9.2, it starts at the receiving dock and stops at the shipping dock. By documenting it, you will discover enough waste to justify a project to eliminate some material handling waste.

To evaluate and prioritize a material handling project, go to budget line items to total all your material handling expenses, including those that are required to transport components for outside processing and those for transporting inventory to your branches. Include your expenses for fuel, maintenance of material handling equipment, and containers or pallets you use to hold batches of material and components within your in-process areas. Next, ask your accountant the current value of your company's investment for material handling equipment. As a starting place, with this information, use the project evaluation form in Chapter 5 to determine how much you can increase ROA for every 10 percent reduction in material handling expense and investment. Create a project to justify investment to automate portions of your material handling processes as a way to reduce lead time.

To find the material handling waste and lead time that can be eliminated, look at it as the processes between other processes, starting at receiving and ending at shipping. Then imagine yourself as a tracking satellite and see how many miles per day you can eliminate. Be sure to include in your study expenses for people who transport shop or office paperwork or who transport tools used in manufacturing processes. Excessive miles traveled each day by personnel is a symptom of poor planning, uncontrolled process flows, and excessive lead time.

Block R—Spare Parts Ship or Storage. If you maintain spare parts close to the customer (with one-minute, one-hour, or one-day customer order delivery lead time), monitor spare parts usage history. Some components or subassemblies are sold only as spare parts. Other components or subassemblies are used both for spare parts sales and as components used to assemble end items. Chapter 11, block 35 (page 177), describes a visual control system called *bin reserve,* which you can consider to be sure you have components or subassemblies on hand to meet spare parts delivery date requirements. The system you use for block C will likely work for processing customer spare parts orders.

Block S—Assembly Shop Order Processing Lead Time. Ignore this if your business doesn't require you to assemble products for customers. As with component shop orders, assembly shop orders should have a start date that isn't started early and is processed in the shortest lead time possible. Assembly processes will likely be able to make use of the lean value stream mapping method in a similar way to its use in processing customer orders and issuing shop orders and purchase orders (blocks C, E, F, G, and H). You should look for cell opportunities during the assembly process to pull components directly from component shop orders without having to pass through the warehouse. This would be for components whose processing lead time is shorter than the customer order lead time shown on a product line's cycle time chart. Other manufactured and purchased components will be pulled from the warehouse. Your assembly process doesn't care from where they are pulled. Look for opportunities for purchased components with lead times shorter than the customer order lead time to be delivered directly to assembly from receiving.

Block T—Product Assembly Processing Lead Time. Ignore this block if you don't assemble products. Figure 9.6, page 126, is a pattern for a product family matrix. It provides steps for grouping each product line or models within each product line. Look at the grouping of these various steps to see which are the logical product families so you can determine how to convert a current assembly process to a cell. If you're already using some form of a cell, the matrix might help you make improvements. Here is another opportunity to reduce the assembly time shown on your cycle time chart from weeks to days or hours.

Block U—In-Plant End Item Storage and Inventory. Ignore this block if you don't assemble products. In Chapter 11, block 18 (page 172), I ask you to document how close to the customer you are required to maintain inventory. In this block, and in the blocks designated by block Z, customize a product family matrix to what actually represents your company. Block U simply indicates that your end-item inventory is sometimes your internal customer.

Some companies eliminate this investment by providing a discount to distributors, dealers, and OEM customers. If you are selling into a distributor network, let a marketing consultant show you how to design a discount structure. This is a financial decision, or project, that can be evaluated using the evaluation form in Chapter 5 to assure that it will increase your ROA.

Block V—Packaging Lead Time. Packaging is its own process and a processing operation that requires lead time upstream of the customer order shipping date. First, ask yourself if it requires significant setup time. If it does, you will likely see batches accumulating ahead of it, creating queue time that will need to be shown on your cycle time chart. If the packaging equipment isn't too expensive, consider adding a parallel station to shorten the lead time. Or look for a minimal setup alternative process. Second, ask if the packaging work schedule is based on shipping dates, and what happens if the shipping date is equal to or earlier than the packaging date. If batches accumulate and there are several people involved, consider a cell. If one or two people are normally required, transfer in personnel to reduce the lead time. Remember, your goal is to shorten lead time in every process in the flow so that more components on the cycle time charts won't have to be ordered until a customer order is received.

Block W—Shipping Lead Time. Perhaps packaging and shipping are one process. If not, try to make them into a cell so that individual shipments move through much more quickly. Shipping is a good place to test your overall system consistency. If the shipping rate isn't about the same every day (versus heavier on Friday than during the week or heavier at the end of the month), you are probably doing considerable wasteful expediting. If you have several major customers who want to give you due dates at the end of each month or at the end of each week, you will want your cycle time charts and master plan to be in daily increments.

You will be surprised how much this policy will satisfy your stockholders with a higher ROA and your customers with shorter customer order lead times. Think about it. Your customers are looking for suppliers who will quote them shorter lead times just like your purchasing function is doing with your suppliers. Shorter lead times eventually translate into increased sales. Personnel outside of the sales department need to realize that they can sometimes do more to increase sales and market share than the sales personnel.

Block X—Invoicing Lead Time. Accounts receivable is one of your company's seven critical business elements listed in Chapter 2. Companies should require customers to pay their invoice within a certain number of calendar days after they ship it. For your financial and credit personnel, this is called the accounts receivable collection period. If there are a batch of invoices mailed once each day, you have an opportunity to make a lead time improvement that would reduce this investment by two or three percent. You might consider including an accounts receivable person in your packaging/shipping cell, even in a remote location. The point I'm trying to make is that the lead time between a shipment and the processing of an invoice should be a matter of minutes, so that invoices can be batched and mailed as many times each day as practical, or may be sent one at a time electronically.

Block Y—Transportation Lead Time. Some customers may use their own truck to deliver their order. That's how important they consider lead time to be. Transportation lead time will also be critical to you if you operate branch warehouses because that transportation time increases the number of days you maintain the shipment as an inventory investment. Your customers are thinking in the same way. You've invoiced them for the order but the product isn't yet available to them when it is shipped commercially.

Think carefully about it before you accumulate enough completed product to make a truckload shipment. Think like a financial businessperson and do the project evaluation that will give you the highest ROA and best availability of your products to your customers.

Block Z—Customer Types. This block is included primarily to get you to identify the types of customers your office and shop processes are serving and to get you to think about the kinds of processes going on in each of these groups.

In your branches, you have a similar kind of reordering process as used for blocks F, G, and W and, in some cases, block S. I encourage you to use something like a bin reserve system (Chapter 11, block 35 [page 177]) at branches, since little paperwork is required and much of the work can be done within the cell by block F personnel.

The reason you provide a discount to distributors is to get them to carry inventory close to the customer and to process the many small customer orders you would have to process if you carried inventory at the factory facility for fast delivery (very short customer order lead time). You are also paying them for maintaining a reordering process for the end items or components they order from you.

A dealer may act very much like a distributor but may also install and service your product when it is utilized on their customers' equipment. They will usually receive the same discount as distributors because you are paying them for essentially the same services.

OEM customers probably have a factory flow similar to yours, with even more opportunities to apply the lean value stream mapping method to shorten lead times and reduce lot sizes. They are usually very fickle, just as you are with your suppliers. They will buy from your competitors if they have the shortest lead time, lowest cost, highest quality, and most reliable delivery promises.

You should bring your major customers and major suppliers into your project teams. Your customers, particularly OEMs, can provide valuable knowledge resources if they are farther along on their mission for "better customer services at a lower cost" than you are.

Including your suppliers on project teams is critical because, at some time or another, you are going to need to get the message across to them that shorter lead times, lower cost, higher quality, and more reliable delivery promises are part of your supplier selection process.

REDUCING DISTRIBUTION AND SERVICE BUSINESS LEAD TIME

The chart in Figures 9.4 and 9.5 is for distribution or service businesses that carry large inventories to meet short customer delivery lead times. As a distribution or service business, if you manufacture some components or products, use the flowchart in Figures 9.2 and 9.3 (pages 106–7) for those items. In this section we are assuming that a distribution or service business purchases all the components it sells.

Reduced office or warehouse lead times help you double or triple your ROA. To implement shorter lead times, customize Figures 9.4 and 9.5.

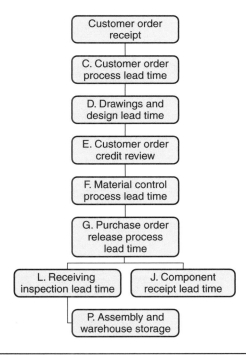

Figure 9.4 Flowchart for distribution and service businesses.

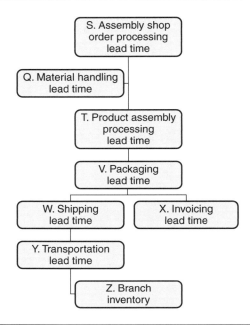

Figure 9.5 Flowchart for distribution and service businesses.

Define office and warehouse processes that apply to processing customer orders between customer order receipt and customer order invoicing.

Blocks C, D, and E. See Reduce Manufacturing Lead Time, page 104.

Block F—Material Control Process Lead Time. In terms of work cells, normal paperwork and data entry can include block F in the blocks C and E cell.

Block G—Purchase Order Release Process Lead Time. If several people work in blocks F and G, consider cells that combine blocks F and G. Some purchasing functions are organized by commodities or suppliers rather than using a cell approach. It could be that block G can be automatically triggered by block F if all quotes and negotiations are completed in advance of the next reorder.

Blocks J and L—Component Receipt and Receiving Inspection Lead Time. If you perform a receiving inspection, consider a cell that combines purchasing, receiving, receiving inspection, and material handling. The goal is to have the shortest lead time possible from the time components or products arrive at the receiving dock until the purchase order is closed.

If purchase order setup costs are reduced as a result of block G improvements, purchases can be made in smaller lot sizes. The combined actions of blocks G, J, and L will result in lower inventory investment.

Some companies only receive shipments during certain hours of the day. This forces batching. The cell wants receipts to flow more smoothly. Even if deliveries can be made any time, there will be some batching. Receipts should be grouped by the oldest due date.

Initiate projects that eliminate counting and receiving inspection. Perform inspection first. If material can't be accepted, why count it? Eliminate counting with sampling processes by supplier and component. Counting is a waste of time if your suppliers can prove they are doing an accurate job. Receiving inspection is a waste of time if you tell your supplier which features on a component concern you most, then require them to provide documentation that they have made these inspections. You should be able to reduce receiving lead time from days to minutes and significantly lower your component inventory investment.

Block P—Assembly and Warehouse Storage. Ignore this block if you don't have assembly operations in your business. The lean value stream mapping method functions best when the setup cost for components is so low that any reasonable lot size can be delivered to assembly as required by a downstream pull scheduling process. If the component lead time is short enough, pull scheduling can be considered.

Block Q—Material Handling Lead Time. Material handling contains lead time. Your material handling starts at the receiving dock and stops at the shipping dock. You should discover and justify projects to eliminate material handling waste.

To evaluate and prioritize a material handling project, go to your budget line items to total all material handling expenses. Include your expenses for fuel, maintenance of material handling equipment, and containers or pallets you use to hold batches of material and components within your in-process areas. Next, ask your accountant to tell you the current value of your company's investment for material handling equipment. As a starting place, with this information, you can use the project evaluation form in Chapter 5 to determine how much you can increase your ROA for every 10 percent reduction in material handling expense and investment. You might even create a project to justify an investment to automate portions of your material handling processes as a way to reduce lead time.

To actually find the material handling waste and lead time that can be eliminated, look at it as the processes between other processes, starting at receiving and ending at shipping. Then imagine yourself as a tracking satellite and see how many miles per day you can eliminate. Be sure to include in your study expenses for people who transport paperwork. Excessive miles traveled each day by personnel is a symptom of poor planning, uncontrolled process flows, and excessive lead time.

Block S—Assembly Shop Order Processing Lead Time. Ignore this block if your business doesn't require you to assemble products for your customers. Look for opportunities for purchased components to be delivered directly to the assembly area from receiving.

Block T—Product Assembly Processing Lead Time. Ignore this block if you don't assemble products. Figure 9.6, page 126, is a pattern for a product family matrix. It is provided so you can look at the steps for grouping each product line. By looking at the grouping, you can see which are the most logical product families and determine if you can convert your current assembly process to a cell. If you're already using cells, the matrix might help you make some improvements.

Block V—Packaging Lead Time. Packaging is a process requiring lead time upstream of the customer order shipping date. If the packaging equipment isn't too expensive, consider adding a parallel station to shorten the lead time. If batches accumulate and there are several people involved, consider a cell. If only one or two people are required, transfer in personnel to shorten lead time.

Block W—Shipping Lead Time. Perhaps packaging and shipping are one process. If not, try to make them into a cell so that individual shipments move through more quickly. Shipping is a good place to test your overall system consistency. If the shipping rate isn't about the same every day or every hour, you are probably experiencing considerable wasted waiting time somewhere.

Think about it. Your customers want suppliers with short lead times just as your purchasing function desires from your suppliers. Personnel outside of the sales department need to realize that they can sometimes do more to increase sales and market share than the sales personnel.

Block X—Invoicing Lead Time. Accounts receivable is one of the seven critical business elements listed in Chapter 2. Companies should require customers to pay invoices within a certain number of calendar days after they send them. For your financial and credit personnel, this is called the accounts receivable collection period. If there are a batch of invoices mailed once each day, you can make a lead time improvement that would reduce this investment by two or three percent. Consider including an accounts receivable person in your packaging/shipping cell, even in a remote location. The point I'm trying to make is that the lead time between a shipment and the processing of an invoice should be a matter of minutes, so that invoices can be batched and mailed as many times each day as practical, or may be sent one at a time electronically.

Block Y—Transportation Lead Time. Transportation lead time is critical if you operate branch warehouses because that transportation time increases the number of days you carry the shipment as an inventory investment. Your customers are thinking in the same way. You've invoiced them for the order but the product isn't yet available to them.

Think like a financial businessperson and do the project evaluation that will give you the highest ROA and best availability of your products to your customers.

Block Z—Customer Types. Identify the types of customers you are serving. Think about the kinds of processes going on within each of these groups. Branches have a similar kind of reordering process as used for blocks F, G, and W. Don't leave them out of the analysis to eliminate small pieces of lead time.

Bring major customers and major suppliers into your project teams. They can provide valuable knowledge. Suppliers are critical because you are going to need to get the message across to them that shorter lead times, lower cost, higher quality, and more reliable delivery are part of your supplier selection process.

APPLY LEAN VALUE STREAM MAPPING

This chapter focuses on lead time reduction and its resulting benefit of reduced in-process inventory investment.

I applaud lean manufacturing for its methods to reduce lead times for your information and manufacturing processes. Value stream mapping provides you with methods that help you reconfigure your information and manufacturing layout to facilitate shorter times to move a product through your facility. To apply lean you need to contact a lean trainer or consultant. I am only showing you how to use lean to discover more verb/noun combination projects. However, lean concepts should be applied only when you can prove to yourself that they will yield the greatest ROA increase.

Minimize Manufacturing Work-in-Process Inventory

Since work-in-process inventory is an investment or asset on the balance sheet, it's natural to look for a verb/noun combination that provides a financial phrase to answer *how* to minimize it. The only way to reduce work-in-process inventory is to reduce manufacturing lead time between the time material is assigned to a shop work order and the time the shop work order is closed and the component is moved to stock, assembly, or shipping.

Chapter 11, block 74 (page 196), shows a formula for calculating how each manufactured item contributes to your investment in work-in-process inventory. You will notice that the quantity you process—the lot size—doesn't affect your lead time or in-process inventory. Lot size does affect finished component inventory. The quantity that affects the in-process inventory formula is the usage, expressed in the same time period as the lead time (days, weeks, months). You can use this formula to estimate an in-process inventory budget or to understand why the company's investment in this asset is as big as it is.

For project teams, the focus must be on reducing work-in-process lead time as the primary way to minimize work-in-process inventory.

You can prove to yourself how important projects will be to reduce your investment in in-process inventory. On any given day, take an in-process inventory audit and estimate its dollar value. Then, assume you can find ways to cut the average lead time in half. You can reasonably estimate that you will have half as many dollars invested in in-process inventory.

Reduce Manufacturing Work-in-Process Lead Time

You're probably already doing some things to reduce in-process lead time. You and your fellow employees could, in less than one hour's time, come up with a multitude of projects to reduce in-process lead time.

Finding creative projects isn't a company problem. The problem is often one of investing in enough personnel to plan and implement projects.

Lead time reduction for cellular manufacturing, covered in Chapter 10, can be a powerful tool. If you have paperwork or manufacturing processing operations located within a cell, and the cell operating times are well balanced, you've greatly minimized the lead time between processing operations, the total time to complete a work order, and the in-process inventory.

Two principles are utilized by cells to reduce lead time that can also be applied to noncellular arrangement of various pieces of equipment in a process flow. Experiment with these two principles in a noncellular environment to test new cell designs.

The first principle is called *paralleling*. In a cell, if you have an operation that takes twice as much time as all other operations within the cell, you simply place two of these machines in parallel within the cell to minimize the time for each part to pass through the cell. For a noncellular process flow, you can do the same if you have the appropriate equipment available and if the setup time required to set up the parallel machine is relatively low.

The second principle is called *overlapping*. This happens naturally in a cell because each part in the process moves from one operation in the cell to the next until all cell operations are completed. If an item or paperwork process is done completely within the cell, the lead time will be about as short as you can hope to get it. For a noncellular process flow, the total quantity of parts on the work order or the total quantity of paperwork forms to be processed can be broken into smaller batches so each operation is overlapped with the next. This means the order is completed in much less time. Overlapping should be considered for long-lead-time processes.

Lean concepts can be applied to office processes to drastically reduce paperwork or information lead times by using value stream mapping to reduce these lead times.

When Can You Best Apply Lean Value Stream Mapping?

Figures 9.2 through 9.5 provide charts you can customize to show the flow of information and products inside your facilities. I suggest places in the flow where value stream mapping is the best tool to reduce lead time. I also show places in the product flow where its concepts don't directly apply to manufacturers and distributors that are forced to carry inventory for fast delivery to customers.

An overly simplified description of lean value stream mapping is that it is a method that causes each process to make only what the next process needs, when it needs it, in a continuous flow, using cells, without detours, and with the finished products and components being pulled through all the processes without batches of inventory or paperwork waiting to be processed. The customer order is sent to only one place in the flow, usually near the end of the assembly process, to control the pull-through of components, all of which are made in daily or hourly lot sizes.

You need to understand that lean manufacturing and value stream mapping concepts are primarily directed at manufacturers that utilize mass production. Our goal in this section is to help smaller-sized businesses that don't use mass production to pick out the lean concepts and ideas that will identify additional profit-producing projects.

There are places in almost every business, particularly in the area of information and paperwork flow, where the value stream mapping method will result in shorter lead times.

Components and raw materials that will not easily fit the lean value stream mapping conditions include purchased or manufactured components whose lead times are longer than the customer order lead time as described in the cycle time chart in Figure 9.1. These need to be controlled by a material control system like the one detailed in Chapter 11. Short customer order lead time requires more components to be carried in inventory in anticipation of future customer orders.

Lean value stream mapping doesn't care whether the process is for a service business, an office or information process, or a manufacturing process. Each of these businesses either has paperwork and information processes, purchased products, or manufactured products. Also, each process has either internal or external customers who want the processing time to be as short as economically possible. The same mapping steps are used for all processes.

Before You Start Lean Value Stream Mapping

Since my audience is distributors, service businesses, and manufacturing job shop operations, not mass production operations, I have arranged my interpretation of lean concepts in a framework that can most directly be applied to operations currently forced to maintain inventory to meet customer delivery lead time requirements.

I treat lean value stream mapping as just another logical tool to identify a large number of projects to reduce lead times. However, most of your paperwork processing can best be improved by seeing paperwork as a mass production operation.

If you are already experienced in lean concepts, I hope this book will give you knowledge that will help you implement lean concepts more profitably, particularly as they relate to component lot sizing, lead times, and the seven critical financial elements in a business.

If you plan to apply lean concepts, I want to encourage you to get started by supplementing lean with the cautions I mention at various places in this book.

Right or wrong, my personal conclusion is, lean concepts work best for small- to medium-sized manufacturers in their efforts to streamline assembly and office flow. They fit best for manufacturers who have precisely known future demand, usually because there is a customer contract for a given quantity to be delivered every day over a long period of time. They don't fit as well with manufacturers who have a broad product line for which the receipt of customer orders is relatively unpredictable and for which the customer order lead time is very short in comparison to component purchasing and manufacturing lead times.

None of these comments about the limitations of lean should deter you from utilizing lean concepts that fit your particular business.

While most of my manufacturing audience will be primarily oriented to job shop lot sizes, manufacturers and distributors will want to use lean concepts to identify projects that won't be discovered without them.

Advice from Some Authors of Lean Thinking

The authors of MEP's value stream mapping resources warn against plunging into waste reduction projects without first doing work on manufacturing and paperwork flow. They say, "To reduce the lead time from raw material to finished goods, you need to do more than eliminate obvious waste. Too many lean implementation efforts have been waste scavenger hunts. While it is good to be aware of waste, your future continuous flow designs need to eliminate the causes of waste in the old flow stream. Once process flow can be seen in a way that reveals these root causes, your company can work at finding original solutions."

These authors of lean thinking offer a five-step process to improve both information and product flow.

First, "Find a change agent." This is a person who can constructively create an atmosphere of dissatisfaction with the existing scheduling and processing practices and then create excitement and inspiration to convert to new practices, such as continuous-flow processing of products and information.

Second, "Find a teacher whose learning curve you can borrow." Invest in training and hiring to get the precise knowledge resources required to implement, year after year, continuous process improvement to reduce product and information lead time and changeover time.

Third, "Seize or create a crisis to motivate action across your firm." Henry Kissinger said, "Policy emerges when concept meets opportunity." A crisis, or opportunity, will often occur when your company is facing a financial crisis or missing sales because your lead times and costs are too high. You and your stockholders should recognize this as a crisis when you have made yourself aware that you can double or triple your ROA and aren't investing in projects and knowledge resources to make it happen.

Fourth, "Map the value stream for all your product families." You map your manufacturing and paperwork flow as they are now, perhaps using the flowcharts from Figures 9.2 through 9.5, and as they will be after the wastes are removed.

Fifth, "Pick something important and get started removing waste quickly, to surprise yourself how much you can do in a very short period."

Use verb/noun combinations to name, evaluate, and prioritize projects that will reduce lead time, changeover time, and their waste costs.

The authors of lean thinking continue, "Unfortunately, we have found that very few of our readers have followed our advice to conduct value stream mapping before diving into the task of waste elimination. Instead, in too many cases we find companies rushing into big waste elimination activities. These well intentioned exercises fix one small part of the value stream. The net result is no cost savings reaching the bottom line, no service and quality improvement for the customer, and another abandoned program."

After You Decide to Do Lean Value Stream Mapping

Most lean courses picture mass production as a chain of islands with product batches (or stacks of paperwork) delivered from the preceding island in the process flow. The people on each island perform their work and when they complete a batch, deliver the batch across the water to the next island. Each island may require its own "push" scheduling system to attempt to get operations completed soon enough that the remaining processing operations will be completed in time to meet the delivery promise made to the customer.

To convert to continuous flow and greatly reduce the lead time and batch inventory on each island, islands are all pulled next to each other so that the batches can be eliminated and operations performed on each island can be moved from one island to the next, one part or operation at a time. Now, only the last island in the process needs to be scheduled since it is "pulling" the process, one part or operation at a time, through the complete process.

For the flow to be smooth and without wasted time, each step in the process is designed to use about the same amount of time so the "make one, move one" concept works as planned. This flow requires less lead time and inventory. Lead time is reduced further by placing appropriate operations of the flow in parallel. Cost and lead time may be further reduced by designing cells that will reduce both lead time and personnel costs.

I suggest you use your paperwork processes to more easily visualize the application of value stream mapping. Look for places where the concepts can be applied to your assembly and component manufacturing areas. You will see how easily value stream mapping can be applied to a service business or distribution business.

Consider paperwork flow when you receive a customer purchase order. Information is flowed through the company, often in batches, from one department or island to another. Some information may flow for credit review, engineering actions, inventory control, purchasing, shop orders, assembly scheduling, invoicing, and accounts receivable. Then imagine how you can reduce paperwork lead time by converting to continuous flow, with appropriate cells to reduce both processing cost and time.

Value stream mapping should be done for each product family. A product family could be physical products made from similar components assembled in the same sequence using the same equipment or assembly station. A product family could be paperwork from a customer order used to generate paperwork for the purchase and manufacture of components that will be assembled into a product. Or a product family could be a customer who walks into the door of a service business, or your branch office, and expects to be quickly greeted so that their request for service can be processed in a shorter amount of time than your competitors are able to consistently achieve.

Once you have identified the product family, the mapping process is very simple:

- Prepare a flowchart that shows the current steps required to process the product. Lead time, processing time, queue time (in minutes, hours, or days), and batching are documented for each step of the process, including any of the other wastes and their causes that were covered in Chapter 8. I've given you my imagination of your process flow in Figures 9.2 through 9.5.

- Prepare a flowchart that shows the future continuous-flow process, with wastes eliminated and appropriate cells added. Estimate the new shorter lead times and processing times for each step in the process. For paperwork, you should expect times to be reduced from days to hours and from hours to minutes or seconds.

- Evaluate, using the form in Chapter 5, the expected ROA increase for each improvement in the new flow diagram so you can determine the part of the process to change first. Remember, mapping is a continuous improvement exercise. You should never be satisfied as long as you can creatively find ways to reduce lead time, reduce setup or changeover time, or do all your scheduling based on the customer order.

- Get started on the most profitable project without delay, hiring and investing in additional people resources as required to implement projects in the shortest time possible.

More About Product Families for Assembled Products

Figure 9.6 shows how to use a grid to group product or paperwork families. In an assembly line, it's often obvious how to separate your products into families. You may already have separate assembly stations for each of them, depending on the difference in the components that go into each of them.

Start by randomly entering products on the grid and rearrange them so they are more logically grouped, based on the process steps and equipment. If you feel a grid will be helpful to rationalize your products or paperwork, this pattern may give you an idea of how to construct your own. You might have an interesting opportunity if column 3 represents a very expensive piece of equipment since it can be used on all of the product families.

You can easily agree to a goal to dramatically shorten the paperwork processing lead time from the time a customer purchase order is received until purchase orders and shop orders are released. Maybe this paperwork currently must pass from sales to credit to engineering and then to inventory control and purchasing, in batches, before the process is complete. You can make a dramatic impact if you redesign your information system to automatically trigger purchase orders and shop orders instantly when customer orders are input upon receipt by a salesperson, or by a sales order/material control cell.

In a service business, where information or paperwork is the product, the transactions and transacting personnel may be configured in a grid, like Figure 9.6, to discover transaction families.

Products or paperwork processes	Process steps and equipment									
	1	2	3	4	5	6	7	8	9	
A	X	X	X		X	X				Product family ABC
B	X	X	X	X	X	X				
C	X	X	X		X	X		X		
D		X	X	X				X	X	Product family DE
E		X	X	X				X	X	
F	X		X		X	X		X		Product family FG
G	X		X		X	X		X		

Figure 9.6   Product family discovery.

More About Your Current Flowchart

In an assembly function, a manufacturer may have one workstation where one or more assemblers build a large number of components into a relatively large end-item product. Or you may have low-volume, smaller products that can be assembled at a workstation by one person. These operations don't particularly lend themselves to lean value stream mapping and its goal of continuous process flow in which you "make one and move one" in lot sizes of one. However, even in these assembly operations, you can identify projects that will eliminate waste.

For paperwork functions, in your current flowchart, look for flow that looks like mass production with its islands or batches of paperwork. When you see this in your current flow, you have a probable opportunity to make significant continuous-flow lead time improvements.

More About Your Future Flowchart

Your future continuous-flow chart can be viewed in two stages. Ideally, you are going to attempt to pull all the islands together and eliminate all the inventory batches staged between each island. Also, you are going to look for opportunities to place some of the islands in parallel as if they were now only one island.

Another key element of your future continuous-flow chart is to identify one of the islands, usually near the end of the island chain, to use as the only island for which you provide a customer delivery schedule. This island sets the pace for all the other islands and allows all the preceding workstations to "pull" their needed components by using visual controls such as cards, flags, or lights.

My interpretation of lean value stream mapping is purposely not as detailed as an MEP course would normally be. The reason is I am primarily trying to trigger more verb/noun or verb/phrase combinations to discover more projects for paperwork and product cells and other lead time reduction.

You can locate many books and consultants to teach you more detail about lean concepts. Just use this book and its interpretation of lean to make their approach financially sound.

10

Projects to Reduce Setup Cost and Inventory

In each section of this chapter we will focus on lot sizing principles that will help maximize your ROA. I will encourage you to decide on a lot sizing formula for those components that require forecasting or those components that, by formula, require a lot size greater than is specified on an individual customer order.

Even if the lead time for a standard component is less than the customer order lead time, a financially sound lot sizing formula may require the purchase or manufacture of a quantity greater than required by an individual customer order. The reason for this is that lead time is purely a time decision and lot sizing is purely a financial decision requiring a financially sound formula.

This chapter provides detailed information for you to reduce component inventory by reducing setup costs.

SETUP COST AND COMMONSENSE LOT SIZING

This chapter and its seven sections are most valuable to manufacturing businesses that have both purchase order and shop order setup costs. For distribution and service businesses its value will depend on the setup costs related to purchased components sold to customers.

Lean manufacturing enthusiasts might be tempted to arbitrarily reduce lot sizes before making the appropriate reductions in setup and changeover costs. This arbitrary action usually results in a lower ROA because costs go up faster than inventory investment goes down.

In this chapter I show project teams how to avoid this mistake. By linking setup cost reduction with lead time reduction, you can move closer to the goal of scheduling work orders and purchase orders from customer orders. The goal for purchase order and shop order setup cost reduction is to dramatically reduce component inventory investment.

Commonsense Item-by-Item Lot Size Decisions

Many lean manufacturing practitioners will promote the concept that, as an ideal goal, the only reasonable lot size is a quantity of one. I don't have any argument with that conclusion, as long as setup cost for every component is very small in comparison to unit cost. For manufacturers, this will mostly occur in assembly operations, where the setup cost is usually less than 10 percent of the cost of all the assembled components for one end item or finished product.

The goal I encourage you to embrace is to reduce your component setup costs, item by item, until the setup cost for each purchased or manufactured component is less than 10 percent of the component's unit cost. This will be a very challenging but financially rewarding goal.

Because of variables such as unit cost, setup cost, usage rate, and the various costs to carry components or end items in inventory, common sense tells you that every purchased and manufactured component must have its own individual lot size. I will prove to you that unless the setup cost for any component is less than 10 percent of that component's unit cost, management needs to approve a method to calculate a financially sound lot size.

This 10 percent rule of thumb is the reason you can financially justify very small quantities for assembly shop orders. The setup cost to assemble a product or end item is usually much less than the total cost for all the components that go into one assembly. However, for most components, particularly those made from castings, it is unusual that the combined paperwork and machine setup cost will be less than the component's unit cost unless you can financially justify a dedicated machine or CNC machine that requires minimal setup/changeover time.

For example, it is common sense you wouldn't decide on a component lot size of one or two parts when the setup cost is ten times the unit cost. Common sense tells you that if you persist in arbitrarily setting very small lot sizes for components that require considerable setup time, your unit costs and selling prices will be too high to be competitive. Your inventory investment would be very low but it wouldn't offset the excessively high unit costs.

Common sense also tells you that your unit cost will be lowest if you arbitrarily run large lot sizes. Your unit costs would be very low but won't offset the excessively high inventory investment.

In between these two extremes is an optimum quantity that will give you the lowest total component cost. Therefore, common sense tells you it will be financially dangerous to arbitrarily guess at a lot size. Common sense demands a rational calculation method that is financially sound. The lot sizing method you use must either show you how to identify the quantity that will give the lowest total cost (unit cost plus inventory carrying cost) and the highest ROA.

In other words, your lot sizing decision is a financial decision and must be guided by your company personnel who are most directly charged with financial results. These personnel must provide or approve a formula and material control procedures that will allow material control personnel to quickly and automatically make these financial decisions about lot sizing. I encourage your material control personnel and your finance personnel to reach a consensus that lot sizing is a joint decision between these two company functions.

FINANCIALLY SOUND LOT SIZING

This is a vitally important section if you are serious about selecting the most financially sound lot size. This isn't a quantity that can arbitrarily be pulled out of the air to satisfy concepts of lean manufacturing courses. If your lot sizing method doesn't do something to bring a financial balance between inventory carrying cost and setup cost, I can assure you, and will prove to you, that you are not maximizing your ROA.

EOQ, the Traditional Lot Sizing Formula

We will use the traditional *economic order quantity* (EOQ) lot sizing formula as an example of a formula that will calculate a quantity that will give you the lowest total cost (unit cost plus inventory carrying cost) and the maximum net profit for every single manufactured or purchased component.

I like this formula because it includes all the elements required to find the lowest total component cost, setup cost, usage rate, inventory carrying percent, and unit cost. The traditional EOQ formula is as follows:

$$\text{EOQ} = \sqrt{\frac{2 \times \text{Setup cost} \times \text{Annual usage rate}}{\text{Inventory carrying percent} \times \text{Unit cost}}}$$

$$\text{or EOQ} = \sqrt{\frac{24 \times \text{Setup cost} \times \text{Monthly usage rate}}{\text{Inventory carrying percent} \times \text{Unit cost}}}$$

$$\text{or EOQ} = \sqrt{\frac{104 \times \text{Setup cost} \times \text{Weekly usage rate}}{\text{Inventory carrying percent} \times \text{Unit cost}}}$$

I present the EOQ formula as an option your company can use to determine lot size, or as a pattern by which your material control and finance personnel can design their own method to authorize financially sound lot sizes. It just happens that this is the formula I would use if I were a stockholder in a manufacturing business that had a goal to maximize ROA.

The formula was derived by putting the elements that determine inventory carrying costs on one side of an equation (like putting them on one end of a teeter-totter) and by putting elements that determine setup costs on the other side (or the other end of the teeter-totter). The idea is to make both sides of the formula equal (or to put the teeter-totter into balance).

When the setup cost and inventory carrying cost are equal, you end up with the lowest total cost for that particular component shop order quantity or purchase order quantity.

In the mathematical derivation of a formula, we put everything but the EOQ on one side of the equals sign. As we do this we get EOQ times EOQ (or EOQ squared) on one side of the equals sign. Therefore, we take the square root of both sides of the equation so that we have just the EOQ on one side of the equation. The square root sign covers everything else on the other side.

If you don't like arithmetic just take my word for it. I didn't invent the EOQ. It's a formula that has served many manufacturers well since the early 1900s. The importance of this formula is that it provides a way to get the lowest cost in your profit and loss statement and annual budget for inventory carrying costs and setup costs in total. It helps see the four elements or facts you need to know to determine a lot size for every component.

Setup Cost. For manufactured components this is the total accumulated shop order paperwork cost, plus the setup time for all operations for a given component, multiplied by the appropriate hourly shop rate, including overhead. For purchased parts, setup cost is the paperwork cost for processing purchase orders. Calculating setup costs for purchased and manufactured components is detailed later in this section.

Usage Rate. This is the best estimate of future annual, monthly, or weekly usage. For a usage rate I prefer to use the quantity of the last one or two lots and the time period it took to consume this quantity to get a monthly or weekly usage rate. This method is described in greater detail in Chapter 11. If you want to use an annual forecast, you may have to use the past 12 months' usage multiplied by a trend for the future. The most recent past is usually the most reliable estimate of the short-range future usage. I don't like to use annual sales forecasts.

The 2 in the EOQ Formula. The 2 is there because your average quantity in inventory at any given time is one-half of the most recent lot size. If you use a monthly usage value, the 2 in the formula is multiplied by 12 and becomes 24. If you use a weekly usage value, the 2 is multiplied by 52 and becomes 104. In other words, the formula treats usage rate and inventory carrying costs in annual terms.

Unit Cost. This is the cost of each individual component, including material, direct labor, and overhead, including setup cost. Actually, purchased components should absorb some of the shop overhead but most manufacturing businesses absorb all the overhead into shop orders. Our definition of unit cost is the cost of each component, including setup cost, as the components go into stock or into assembly.

The Inventory Carrying Cost Percent. This is a value that represents the total of the many costs for carrying inventory, divided by the annual average total inventory investment. Normally it is about 25 percent, which is another way of saying that an item held in inventory will eat up its own value within four years (100 percent divided by 25 percent). This percent is seldom less than 15 percent in most manufacturing companies. Details for calculating the inventory carrying cost are shown later in this section.

As you implement each project to reduce lot sizes, the inventory carrying costs automatically disappear from operating budgets at the same time your inventory investment reduces. Net profit increases as your inventory investment goes down and, as a result, your ROA increases. That's why you should continuously have many projects to reduce setup cost and lead time on individual components (or groups of very similar components). The goal is to continuously have more components that can be ordered after you receive customer orders because their setup cost is less than 10 percent of the part's unit cost.

Note: Normally you also invest in capital equipment or tooling expense to obtain an inventory investment reduction as you implement projects to reduce setup time and lot size on various components. When evaluating a project (with the forms in Chapter 5) to reduce setup cost and the inventory investment on a component, or a family of similar components, be sure to include the investment for the required capital equipment or the expense for tooling that won't be capitalized. The equipment or tooling cost is usually less than the reduced average inventory value.

Inventory Carrying Cost Expenses

The lines in the list in Figure 10.1 are the expenses needed to estimate the inventory carrying cost percent. You need to have an idea about how many cents in expense you have buried within other expenses just to maintain each dollar of inventory investment for components and finished products. This means that when you reduce setup cost so that you can reduce inventory investment, you also receive an expense reduction bonus of 15 to 25 cents for each dollar you reduce inventory.

Just go to your annual budget and gather all the costs that relate to each of the lines in the list. Next, total lines 1 through 12 and enter this total on line 13. Line 13 is the total annual cost to maintain your current level of inventory for components and finished assembled products. On line 14, enter the total asset investment for all component and finished product inventory. Then divide line 13 by line 14 to get a percent, which you enter on line 15, as a factor to represent the cost to maintain each dollar of your

Line	Inventory carrying cost
1	Rework or scrap because of design changes
2	Change of inventory value from reevaluation
3	Rework or scrap from deterioration or damage
4	The current interest percent even if you're not currently borrowing
5	Warehouse labor, including supervision.
6	Receiving and shipping labor, including supervision
7	Depreciation or rental cost for warehouse, shipping, and receiving floor space, storage racks, and material handling equipment
8	Property taxes related to the inventory value
9	Real estate tax for warehouse, shipping, and receiving areas
10	Insurance premiums for inventory
11	Insurance premiums for warehouse, shipping, and receiving areas
12	Workmens compensation insurance for warehouse, shipping, and receiving personnel
13	Total inventory carrying expense
14	Total component and assembled end-item inventory investment
15	Percent for line 13 divided by line 14

Figure 10.1   Expenses needed to estimate inventory carrying cost percent.

inventory investment. For most businesses, this percent factor will be 15 to 25 percent.

This calculation should give you clear insight into the expenses that will systematically evaporate as setup costs and lead times are reduced, resulting in even smaller lot sizes and a lower inventory investment.

The EOQ formula is a result of placing the inventory carrying costs on one end of a teeter-totter with setup cost on the other end of the teeter-totter to see what lot size quantity will bring the teeter-totter into horizontal balance.

Each line is self-explanatory. You will need to ask your accountant to help you use the budget to estimate these values. This carrying cost percent will apply to both purchased and manufactured components.

Setup Costs for Purchase Orders and Shop Orders

The next list of expenses (Figure 10.2) are those needed to cover paperwork setup costs related to processing purchase orders, receiving costs for purchased items and outside processing, or shop order paperwork processing,

Line	Setup cost expenses
1	Inventory control salaries
2	Portion of purchasing salaries related to product sales
3	Receiving salaries related to counting and paperwork, excluding material handling
4	Receiving inspection salaries
5	Production control salaries
6	Physical inventory and/or inventory cycle counting
7	Data processing allocated to the above functions
8	Total dollars allocated to purchase orders
9	Total number of purchase order line items plus blanket order releases
10	Paperwork setup cost for each purchased component ordered
11	Total dollars allocated to shop orders
12	Total number of shop orders
13	Paperwork setup cost for each manufactured component ordered.
14	Machine setup cost or process changeover cost

Figure 10.2 Expenses needed to cover paperwork setup costs.

shop scheduling paperwork costs, and machine setup or changeover costs for manufactured items.

For this list of expenses, look at your annual budget and identify the departments that perform duties related to inventory control, purchasing, receiving, receiving inspection, production control, data processing costs allocated to these functions, and physical inventory or inventory cycle counting.

Purchased items have paperwork setup costs that must be considered to decide ordering quantities, and manufactured items have shop order paperwork costs and machine setup costs to decide lot or batch sizes.

The values in this list should be the amounts shown in the current annual budget or the actual annual values from the preceding year.

Again, I encourage you to utilize the facts gathered and recorded by accounting personnel for other business purposes to support project teams as they look for facts to improve the ROA.

Use the list in Figure 10.2 to make a list that relates to the way your company is organized and/or the way your budget is formatted. If you are a small company, you may have one person who performs several of these functions. Study the following instructions for each line and, with the help of your accountant, make the best estimate you can for each line.

Accumulate the values for these lines to design a financially sound lot sizing formula. If your estimate is too low, order quantities and inventory will be smaller than a formula would recommend. If your estimate is too high, order quantities and inventory will be larger than a formula would recommend.

Line 1. This line is for salary expenses of the inventory control function. This is the function through which sales order quantities, or forecast quantities, are translated and communicated to the purchasing and shop scheduling functions. Then, after purchased and manufactured items are received into stock, this function may be responsible for maintaining accurate records of quantities on hand until issued for assembly shop orders or shipping orders. For manufacturers, part of this dollar amount will be allocated to purchase orders, and the remainder will be allocated to shop orders. For distributors or service businesses, all of these costs will usually be allocated to purchase orders for products inventoried and sold to customers. To make the allocation, you can count the number of inventory items that are purchased and the number that are manufactured, total them, and use the two totals as the divisor to get the percent of salary costs that should be allocated to each group. You can save time by counting every tenth component and then multiply by 10.

Line 2. Salary dollars for this line will be allocated only to purchase order setup cost. Look in your budget at the salaries for your personnel who process quotations, place purchase orders, and follow up on open purchase orders for product components. You might include some or all of a department manager's salary. Don't include any salary expense for processing purchase orders for plant and office supplies. Do include purchase orders to process manufactured components outside.

Line 3. The salary dollars for this line will be allocated only to purchase orders. Include salaries and wages for receiving used for counting and processing paperwork. Don't include material handling into or out of the receiving area.

Line 4. Include inspector expenses to accept or reject incoming components or incoming outside processing.

Line 5. For manufacturers, production control activities control shop orders, after being triggered by inventory control, until parts are delivered to assembly, stock, or shipping. This function does shop order planning, scheduling, and expediting. In some shops, much of a supervisor's time may be used to schedule and expedite orders. This salary can be rightfully included. These activities relate to in-process inventory investment.

Distributors and service businesses may have a schedule control system incorporated into the costs for purchase orders.

Line 6. If you must maintain inventory for some items, you must keep an accurate quantity count for both accounting purposes and reordering purposes. If you perform an annual physical inventory, or rely on ongoing random cycle counting, you should include salaries and wages used to do both. Manufacturers will need to allocate the cost from this line for purchase orders and shop orders in the same percentages as used for line 1. I recommend eliminating annual physical inventory in favor of random cycle counts, because random cycle counts are much more accurate. In Chapter 11, I will suggest to you the best time to take a physical inventory count.

Line 7. It may be difficult to accurately define a percent of total data processing costs for inventory, purchasing, and production control activities. Personnel in data processing can make the best guess possible about what percent of their total budget could be charged to these functions. Allocate the total cost between purchase orders and shop orders the same as you did for lines 1 and 6.

Line 8. The sum of lines 1, 6, and 7, times the percent from line 1 allocated to purchase orders, plus lines 2, 3, and 4.

Line 9. For the same period of time you estimate the dollar values, you can take every tenth purchase order for purchased components, count the number of line items found plus the number of blanket order releases, and multiply by 10.

Line 10. Divide line 8 by line 9. This will be the purchase order setup cost you will use if you decide to use a financially sound lot sizing formula for purchased items.

Line 11. This is the sum of lines 1, 6, and 7, times the percent from line 1 allocated to shop orders, plus line 5.

Line 12. Manufacturers should count the number of released shop orders for the same period of time used to estimate dollar values.

Line 13. Divide line 11 by line 12. This is the shop order paperwork setup cost in the lot sizing formula for manufactured items.

Line 14. For manufacturers, machine setup cost for each manufactured component should be the historical average time it takes to set up or change over a machine or process, times the hourly shop rate. Hourly shop rates can run as much as $40 to $75 per hour, or more. If you don't have a logical setup cost calculated for each component in your cost accounting system, you may have to rely on shop or accounting historical averages or on process engineering or supervisor estimates for setup hours.

Often, shop hourly rates include overhead for receiving costs for material. Consider only including overhead related to the processing departments to set the hourly shop rate for setup cost.

The EOQ formula doesn't do anything to lower your inventory investment. It only gives you the lowest-cost inventory level. You only lower your component inventory investment by lowering your setup cost, component by component. It may take several years to complete all the potential projects.

Experimenting with the EOQ Formula

Here's a simple way to experiment with the EOQ formula to determine the weeks' or months' supply you will make, based on your own setup costs, unit cost, and usage rate.

You can increase your ROA by increasing your inventory investment if your lot sizing formula tells you to begin making components less frequently than you do with your current lot sizing method.

Let's use the EOQ formula based on monthly usage and simplify it slightly by pretending that your inventory carrying cost percentage is 24 percent. The formula becomes, after dividing 24 percent into the 24 in the numerator:

$$\sqrt{\frac{24 \times \text{Setup cost} \times \text{Usage}}{24\% \times \text{Unit cost}}} = \text{Lot size}$$

or, by dividing 24 by 24 percent,

$$\sqrt{\frac{100 \times \text{Setup cost} \times \text{Usage}}{\text{Unit cost}}} = \text{Lot size}$$

Do your experimenting by using round numbers such as 10, 100, or 1000.

$$\sqrt{\frac{100 \times \$100 \times 100 \text{ quantity}}{\$10 \text{ Unit cost}}} = 316 = \text{Lot size}$$

$$\text{Inventory investment} = \frac{316}{2} \times \$10 = \$1580$$

$$\text{Setups/year} = \frac{100 \text{ Usage per month} \times 12}{316} = 3.79$$

$$\text{Setup cost/year} = 3.79 \times \$100 \text{ per setup} = \$379$$

$$\text{Inventory carrying costs/year} = \$1580 \times 24\% = \$379$$

These calculations should prove to you that the formula does balance setup costs with inventory carrying costs. The EOQ formula gives the lowest total cost for carrying inventory and making setups. Then, as you reduce setup costs, both your expenses and your inventory investment go down at the same time, giving you a double kick to your ROA.

For example, in the above exercise, if you reduced the setup cost to $50, the EOQ would be 223. Every time you can cut a setup cost in half, the lot size and inventory investment is 70.6 percent, or (223 ÷ 316 = .706) of what it was previously for that component.

Stockholders in your company should insist that the EOQ formula be used to communicate to material control personnel how to make the lot sizing financial decision to govern component inventory levels.

If you're able to get all your setup costs down to 10 percent of each component's unit cost, no lot sizing formula will be needed. You can experiment with the formula and prove to yourself that this 10 percent rule of thumb would be financially acceptable.

PRODUCT AND PROCESS DESIGN TO REDUCE LOT SIZES

Calculating Lot Sizes for Families of Components

Whether you use cells to reduce setup costs, or whether you decide to group similar components until you can justify cells, you still have a financial decision to make each time a quantity of individual parts is processed.

Be sure the lot sizing formula you decide to use can be utilized when you decide to run a group of similar components, one behind the other. The EOQ formula can easily be used to calculate the lot sizes for a group of components using almost the same setup. The easiest way to explain this is with an example.

Let's say you have a group of six components whose tooling and sequence of four operations are almost the same. They are made from the same or similar castings and are processed on the same holding fixtures. Each component has some unique dimensional feature that makes its setup slightly different from the others. When run individually, the setup time for the four operations is eight hours each. When two or more components can be run on a common setup, the changeover from one part to another totals three hours.

- For two parts, the average setup will be $(8 + 3) \div 2 = 5.5$, a 31 percent setup time reduction.

- For three parts, the average setup will be $(8 + 3 + 3) \div 3 = 4.7$, a 41 percent setup time reduction.

- For four parts, $(8 + 3 + 3 + 3) \div 4 = 4.3$, a 46 percent reduction.

- For five parts, $(8 + 3 + 3 + 3 + 3) \div 5 = 4.0$, a 50 percent reduction.

The process begins each time one of these six parts is reordered. At that time, the material control system predicts which of the other five components will be reordered within the next two weeks (or another short time period). Assume that three components can run together as a group. One full setup and two partial setups will be made. From the preceding paragraph, you use the setup cost of 4.7 hours for each of the three components, rather than 8.0 hours for a full setup for each. The inventory investment for this combination of three parts would be 77% ($\sqrt{4.7 \div 8} = .77$) of the investment if all three components were processed on separate setups.

A more detailed proof of this simple calculation is as follows, using the preceding example on page 139:

$$\sqrt{\frac{100 \times \text{Setup cost} \times \text{Usage}}{\text{Unit cost}}}$$

$$\sqrt{\frac{100 \times \$100 \text{ Setup cost} \times 100}{\$10}} = 316 \text{ Lot size}$$

The average setup time for parts run separately is eight hours each. When three are run together the setup time is 4.7 hours each. Therefore, in the above example, the setup cost for 4.7 hours would be 58.75 percent of the setup cost for eight hours (4.7 ÷ 8 = .5875 or 58.75%).

The above lot size calculation would become

$$\sqrt{\frac{100 \times \$58.75 \text{ Setup cost} \times 100}{\$10}} = 242 \text{ Lot size}$$

For a 4.7-hour average setup time, the inventory investment would be 77 percent of what it would be for an eight-hour setup for each part (242 lot size ÷ 316 lot size = .766 or 77%). Thus

$$\sqrt{4.7 \div 8} = \sqrt{.5875} = .766 \text{ or } 77\%$$

This example illustrates how to reduce setup costs and inventory investment without making improvements in the setup itself. It also illustrates how much lot sizes can be reduced by manufacturing cells or by experimental cells using paralleling and overlapping techniques explained in blocks 59 and 60 of Chapter 11.

Reducing Changeover Time by Shortening Pit Stop Time

Later in this chapter lean quick changeover and cellular manufacturing are covered. In this section we cover setup and lot size reduction in a general way to discover project opportunities.

Focus some setup cost reduction on reducing your operator's time "in the pits." Observe the operator between shop orders to see how you can have other personnel prepare replacement tools ahead of the pit stop (changeover) and then gang up on the processing equipment to get it back into production in the shortest time, hopefully in minutes. This doesn't always mean that the total personnel direct hours won't be the same as before. However, the cost per machine hour will go down dramatically and machine utilization percentages will increase.

Can you imagine a NASCAR race where at a pit stop the driver gets out of a car to change the tires and fill the fuel tank? Yet the same thing probably happens every day in your shop. Every setup should be treated as a portion of a race, with ROA points that count toward the championship. Every setup should have a "pit crew" to plan and prepare for the next time the machine operator finishes one shop order and comes into the pit to start the next. A racing team knows that the race car needs to get back out on the track quickly or it will get behind and not place well in the race or the point standings. The same applies to expensive shop equipment. The longer a machine stays in the pits between shop orders, the less chance it has to maximize the quantity of product it can produce per hour and per year, increasing its utilization rate and eventually reducing the investment required for capital equipment.

Race teams invest much money in equipment and people to win races and gain customers for their sponsors. They know that many races are won in the pits. The same goes for your shop. Your company's ability to stay in the race against competitors for the championship may depend on how much you invest to reduce setup pit time. Your sponsors, customers and stockholders, will insist on it.

The goal of a setup reduction strategy is that while an expensive piece of capital equipment is completing its last few parts, a setup team is gathering raw material and tooling to be ready to come over the pit wall so they can get the equipment back into the race in the shortest possible time.

Reducing Manufacturing Lot Sizes by Investing in Tooling and Equipment

Many setup cost reduction projects can be initiated with little investment. You will have projects for which your accountant will write off tools as an expense. You will have others that will require major capital investment.

When you discover a project that requires an investment, before completing the Project Evaluation Form from Chapter 5, ask your accountant whether the investment will be treated as an expense in the profit and loss statement or whether it will be capitalized as an asset in the balance sheet. If it will be an expense, include it on line 7 of the form. If it will be treated as a capital asset, include it on line 16 of the form, and on line 7 include its annual depreciation expense.

What you are really doing in setup cost reduction is implementing projects that reduce your inventory investment more than you increase your capital investment. As you reduce your lot sizes by reducing setup time and costs, your inventory investment will go down. To reduce the setup time will usually require an expense or capital investment. This will always be a good investment if you evaluate each project as I have suggested in Chapter 5 and prove that the project will increase rather than decrease the ROA.

Design Setup out of Your Components

In case it isn't part of your product and process design culture, I suggest you establish a design philosophy that focuses on product designs with fewer components and fewer setups on individual components.

Most products made of assembled components contain two or more components that can be redesigned into one. For example, in the original design two different parts may have been designed to be bolted together. As time has passed, casting and machining equipment may have improved to the point where the two parts can now be machined from one casting. Or, it's possible that you can now financially justify a new piece of capital equipment that can machine more surfaces with a single holding fixture.

As a result, two or more machining operations and their setups can be designed out of the original two components. Obviously, if products can be economically redesigned to reduce the number of components or number of setups, this approach can become part of your design philosophy for all future new product designs.

Included in this design philosophy is the approach that new product design becomes a joint venture between personnel who design the product and personnel who design the processes, including the operators who set up and run the process. The processing personnel must be brought in at the initial product design phase to get the best results. Help the design personnel to make it a normal part of their design culture that your stockholders, with their desire to minimize inventory investment, are one of the customers that need to be satisfied with a final product and process design that reduces the investment in inventory. This kind of action is incorporated in Six Sigma improvement programs.

The next piece of this design philosophy is to design components in such a way that they can be processed in the least number of operations and with the fewest number of setups. For example, you might add chucking lugs to a casting so that two lathe operations can be performed on a single setup.

Another example is to design a component so all machining operations can be performed on one setup on a CNC machining center. Or, you might be able to financially justify a machining center that has multiple indexing tables built in so you can run very small lot sizes to feed to assembly operations on a daily or hourly basis.

A bonus from this product and process design culture is the improvement in product quality. If you can do all processing operations with one setup, all dimensional controls are dependent on the repetitive capability of the processing equipment. Each time a component is moved from one operation to the next, dimensional features that depend on each other will often require additional inspection. If all dimensions are obtained in one holding, inspections are minimized or eliminated, particularly if you use preventive maintenance as a tool to maintain the dimensional capability of your equipment. This is another element included in Six Sigma improvement programs.

Another bonus from this design approach is that as you reduce the number of setups for current processing operations, you also reduce the number of stations needed when you design a manufacturing cell.

If you make the investment to send your product and process designers to trade shows, or schedule periodic meetings with equipment sales representatives, you will make it easier for them to discover appropriate equipment to process components with minimal setup. Equipment such as machining centers with multiple pallets to hold fixtures and with multiple cutting tool holders appears to be a very expensive investment until you calculate the reduction in your inventory investment that will result from shorter setup times and smaller lot sizes. Look for these opportunities where the equipment investment plus the smaller inventory investment will be a fraction of your current inventory investment for the components plus your current capital equipment investment.

As you modernize your processing equipment, look for opportunities to dedicate a piece of fully depreciated equipment to a few components that require significant setup time. If you have the floor space available, you may be able to keep the equipment set up for a few appropriate components so you can make them in very small lot sizes, hopefully only when required by a customer order or an assembly shop order.

LEAN QUICK CHANGEOVER CONCEPTS

In this section I refer to lean concepts that relate to setup and changeover reduction. In most lean manufacturing courses, setup reduction is related to changeover that occurs when a mass production line or continuous-flow process is changed over to a different product line.

In continuous-flow processes the products will be grouped in families that use the same equipment in the same sequence. Many of the same concepts can be applied to job shop assembly, component manufacturing, and paperwork or information processing. This section and the next are closely related to the previous material in this chapter that focused on setup cost reduction for manufactured and purchased components.

Components That Don't Mesh with Lean

If you've studied lean manufacturing or attended lean seminars, you may wonder how you can apply lean concepts to your particular business, especially if your customers give you a very short lead time between your receipt of their purchase order and their expected delivery date.

For example, www.mep.nist.gov, the lean Web site, encourages you to, "avoid batches and move toward continuous flow in batches of one." A lean workbook states, "Any supply in excess of a one-piece flow through a manufacturing process" represents inventory waste. This has caused many lean practitioners to arbitrarily reduce lot sizes before they design a lot sizing formula or sufficiently reduce setup cost.

The above quotations relate to manufacturers who are currently utilizing mass production and desire to apply lean concepts to convert to a continuous-flow process. I will clarify this confusion as I show you how to apply lean concepts to businesses like yours, which are forced to manufacture components and assemble products in job shop lots ahead of the receipt of a specific customer order.

Another quote from the lean Web site states, "Pull systems are customer order driven production schedules based on actual demand and consumption rather than forecasting." This has caused some lean practitioners to decide that material requirements planning or other push systems should be eliminated for all components.

The fact is, if a component has a longer purchasing or manufacturing lead time than the customer order lead time you promise to customers, that component requires some method to predict its future usage so it can be ordered before the customer order is received.

Reducing lot sizes and lead time, and using pull systems based on actual customer orders are very good lean concepts and should be applied to as many purchase orders and shop orders as possible, particularly in assembly operations.

Lean Quick Changeover

Quick changeover as presented in traditional lean courses is primarily focused on changing a mass production line or continuous-flow line from one product to another. Since my audience here is small- to medium-sized manufacturers who aren't currently using mass production, my description of lean quick changeover for setup time reduction will focus on applying lean methods to your setup cost (and time) reduction projects. Remember to link the methods described in this section with the principles presented in the previous sections of this chapter, which speak to setup reduction for component manufacturing operations.

The changeover improvement process is an organized sequence of activities that seeks to eliminate the wastes that contribute to excessive setup time and costs:

- *Document all actions** performed during a changeover, including the teardown of the existing setup and actions required after the new setup is complete and until the processing dimensions and specifications are acceptable. Look for other kinds of waste.

- *Analyze the detailed information,* looking for wastes and their causes (see Chapter 9). Think about actions that can be done by people other than the machine operator before, during, and after the machine setup and changeover activities are completed.

- *Implement and experiment* with various changes and numbers of people involved as if they are a NASCAR auto racing team's pit crew members.

- *Standardize the changes,* much as you would in the 5S program for workplace organization described in Chapter 9.

There are quick changeover financial rewards to be gained as you apply lean quick changeover concepts.

Increased accuracy and improved quality become more important as you reduce your setup costs. The reason is because as you reduce setup costs you are financially justified to reduce your lot sizes. When you reduce lot sizes, you make more frequent setups (more setups per year). Those of you who have performed machine setups from bar stock or castings can testify how difficult it is to complete a setup without having to scrap material

---

* Italics in this section signify verb/noun combinations that discover additional team projects.

before making the first acceptable part. This is a waste your setup reduction projects can and must solve.

Decreased costs and increased capacity are issues that relate to setup. The primary cost you will want to reduce is the total cost for shop order cost and machine setup cost. You will want to reduce total setup cost (and time) because that is what financially justifies smaller lot sizes. You also want to get your capital equipment back into the race as soon as possible at each setup pit stop because this results in increased manufacturing capacity for each individual piece of equipment. This is like getting additional capital equipment and manufacturing capacity without making additional investment. Financially speaking, net profit increases (from reduced setup, scrap, depreciation, and inventory carrying costs) and asset investment decreases (lower inventory and capital investment) resulting in a bigger ROA.

Reduced lead time is a reward for both customer and stockholder. As you shorten a component's setup time on one or more operations, you reduce shop order lead time and decrease stockholder work-in-process inventory investment. There are other things that reduce lead time much more than reducing setup time. However, lean quick changeover needs to be given its share of the financial reward.

More flexible response to customer needs from quick changeover may have a dramatic impact on helping you respond to your customers' need for shorter delivery lead time. Remember, if you have component lead times that are less than your customer order lead time, and you have reduced setup cost to less than 10 percent of the total component cost, you will be more flexible in your response to customers because you will only need to make components in the quantity shown on customer orders.

Improved on-time delivery, a major customer satisfaction issue, will be improved by anything that shortens lead time. Though quick changeover on individual components may have little impact on customer delivery, the accumulated results from many components will have significant impact. Since meeting customer delivery promises is so important, every little bit helps. As we all know, often it is the delay of one component that keeps you from meeting a delivery date.

Three stages for lean setup reduction are suggested as an organized way to achieve quick changeover.

Stage #1: Separate Internal and External Setup

Internal setup is changeover that must be performed directly on the equipment used for processing. External setup includes preparation activities that can be performed for the next order while the equipment is processing a current order. External setup also includes such things as returning tools from the preceding order to their designated locations after the new order begins being processed.

Develop and implement changeover checklists for every piece of equipment and each component or component family. A component family is a group of similar components, using the same or similar material, with operations on the same piece of equipment, and with operations performed in the same sequence. You might focus first on those components with the largest setup cost.

Separate the checklist into actions that comprise internal setup and those that comprise external setup. For each item on the two checklists, ask questions such as, What needs to be done? When and where will it be done? Who needs to do it? How much time will it take? What are the correct process settings and can they be partially or completely set externally? and Have checklists been documented on appropriate paperwork or information sources so they will be consistently communicated and used?

Document a checklist to clean and inspect tools and fixtures after completion of each shop order. Have repairs made before the next scheduled requirement.

Stage #2: Convert Internal Setup into External Setup

Do this by standardizing the external activities on appropriate documents.

Show a preparation operation and scheduled date on shop order routers to assure that the raw materials and external activities will be completed and delivered before the internal setup is scheduled to start. This is simplified if dedicated tools, fixtures, and raw materials are stored near the machine or workstation.

Include external process settings, such as dimensions, pressure settings, or temperature settings, on your preparation checklist. Document on your checklists what, when, and by whom something needs to be done, including such things as presetting of cutting tools for length and diameter. Many of these things are solved by making capital investments in CNC machines that provide dedicated pallets with permanently mounted holding fixtures and a large tool conveyor of permanently dedicated cutting tools and holders.

Stage #3: Streamline Internal Setup Elements

Do this by paralleling checklist items.

Separate out internal elements to be performed by someone other than the person who sets the equipment to specific dimensions. Using the time allowance documented for each internal checklist item, you can determine how much time the internal person (machine operator) and the external pit crew will require during the setup pit stop. You can also determine how many internal pit crew members you should assign to complete the internal setup in the least elapsed clock time.

Other ways to streamline internal changeover are to use visual indicators, quick-set mechanisms, or fixed stops to eliminate the need for adjustments.

LEAN CELL DESIGN AND IMPLEMENTATION

Cells don't care whether they are processing paperwork and information or are being used to process components or assemble products. Cells should be applied to paperwork processes as well as machining processes. Contact a lean trainer to learn more. This section is only an overview of what you can learn from lean.

Cells for Manufacturing or Paperwork Processing

Traditional lean manufacturing is primarily about converting mass production processing islands to a continuous-flow process. The islands have batches of inventory or batches of paperwork between each island. In a continuous-flow process, the batch sizes are minimized and the islands are moved closer together so you can "make one and move one," resulting in lot sizes of one. Labor costs, lot sizes, and lead times are drastically reduced.

When the continuous-flow design is completed, there are opportunities to reduce the lead time and labor even further by designing U-shaped cells in which two or more employees, as a team, operate several processing steps or several machines.

U-shaped cells can also be applied to paperwork and processes in a manufacturing, distribution, or service business.

Manufacturers who make components requiring several operations can view each of the operations for each component as a mini mass production operation that needs to be converted to continuous flow provided by a cell. As the many components of a component family are added to the cell, it can still be viewed as the same continuous-flow process that has many frequent changeovers, as if changing from one product to another. The reason a cell can be viewed as a continuous process is that after each changeover all components use the same or similar material, use the same machines, and perform operations in the same sequence. These same principles apply to office processes.

I now show a lean five-step process for developing cells, particularly as it applies to paperwork and information processes. Experiment with machines in their current locations. Use paralleling and overlapping to get an idea of which configuration is best before you actually relocate and reconfigure your machines into a U-shaped cell. See Chapter 11 (blocks 59 and 60, page 189).

The Lean Five-Step Cell Design Process

This five-step design process provides a procedure to gather data about a process and analyze it to discover the best cell layout.

In a continuous-flow process, there will be sections of the flow that better utilize people by consolidating several individual operations into a cell (a mini continuous-flow process) that allows them to flexibly work as a team within the cell, sharing activities that make the whole cell more productive than before.

Step #1: Group Products in a Grid or Spreadsheet

We've already discussed the requirements to identify component families and product families (same or similar raw material, same processing equipment, and same sequence of operations). A sample grid is shown in Figure 9.6, page 126.

- *Customer order processing* can be looked at as the raw material for a continuous-flow process for a standard product. Every operation, department, and piece of equipment within each department, between customer order receipt and invoicing, could be included in the total process. Certainly the scheduling of component purchase orders, component shop orders, and assembly orders would be important elements. Separate but similar customer order processing flow could be customer orders for special products made from standard products, customer orders for a one-time contract for a unique product, or a customer order for a product made to a customer's drawings and specifications. The paperwork flow for these four possibilities will likely be so similar that when shown on a grid it will be clear whether they can be treated as a family. The four possibilities would be listed on four rows in the first column of the grid. The departments or equipment or operations, in their flow sequence, would be the headings for the other columns. By placing an "X" under each of the columns that matches with the appropriate row, you can begin to get a picture of how many rows can be brought into one cell. In addition to deciding which rows can be in the same family, you are also looking for columns that might be pulled together into a U-shaped cell.

- *A service business or a manufacturer's branch office* can use the same grid process for the various kinds of customers who phone, e-mail, or walk in the door for service.

- *Component manufacturing areas* can use a grid with many rows to list component names and part numbers. The columns would be used to list equipment names, types, or machine numbers for the various operations.

Step #2: Do the Arithmetic

For each row and product family you need to know how much is coming into each row (quantity of customer orders for a given time period, rate at which customers come in the door, quantity of components or machine-hours for a given time period) so you can compare it to the daily, weekly, or monthly availability of time from each column or the columns in total:

- *Customer orders,* as an example, might flow into your business at a rate of 50 orders per day. To convert the customer orders into component purchase orders and shop orders may require 25 hours per day total by personnel in various departments. Therefore, the unit processing rate (lean uses the phrase *takt time*) is .5 hours per customer order (25 orders per day ÷ 50 hours per day = .5 hours per customer order). This departmentalized approach may use up three to five calendar days before purchase orders and shop orders are released. However, if you have a cell composed of a maximum of three people, you could easily reduce the calendar time to one day maximum. And, depending on the minimum batch sizes you can arrange for your cell to receive, your order processing time should range between 30 minutes and a few hours. With creativity and automation, the 30 minutes should be further reduced as a cost reduction to require fewer people in the cell.

- *Service businesses or branch offices,* where the customer is involved in processing time, can make the same calculation to shrink the processing time and batch sizes. When customers are involved, by phone or walking in the door, you are interested in the average rate at which customers make contact, such as one every 10 minutes or six per hour. If it takes an average of five minutes to process each customer, there is a low probability that the waiting time will be significant. However, if the average processing time is eight minutes, or a range of five to 11 minutes, there is a higher probability that one or two people will sometimes be waiting to be served.

- *Component manufacturing opportunities* to rationalize the possibility of a cell require a similar calculation approach. You will first decide how many shifts or how many hours per day you must operate the cell for it to pay out financially. A cell will normally be a multi-shift operation. Since each component in the cell or component family won't have exactly the same processing time for each operation, you may find it easier to simply use your grid from step #1 and enter the daily, weekly, or annual hours needed from the cell for each component. This time requirement is the result of multiplying the run time for each operation for each component by the component's usage rate. This will give you the weekly, monthly, or annual hours needed from the cell for each component. Then, as you accumulate the cell time, component by component, you will determine whether you have enough hours to justify at least one cell.

Step #3: Review the Processing Sequence

You broadly described the process operations by name or equipment in the step #1 grid. In this step you are breaking each operation down into its smaller elements to eliminate waste that adds no value to support customer satisfaction. Use the same analysis for paperwork and information processes such as customer orders, service business processes, or component manufacturing cells:

- *Document and study the sequence* of each task the person or machine performs in each separate operation. Analyze the cell and the sequence you recorded on your grid. By moving some operations to a different place in the sequence, you may be able to combine two or more component families into one.

- *Break each operational task down* into the smallest observable elements. For manufacturing parts, challenge the necessity of design features or close tolerances that add no value. For paperwork processes, ask whether some actions, such as redundant approvals, are really required.

- *Minimize the non-value-added elements.* Identify which of the elements are non-value-added elements. Eliminate those wastes on which your project team can reach consensus.

- *Refine the cell's capacity* by reducing the times recorded on the grid for non-value-added elements that have been eliminated. Also be sure that every line has an estimate for the number of changeovers each year based on the best estimate of lot sizes calculated by a financially sound lot sizing formula. Also, estimate a time period for scheduling preventive maintenance for the cell equipment.

Step #4: Combine Operations to Balance a Process

In step #2, you looked at ways to arithmetically relate the work flowing into each paperwork or manufacturing process (such as 50 customer orders per day) with the work time available (such as 25 hours per week) to determine the processing rate (such as .5 hours per customer order).

The total processing time is made up of highly variable times for each operation in the total process. The longest operation may take five times as many minutes as the shortest operation. This variation isn't a big problem in a cell where the operations are done by hand by people. However, in manufacturing cells where operations are performed by machines, it requires more thought and creativity to decide how to combine operations to balance the process with the number of people required in the cell. For paperwork or service business cells, your goal is to share the work equally among the personnel in the cell. For component cells, your goal will be to minimize the work done in the cell with the longest time requirement by moving the work to a different machine in the cell, and attempt to sequence the machines next to each other that have the shortest time requirements.

- *Customer order processing* in many companies is done by several departments such as sales, inventory control, purchasing, and production control. Together they consume excessive lead time. However, if converted into a cell that flexibly combines the tasks of several departments, and by reducing the batch sizes, the cycle time for each customer order can be reduced from days to minutes. It's only necessary to train the few people in the cell to do most or all of the tasks so the task times can be broken into equal parts for the number of people required.

- *Service businesses or branch offices* include customers as one of the participants in the process. One goal is to reduce the batch size of customers waiting in queue to be serviced. The other goal is to reduce the processing time previously required to process each customer, or reduce the lead time to do the work performed for them.

- *Component manufacturing families* shown on your grid may have enough operations to require six or seven machines that will require only two or three people when combined in a U-shaped cell. If the cell is designed to reduce setup or changeover time, batch sizes will be much smaller than before and, internally within the cell, you will be able to "make one and move one." As a result, the cycle time for individual components can be reduced from days to hours or minutes to help shorten the lead time and get components to assembly or the shipping dock daily or hourly.

Step #5: Design and Implement the Cell

Using the facts documented and analyzed in the first four steps, your project team is ready to bring their knowledge together to implement the cell. If you want to, your team can cut the lead time it takes to complete the first four steps by dividing the team into three or four leaders of three or four other project teams to get the first four steps done in weeks rather than months.

If a cellular project is prioritized by a high ROA when evaluated by the form in Chapter 5, your company will be ahead of the game if you allow the teams to concentrate full time to complete these steps in the shortest lead time. That's why I suggest you invest in additional personnel if you expect to quickly double or triple your ROA using lean and the verb/noun project discovery process.

In this step you want to go back to Chapter 8 to look again at the various wastes and their causes to identify wastes you can eliminate. Also, you will want to review the lean building blocks, also in Chapter 8, for such subjects as point-of-use storage and visual controls.

- *Agree about design goals* as a team. Use the facts you've gathered to establish cell design goals. This activity will reveal whether you need to gather additional facts when the team is having trouble reaching consensus. Test goals as you would test a new product prototype. Make several U-shaped layouts to see whether adding one or two extra machines would allow you to draw additional component families into the cell.

- *Simplify the flow* using concepts from Chapter 9 under Apply Value Stream Mapping. Minimize the need for operations that interrupt one-way flow. Don't avoid minor interruptions in the flow if that maximizes the number of hours the cell is used or allows you to bring additional component families into the cell. Integrate process operations so that the cell is seen as a single piece of equipment. For paperwork processes where several people are operating the cell, your goal should be to make it appear as if the cell were one person.

- *Design-in preventive maintenance* procedures. Include a maintenance person on the team during changeover activities. Train maintenance personnel to assist with preventive maintenance during changeover pit stops between component shop orders.

SUPPLIER SETUP COST CONTROL AND REACTING TO PRICE BREAKS

When you get supplier quotes with quantity price breaks, in most cases they are telling you that they have significant setup cost for that particular component. Your first reaction to this information should be to work with that supplier and insist that they allow you to help them reduce their setup cost. Your other option is to get quotes from alternative suppliers who will work with you to reduce setup costs so you and they can reduce lot sizes.

Your obvious reason for building this kind of relationship with your suppliers is for both of you to understand that they have great control over your component inventory investment and, therefore, must work with you to reduce their setup costs and lot sizes. This simply means that with a little investment in setup cost reduction by you or your supplier, unit prices for the affected components will also be reduced as soon as the investment is paid off. This is a place where you will use the project evaluation form in Chapter 5 to determine whether the investment will increase the ROA.

Put another way, you won't maximize your ROA if the 20 percent of your suppliers that supply 80 percent of your components with price breaks don't implement projects to reduce their paperwork and manufacturing lead time and projects to reduce setup costs. They must be required to do this so they can minimize their in-process inventory investment and your component inventory investment and pass less than the cost of inflation on to you.

You must work with suppliers to reduce setup costs, even if you must invest in tooling to force down their setup costs so lot sizes can be minimized. The results will be a lower unit cost and a lower inventory investment. Keep this fact in mind as you look for projects to increase your ROA, because some of your best projects are hidden from your view in your suppliers' processes.

Here's a checklist of things you should expect from all your suppliers:

- Increase their prices at a rate lower than inflation

- Follow continuous improvement principles so they can also increase their ROA year after year

- Reduce their setup costs so your unit costs will be lower and, by running smaller lot sizes, your inventory investment will be much lower

- Have minimum variation in the lead time of each given component they supply so you won't have to invest in as much inventory for safety allowance

- Deliver the full quantity ordered on the day promised

- Follow a documented quality system so they can minimize dimensional variation and perform inspection and part counts at their location so that you can eliminate these activities at your location

- Reduce their ratio of salary and wage costs and overhead costs divided by sales so they can pass some of the savings on to you

Quantity Price Break Financial Evaluation

Until you and your supplier achieve a significant reduction in their setup costs, you need a way to separate their setup cost from the price they give you for each quantity.

You can always justify an EOQ quantity or the quantity from your own financially sound lot sizing formula.

Remember, a financially sound lot sizing formula, such as the EOQ formula, is your tool to prove that you have the lowest possible cost for inventory carrying costs and setup costs in your annual budget and profit and loss statement. This also means the formula will cause you to maximize your net profit.

Therefore, when a supplier gives you a quantity price break, your first action should be to determine the dollar value of the setup cost in each of the price breaks. If you have a good working relationship with the supplier, you can ask them to tell you the dollar value of the setup cost in each quantity. The reason you need the setup cost on each individual component with a price break is so you can compare it with other projects to reduce setup cost on other specific components and decide which project will improve the ROA most, using the project evaluation form in Chapter 5.

This is going to look like a lot of work. However, the math is simple and a computer can make these calculations on a moment's notice and store them until one of the values changes. If you're serious about selecting the right lot sizes so that you will maximize net profit and ROA, you just have to accept that this is a necessary process.

Let's assume a supplier provides you with the following price break schedule for a particular component:

Quantity	Price
10	$150
20	$100
25	$90
50	$70
100	$60
200	$55
250	$54

You are always financially justified to buy an EOQ if you have all the required values to insert into the formula. For annual usage the EOQ formula is:

$$EOQ = \sqrt{\frac{2 \times \text{Setup cost} \times \text{Annual usage rate}}{\text{Inventory carrying percent} \times \text{Unit cost}}}$$

For this particular part, assume that the annual usage rate is 200 per year and that you have calculated your inventory carrying cost and found it to be 20 percent. However, you can't calculate the correct lot size because you don't know which quantity and price to pick. Therefore, if your suppliers won't or can't tell you the setup cost, you must calculate it for them. To calculate the setup and run costs requires you to solve a simultaneous equation like the ones you should have learned in math or algebra classes.

The equation you will use is:

Setup $ + Price break quantity × Run $ = Total lot $

For this simultaneous equation solution, use the values from the price break schedule for quantities of 20 and 25.

In case you don't remember how to solve a simultaneous equation, here are the detailed steps you could design into a spreadsheet and let it do the calculations for every price break quote you receive.

Step 1: Revise the preceding formula to say: Setup $ + Price break quantity × Run $ = That quantity × Its price.

Step 2: Pick any two price breaks.

Step 3: Enter the values into the step 1 formula for the smaller quantity.

$$\text{Setup \$} + 20 \times \text{Run \$} = 20 \times \$100 \text{ Total lot \$}$$
$$\text{or Setup \$} + 20 \times \text{Run \$} = \$2000 \text{ Total lot \$}$$

Step 4: Enter the values into the step 1 formula for the larger quantity.

$$\text{Setup \$} + 25 \times \text{Run \$} = 25 \times 90 \text{ Total lot \$}$$
$$\text{or Setup \$} + 25 \times \text{Run \$} = \$2250 \text{ Total lot \$}$$

Step 5: Set up and solve the simultaneous equation by changing the step 3 equation positive values to negative values and placing it beneath the step 4 equation:

$$\text{Setup \$} + 25 \times \text{Run \$} = \quad \$2250 \text{ Total lot \$}$$
$$\underline{- \text{Setup \$} - 20 \times \text{Run \$} = -\$2000 \text{ Total lot \$}}$$
$$0 \quad 5 \times \text{Run \$} = \quad \$250 \text{ Difference}$$

The setup dollars become zero, $25 - 20 \times \text{Run \$}$ becomes $5 \times \text{Run \$}$, and $\$2250 - \$2000$ becomes $\$250$.

Step 6: Move the 5 difference between the two quantities to the other side of the equals sign.

$$\text{Run \$} = \$250 \div 5 = \$50 \text{ Run price}$$

Step 7: Insert the $50 Run price into the step 3 equation and it becomes:

$$\text{Setup \$} + 20 \times \$50 \text{ Run} = \$2000 \text{ Total lot \$}$$

Step 8: Reconfigure the step 7 equation so only setup $ is on one side of the equals sign.

$$\text{Setup \$} = \$2000 - 20 \times \$50$$
$$\text{or Setup \$} = \$2000 - \$1000 = \$1000$$

Now we have setup and run values we can insert into the EOQ formula to make a good judgment about lot size. If the supplier knows what they're doing, any pair of the price breaks will give the same answer. If various pairs don't give the same answer, that supplier may be just guessing or may be arbitrarily increasing some of the price breaks so they can make a higher profit if you happen to select the one that favors them. Start with the price break that approximates a one-month supply:

$$\text{EOQ} = \sqrt{\frac{2 \times \$1000 \times 200}{20\% \times 90}} = 149$$

Next, contact the supplier to get a price break for 150 parts or just calculate it for yourself:

$$\$1000 \text{ Setup} \div 150 = \$6.67 + \$50 = \$56.67$$

Finally, get with this supplier and decide what you are going to do together to reduce the lot size and inventory dollars.

$$\text{Inventory investment } \$ = 150 \div 2 \times \$56.67 = \$4,250.25$$

The whole reason for taking the time to perform this calculation on each component that your supplier prices with a price break is to find the lowest total cost for a component so that you will make the best decision about the right lot size. It's just another tool to be sure you know you will make the highest ROA on each individual component.

DISPOSE OF SURPLUS INVENTORY

Almost every business has money invested in inventory that it will never sell. Many managers are reluctant to dispose of surplus and obsolete inventory because in the year it is written off as an expense the net profit for that year will be lower than desired. However, managers must think of the two other offsetting financial issues that temper the lower net profit for that year:

- First, the inventory asset investment is lowered by the same amount as the expense that is written off, tempering the impact on the ROA.

- Second, all the expenses for the inventory carrying costs listed in this chapter will be reduced to offset the write-off. If your inventory carrying percent is 25 percent, for every surplus or obsolete dollar of inventory you keep you are paying 25 cents each year just to hold on to it. That means in four years you will have had expenses equal to the value of that inventory item.

Consider disposing of surplus and obsolete inventory every year, as soon as it's obvious that you will not sell it within the next year or two. For some spare parts components you might be able to justify keeping a seven-year supply when you make this decision.

It will be almost impossible to avoid having some surplus or obsolete raw material or finished components.

Surplus usually results from inflated inventories near the end of a company's business cycle. You may have been operating for several months at nearly full capacity when your customers' sales begin to fall off and they begin to shut off their orders to you. Meanwhile, the same thing is going on between them and their customers. You don't recognize soon enough that your company business cycle is turning down. Therefore, you don't shut off your shop orders and purchase orders soon enough to avoid an inventory surplus.

At this point I hope you will ask yourself why you haven't been monitoring your company business cycle, as will be described in Chapter 14.

Surplus inventory implies that the inventory will eventually be consumed when you start getting new customer orders. However, it's not impossible that you will have several years' supply on some components or raw material. If your inventory carrying cost percent is 25 percent, you should retain less than a four-year supply (100% ÷ 25% = 4). If it is 20 percent, your retention time would be less than five years.

Obsolete inventory is often a result of product design changes or as a result of a product being discontinued by you or your customers. You need an ongoing project that monitors your surplus and obsolete inventory. You can use the evaluation form in Chapter 5 to calculate the additional expense and reduced net profit to write off the unnecessary inventory. The project evaluation may show, even with the reduced inventory investment, that this action will negatively impact your ROA for that year. However, it will certainly increase the ROA for all future years or future business cycles.

The only solution for obsolete inventory is to dispose of it as soon as possible at the best price you can get for it.

If you have a sizable amount of sales of spare parts, there will be personnel in your sales or service department who will want to keep several years' supply of spare parts items declared to be surplus, particularly if they are no longer being manufactured. As a rule of thumb, once you have material or components in your inventory to service anticipated future customer demand for spare parts, you should avoid keeping more than a four-year supply. The reason for this is that it costs about 25 percent of the value of a part just to hold it in inventory for a year. Therefore, if a quantity of a part is likely to be in stock more than four years, it would probably be a good financial decision to dispose of the excess as soon as possible, or sell it at a very low price to a customer who might be able to use it.

11

Rationalizing a Material Control System

I've done two things to make reading this chapter easier for those who only need an overview of what material control must do to consolidate the basic elements of shipping customer orders on time, controlling lead times, controlling lot sizes, and doing all of this at the lowest possible cost. First, I have summarized several very detailed flowcharts into one flowchart that contains the bare essentials about what a material control system must contain. Second, in the detailed explanations about each block in the flowcharts, I've italicized the few sentences that give a short description of each block. The fully detailed description is for those material control professionals who must make decisions about all the various things a material control system could and should do.

RATIONALIZING A MATERIAL CONTROL SYSTEM

Material control and scheduling systems will be most complicated for a manufacturing business and most simple for a service business. Systems for distributors fall somewhere in between these extremes. Detailed charts and formulas are provided to help employees discover whether there are critical gaps in your material control system that need to be corrected before projects to reduce lead times and setup costs can be effectively implemented.

The cause of these gaps may be disconnects between the material control system and accounting or data processing systems. Other gaps may exist because employees don't embrace or haven't been trained in the most basic inventory and production control principles and formulas.

I will explain the basic material control principles by which you can plan and schedule for the shortest lead times and determine the most profitable lot sizes. All the major ways to double or triple your ROA will be significantly limited by an incomplete or poorly managed material control system.

If you are a manufacturer, you need to study this section very thoroughly as summarized on the flowchart in Figure 11.1. If you are a distributor, you will want to look at all of the chart except the part that has to do with the scheduling and control of manufacturing shop orders. As a service business, how much of the chart you will need to consider will depend on those elements that have to do with delivering product or services on time, how large a purchasing function you require to deliver product to your customers, and how much manufacturing you do.

If you have a significant number of weaknesses in your material control system, you won't get the maximum ROA improvement from implementing projects generated by any kind of continuous improvement process, whether you use my approach, the lean manufacturing approach, the Six Sigma approach, or implementation of a quality system such as ISO 9000.

Before I cover Figure 11.1 in detail, I will cover some basic principles of material control systems to help you decide how important this chart is to your business.

Material control financial arithmetic is very important and very simple. If I hadn't provided the financial formulas and financial mathematics, you would have said my claim that you can double or triple your ROA is just bold bragging. The same applies to my claim that lead time and setup cost reduction projects can't be successful with a poor material control system.

The mathematics of material control is just as important as accounting and financial mathematics. Many material control professionals don't know how to effectively apply financial and material control formulas to their daily decision making. Even fewer top management or financial people realize that setting policies about manufacturing and purchasing lot sizes is a financial decision rather than a material control or manufacturing decision.

My point is, every time you make a decision about a purchase order or shop order quantity, you are making a high-level financial investment decision about the size of your component and product inventory investment.

Therefore, this chapter and its four sections are organized around a small number of material control formulas, the names of the values that go into them, and an explanation of the principles behind them. Don't reject these formulas because they appear to be old-fashioned. I simply use them to prove that any material control system, no matter how sophisticated, requires this arithmetic to make financially sound decisions.

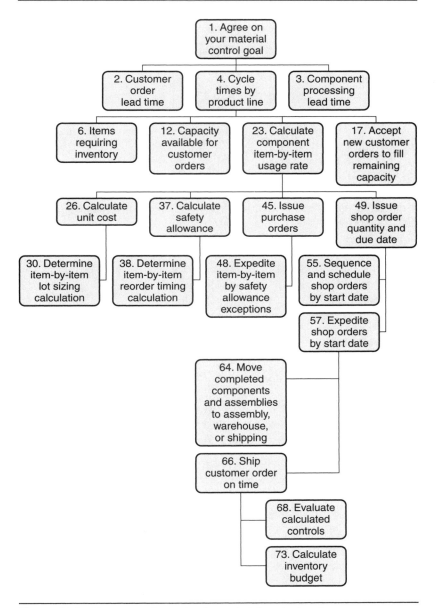

Figure 11.1 Necessary elements of a material control system.

The Ideal Material Control System

The ideal material control system defends against imperfections in systems used by customers, suppliers, and yourselves. For example, most small- or medium-sized manufacturers have few processes with negligible setup or changeover time and few have situations where all components of an assembly have combined customer order processing, purchasing, and manufacturing lead times shorter than the delivery lead time customers will accept.

I provide you with material control arithmetic, formulas, elements of the formulas, and explanations about control of elements for businesses that currently have purchasing and manufacturing lead times that are too long, setup costs that are too high, and customer orders that are shipping too late. I will show you what I consider to be requirements of an ideal production and inventory control system and how to implement projects that make adjustments to your current system.

Elements of your existing material control system may be working well to help you minimize stock-outs at low material control costs and at the lowest possible inventory investment. Use this chapter as a checklist to discover projects that will help you evaluate your current system. I promise that you will discover improvements that will increase your ROA.

Much of what I present in this chapter, and presented in Chapters 9 and 10, was gleaned from books written by Robert L. VanDeMark, titled *New Ideas in Materials Management, Inventory Control Techniques,* and *Production Control Techniques.*

The numbered blocks in the flowcharts in the remaining three sections of this chapter can be basically divided into three main groups. Descriptions for each block in the chart in Figure 11.1 begin in the next section.

- Blocks 1 through 44 represent an inventory control system that begins when a customer purchase order is received and ends when it's time to issue purchase orders and shop orders.

- Blocks 45 through 66 represent a production control system that begins when it's time for your purchasing function to release purchase orders for material and purchased components and when shop orders are released to the production control function. The production control system ends when a customer order is shipped.

- Blocks 67 through 76 represent a system to check and evaluate how well the overall system controls lead times, lot sizes, and on-time shipment of customer orders.

IMPROVING INVENTORY CONTROL

The chart in Figure 11.1 is a summary of the other charts in this chapter. There is much detail in this chapter because material control is a complex practice for businesses that must carry inventory because customers demand on-time delivery. Keep your system as simple as required to consistently make on-time shipments at the lowest possible cost.

This chapter is primarily designed for sales order processing, inventory control, purchasing, and production control personnel. However, we will point out places where personnel in other departments impact your company's ability to make on-time deliveries at the lowest possible material control costs.

Look at Figure 11.1 to see the benchmarks for a complete material control system. When you recognize that you have a material control problem, go to the more detailed charts in the remaining sections for answers.

Use the detailed charts as checklists to document the current material control system. Rationalize the things that interest you and identify projects that will result in cost reduction or better customer on-time delivery. Decide what changes can be made, what benefits would result, and what investment would be required so you can rank your material control project ideas with other projects.

Don't worry about a major improvement program as much as improving the bits and pieces. Likely your current system is serving well. Don't destroy the methods you now use. Let your improvements be an evolution process by considering suggestions I will make as you read the explanation for each block. We'll begin with the flowchart in Figure 11.2.

Block 1—Agree on Your Material Control Goal

Customers expect you to provide delivery within a competitive time frame. Their suppliers, such as your company, with the shortest lead times often get the sale. Your stockholders realize this fact and expect you to increase sales levels by providing better lead times than your competition, at a cost lower than your current cost. A good starting place to improve material control will be for your company management to agree about your mission. A short, simple goal might be, "Better customer service at lower cost."

Block 2—Document Your Customer Order Lead Time Policy

If your customer expects product delivery the same day as ordered, you know you must carry inventory at your plant, a branch warehouse, or with

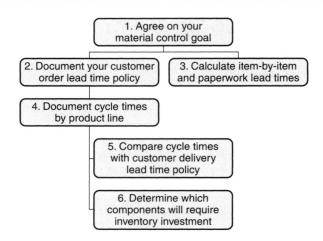

Figure 11.2   Inventory control system.

a distributor. If you were given six months lead time for standard products, you would need minimal inventory and could do almost all your purchase order and shop order scheduling based on customer orders only. Your situation may be somewhere between these two extremes.

Be sure your personnel who influence paperwork and information lead time as well as purchased item and shop order lead time know the customer lead time restrictions under which you must operate. They need to know the customer lead time restrictions to limit the number of components and end items for which inventory must be maintained. *Your particular market has likely determined the maximum customer order delivery time it will allow and, therefore, forces you to carry some components in inventory. To get an advantage over your competitors, you must implement projects that will minimize lead time before your competitor beats you to it.*

Block 3—Calculate Item-by-Item and Paperwork Lead Times

When you receive a customer order, your personnel must get information about the customer order to the shop and purchasing functions in the shortest time practical. Therefore, *you must document the lead time required for the flow of information* so the required actions are quickly handed off to purchasing and manufacturing. Then, *you need to know the historical lead time required for purchased and manufactured components on an item-by-item basis.* The most reliable way to get an idea about the lead time for these various activities is to measure the time each has been taking in the most recent past. You're going to discover that most of the functions are actually taking more time than is required. *Eliminating the difference between "taking" and "required" for information flow is your first group of material control improvement projects.*

For the information flow lead time facts, take a sampling of the most recent customer orders and subtract the order receipt date from the date the information was received by your inventory control function. If this isn't less than one calendar day, break this part of the lead time into controllable pieces. Next, sample information flow from the inventory control function to the issuing of all the purchase orders and shop orders triggered by customer orders. If these lead times aren't reasonably short, you have found some more improvement projects.

For component lead times, make the calculation item-by-item for every component. To complete blocks 4, 5, and 6, sampling will be adequate. However, when your system analysis gets to blocks 24 and 49, you will need to calculate the lead time for every component you buy or make. *Your most reliable way to keep item-by-item lead times up to date is to maintain a record of the last three receipts for all purchase orders and shop orders.* For most inventory control purposes, the recent past is the best predictor of the future. This calculation will gradually adjust lead times downward as you implement projects to reduce purchasing and manufacturing lead times.

Block 4—Document Cycle Times by Product Line

Figure 9.1, page 100 shows you a pattern you can use to *create a cycle time chart so you can graphically illustrate the mismatch between your customer and manufacturing lead times. This is a necessary step in identifying specifically which end items and components you must maintain in inventory to consistently meet customer delivery date promises.*

A cycle time chart shows the accumulated paperwork, purchasing, and manufacturing lead times drawn on an exploded material list. The list shows each component in an assembled end item along with the raw materials and/or subassemblies. *A cycle time chart should be made for a typical model in each product line.* In some cases, there are some common components in each product line.

Block 5—Compare Cycle Time with Customer Delivery Lead Time Policy

After the lead times are drawn horizontally on the charts in the appropriate sequence, the lead time that must be promised to customers is drawn as a vertical line. *Any assembly, subassembly, raw material, or component whose lead time is to the right of the vertical customer lead time line will require an investment in inventory if you expect to consistently make on-time customer deliveries.*

Block 6—Determine Which Components Will Require Inventory Investment

A cycle time chart will serve as a powerful motivator for personnel in charge of information regarding purchase order and shop order flow to *implement projects that will dramatically reduce the accumulated lead times for all of the items shown on the chart list.* Then, coupled with reduced setup cost for purchased and manufactured items, you will start seeing a significant reduction in your inventory investment.

Update the chart every year to dramatize the "before and after" progress your project teams are making.

Block 7—Calculate End Item Usage Rate by Product Line

In block 3, to predict future lead time, I said the most reliable information is found in the most recent lead time history. I say the same for predicting future usage for end items. By knowing your end item usage, you can do a better job of deciding on your manufacturing capacity for accepting new customer orders in blocks 8 and 12, for component reorder timing, and for calculating lot sizes (see Figure 11.3). If most customer orders are for customized products, you may have to use man-hours or machine-hours to decide when you exceed your capacity for a future time period.

Most sales forecasts show a smooth month-to-month demand on an annual basis and may even predict seasonal demand if that is normal for your business. *Sales forecasts are usually more optimistic than your most recent history. They should only be looked at as a guide.*

Since actual demand for each end item tends to be erratic, monitor your end item usage each month, based on the most recent time period. This is a good starting place and will help material control see trends or normal seasonal expectations.

If you have accurate data about equipment-hours for each product, you may have a starting place to get a feel for when in any given week or month you should not schedule any additional orders. You may also look at your most recent peak business cycle to get a feel for maximum capacity levels that might be achieved again by adding man-hours to existing equipment.

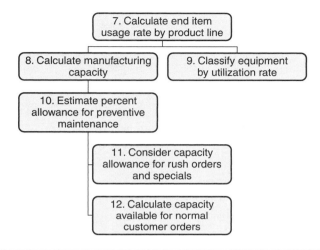

Figure 11.3   Inventory control system.

Block 8—Calculate Manufacturing Capacity

Manufacturing capacity is defined by processing bottlenecks. Capacity is a pipeline with departments or machines that have various diameters. The smallest diameter determines your capacity to accept customer orders. To improve the odds that you won't accept more customer orders than you have machine-hours, consider relating machine-hour requirements for each end item to the usage of each end item from block 7. You divide the annual usage for each component by the number of shop orders for each component to estimate machine setup hours. With this data, you can get a feel in advance for when to expand bottlenecks to help make on-time delivery.

Block 9—Classify Equipment by Utilization Rate

By using the facts from block 8, or a sampling method as in blocks 61 and 62, *identify existing and potential bottlenecks by monitoring the increase in the utilization percent for each machine.* It will be obvious which machines have low utilization rates and are candidates to be sold to reduce capital investment.

Block 10—Estimate Percent Allowance for Preventive Maintenance

Preventive maintenance to control process capability is important to connect product design with process design. Product designers must not design-in tolerances that exceed the capability of the machine or process. *Preventive maintenance is the function that maintains or improves the capability of the machine to hold design tolerances consistently. You will be wise to rationally set aside a certain percent of a machine's capacity for preventive maintenance.*

Block 11—Consider Capacity Allowance for Rush Orders and Specials

I include this as a consideration if your real world has customers or sales staff who thrive on this kind of excitement. It's not fair to your customers who plan well enough to avoid it. *Set a little time aside so you don't add to the problem by delaying other customer orders when you have to run in a rush order.*

Block 12—Calculate Capacity Available for Normal Customer Orders

You may already be doing blocks 7 through 11, or something like them. Keep blocks 7 through 11 in mind if your customer order scheduling or your product lines get more complicated.

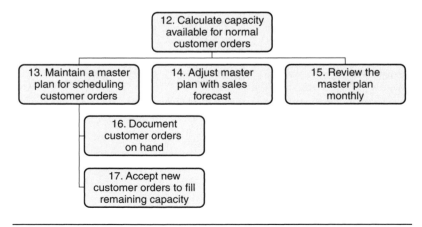

Figure 11.4 Inventory control system.

Block 13—Maintain a Master Plan for Scheduling Customer Orders

Planning is the least expensive form of control. Your master plan is the time and quantity coordinator for all company operations. I recommend some form of master planning that will accurately connect your acceptance of future customer orders with your current manufacturing capacity plan. Review the plan monthly with key sales and management personnel to make adjustment up or down based on the most recent usage or known future demand. The time period covered by the master plan should be slightly longer than the cycle time from block 4 for each of your product lines. The individual time periods shown on your master plan should be in the days, weeks, or months you use to make delivery promises.

The quantities should be broken down by product line or models within each product line. *A master plan should be a communications and discipline tool between sales and manufacturing. Much expediting expense will be eliminated by this tool and blocks 48 and 57.*

Block 14—Adjust Master Plan with Sales Forecast

As mentioned in block 7, use sales forecasts as guides to make adjustments to the master plan. Use the most recent usage over a cycle time period to make initial estimates for future usage. Make adjustments in consultation with a key sales person.

Block 15—Review the Master Plan Monthly

A master plan establishes customer delivery promises for future time periods for each product line. It isn't only a guide for customer shipping promises. It also serves as the guide for capacity improvement as sales trend upward. Since business conditions often change quickly, the master plan must be reviewed monthly by key planning personnel. The monthly review also forces planners to evaluate material control system performance each month by counting the number of past due orders so additional capacity can be added as required.

Block 16—Document Customer Orders on Hand

If the master plan covers a complete cycle time for each product line, on any given day *you will have some accepted customer orders scheduled for some or all of the future time periods.*

Block 17—Accept New Customer Orders to Fill Remaining Capacity

You're now ready to start filling your planned capacity by *making delivery date promises for customer orders based on the remaining available capacity.*

Block 18—Maintain Inventory Close to Customers

Proximity to customers is measured in minutes, hours, days, or weeks (see Figure 11.5). It can also be measured by shipping time from the plant to the customer. If competition requires it, or you desire to increase sales, you may move it closer by setting up branch warehouses or get distributors to carry an inventory. If you must maintain branch inventories, I will suggest, in block 35, a visual reorder method you can utilize to know when to reorder.

Block 19—Decide on End Item Reorder Method

This block primarily relates to blocks 20 through 22. You won't need blocks 20 and 21 unless forced by customers to deliver assembled end items from the plant on short notice. If components are carried in inventory, stocking for quick delivery will depend on assembly lead time and daily usage

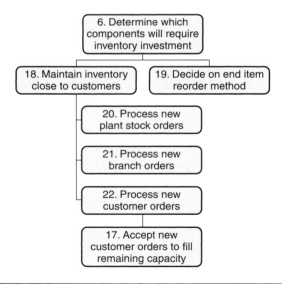

Figure 11.5   Inventory control system.

demand. Visual bin reserve methods can be used, or detailed perpetual inventory records may be required to cover for components requiring long lead times.

These blocks dramatize the conflict between pull material control systems, preferred by lean, and the MRP push methods you may be using.

Blocks 20, 21, and 22—Process New Plant Stock Orders, New Branch Orders, and New Customer Orders

All new customer orders, branch orders, or plant stock orders should be given equal priority because each is intended to get your product as close to the customer as you decided was necessary in block 18.

Block 23—Calculate Component Item-by-Item Usage Rate

By dividing the most recent one or two lot sizes of each component (block 24) by the period of time it took to consume it (block 25), you will have a weekly or monthly usage rate that you will use to determine lot sizes in block 30 and reorder timing in block 38. See Figure 11.6.

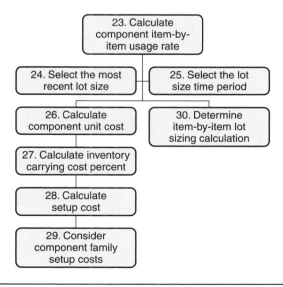

Figure 11.6 Inventory control system.

Blocks 24 and 25—Select the Most Recent Lot Size and Lot Size Time Period

You're now ready to explode the master plan and firm customer orders into the components required for product assembly. *Item-by-item usage is needed to determine quantities and timing for purchase orders and shop orders* released by blocks 45 and 49. Our suggestion for estimating future usage requires the combination of blocks 23, 24, and 25.

In block 7, I told you that *the most reliable way to predict future usage is to start with history for the most recent past.* You must decide how far back into the recent past to look. You can get the best usage quantity by *going no further back into history than the period of time it took to consume the last one or two lot sizes.* The lot sizes will be good for determining usage only if they are determined by some financially logical calculation similar to block 30.

Block 26—Calculate Component Unit Cost

Unit cost for each component is required to calculate the lot sizing cost in block 30 and to classify components in block 32. *Our definition of unit cost is the total material, direct labor, and manufacturing overhead cost of components, including equipment setup or changeover, as the components go into stock or assembly.* It may be the same cost your accountant uses for cost accounting.

Block 27—Calculate Inventory Carrying Cost Percent

Blocks 26 through 29 are the ingredients for the lot sizing formula in block 30. In Chapter 10, I showed the costs for carrying inventory and the inventory carrying percent.

Inventory carrying costs are expenses that are hidden in a financial budget and P&L statement. These are expenses that components accumulate when they are held in inventory. Expenses such as depreciation, obsolescence, borrowing cost, storage area costs, taxes and insurance for both property and inventory, and a small amount of material handling attach themselves to each inventory item waiting to go into an assembly or to be shipped to a customer, branch, or distributor.

These costs will automatically drop from budget expenses as you reduce component setup time and cost, and as you reduce lead times. This should motivate you to aggressively initiate projects that will reduce setup costs and lead times when you study Chapter 10.

Block 28—Calculate Setup Cost

Purchased component setup cost is the cost of processing and receiving each purchase order. For shop orders, it is a combination of the cost to process, schedule, and control each shop order plus the cost of the time required to set up equipment between shop orders. The calculation of these costs is covered in Chapter 10.

Block 29—Consider Component Family Setup Costs

If you have components that fit into families because they look alike and have very similar processing operations, you can cut the lot sizes in half, rather than processing them in separate setups. For cellular manufacturing, see Chapter 10.

Block 30—Determine Item-by-Item Lot Sizing Calculation

In Chapter 10, *I proved that you need to calculate a lot size for all components until their setup cost,* from block 28, *is less than 10 percent of the component's unit cost* from block 26.

Common sense tells you not to make just one or two parts at a time if your machine setup time is several hours and the current unit cost is only a few dollars. The result of arbitrarily setting small lot sizes for components that require considerable setup time is an excessively high unit cost. Common sense and experience also tell you that your unit cost will be lowest when you run larger lot sizes. In between these two extremes is an optimum quantity that will give you the lowest total cost for setup cost and inventory carrying cost.

Remember, *lot sizing is a financial decision that must be governed by a formula used by material control personnel and approved by top-level financial managers. Setup costs should determine lot sizes because lot sizes determine the investment for component inventory.*

Block 31—Calculate Usage Value for Each Component

Usage value is equal to a component's unit cost times its usage rate per month or annually. Usage value is only important when it is compared to the usage value for all other components for which inventory is required. See Figure 11.7. The combination of a high-cost component with a very

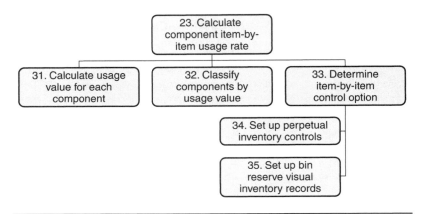

Figure 11.7 Inventory control system.

high usage rate will result in a high usage value. *These are items you will want to control very carefully because they represent the 20 percent of the components that make up 80 percent of the inventory investment.* Conversely, your components with low usage values are the 80 percent that represent 20 percent of your total inventory investment and can be controlled by less expensive methods.

Block 32—Classify Components by Usage Value

Divide components into at least three (ABC classification) or four (ABCD classification) categories, depending on the different levels of control you believe will yield the lowest material control costs. If you calculate by computer you can know the usage value for every component and arrange them in order from the largest usage value to the smallest. With this data you can classify components into ABC or ABCD groups. The percent of components or the percent of total usage value in each group is arbitrary. Experiment with various combinations until common sense makes the decision for you.

For ABC classification, you might settle for combinations with "A" classification to be 70 percent of the total usage value representing 15 percent of the components. For "B" classification it could be 20 percent of usage value representing 30 percent of components. For "C" classification it could 10 percent of usage value for the remaining 55 percent of components. For ABCD classification, break the groups into smaller percents if you want a greater variety of control options.

Block 33—Determine Item-by-Item Control Option

Inventory control is item-by-item control to assure that you will deliver customer orders on the promised date. Let's look at options by which you can use item-by-item classification to lower your costs and investment.

The variables you can use to determine your ABC control options are lot size (block 30), safety allowance (block 37), and record keeping method (blocks 34 and 35).

Using a financially sound lot sizing formula, as proposed in block 30, *lot sizes will automatically tell you to look more frequently at the 20 percent of your items that make up 80 percent of the inventory investment.* View lot sizes as the number of months' supply rather than a specific quantity. A good lot sizing formula will tell you to make your highest usage/highest cost items more frequently.

For "A" class components, you automatically review the major part of the inventory investment more frequently. Because of the short reorder frequency, you might decide to minimize your safety allowance inventory investment. On an exception basis, *expedite when the on-hand quantity reaches one-half the safety allowance.* You should maintain control using perpetual or computer records.

For "B" class components, the lot size will also control reorder frequency. You can use the full calculated safety allowance to expedite by reporting exceptions when the on-hand quantity reaches the safety allowance. Maintain perpetual or computer records.

For "C" class items consider visual controls such as a manual bin reserve system rather than computer records. In visual control systems you relate the lot sizing calculation with usage values and arbitrarily assign lot sizes as a number of months' supply up to a maximum of 12 months' supply for very low usage value "D" class components. You can double the safety allowance without greatly increasing the inventory investment. This can be the 55 percent of your components that account for only 10 percent of your component inventory investment.

Blocks 34 and 35—Perpetual Inventory Controls versus Visual Inventory Controls

These blocks connect with block 33 because at this point you evaluate whether you have the lowest-cost system to determine lot sizes and reordering of components that must be carried in inventory (blocks 30 and 38). Use blocks 32 and 33 to make your item-by-item decisions for each component in block 38. See Figure 11.8.

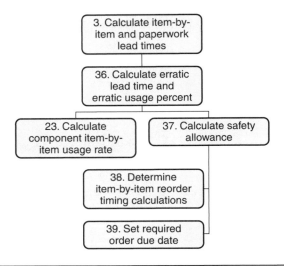

Figure 11.8 Inventory control system.

Block 36—Calculate Erratic Lead Time and Erratic Usage Percent

If you must carry a component in inventory, you need a rational way to calculate a safety allowance for it. Safety allowances are required because the usage rate and lead time for a given component varies from one purchase order or shop order to the next. *With no safety allowance for components, you will miss many customer delivery dates. Safety allowance becomes a permanent investment that must be reduced by shorter and more consistent lead times for both purchase orders and shop orders.*

You need a percent by which to multiply a component's usage rate to obtain a reasonable quantity that will act as a cushion when the lead time is longer than average and/or when the usage rate is significantly increased or decreased by actual customer demand. A large percent will be your signal to initiate projects to shorten lead times and make them more consistent from order to order.

I recommend that you start with a percent based on the following formula to cover both erratic lead time and erratic usage. You can adjust it up or down based on your system evaluation as described in blocks 68 through 71. I recommend that you use as the lead time the three most recent lead times from purchase orders or shop orders for each component.

$$\text{Safety allowance } \% = \frac{\text{Maximum lead time} - \text{Average lead time}}{\text{Average lead time}}$$

This percent will likely range between 15 percent and 50 percent.

Block 37—Calculate Safety Allowance

My suggested safety allowance formula is as follows and *must be calculated item-by-item each time it is reordered:*

Safety allowance quantity = Usage rate × Safety allowance %

Block 38—Determine Item-by-Item Reorder Timing Calculations

Normally you will want to release a new purchase order or shop order for a component when there is just enough material on hand to last until a new customer order is received. The suggested formula below uses information from blocks 23, 3, and 37.

Reorder quantity = (Usage rate × Lead time) + Safety allowance

If you didn't have the cycle time problem described in block 4 and Chapter 9, you could wait to release new orders based on actual customer orders. However, *you have to face the reality of needing to issue these new orders before you actually receive your customer purchase orders.*

Neither your usage rate nor your lead times can be relied on to be exactly right. That's why I believe your most reliable estimate of the future will come from the most recent past as described in blocks 3 and 23. The better your estimates, the better you can gamble that you will minimize your inventory investment and meet customer delivery dates. Then, since you know that your estimates for usage rate and lead time for each component are going to be wrong, you will want to add a safety allowance.

Gambling isn't a consistently profitable activity in either a business or the most colorful casino you can imagine.

Relatively small investments in safety allowance will create large decreases in stock-out rates. As you keep increasing the safety allowance, there is a point between five percent and one percent stock-out rate where the safety allowance investment becomes prohibitive. I give you this warning so you won't expect more from a material control system than it is statistically able to deliver. Just evaluate your controls, using block 68, and make logical changes in the formulas to improve future system performance.

Block 39—Set Required Order Due Date

This is the simple calculation of adding lead time to the reorder date to inform purchasing or production control when an order must be delivered to the warehouse, assembly, or shipping to assure that customer delivery promises will be met. Along with due date, the inventory control function also communicates the order quantity authorized by block 30.

Block 40—Adjust Component Usage Exceptions Upward Based on Actual Customer Orders

The only reason I include this block is to recognize the possibility that actual customer orders might introduce an unusual demand pattern such that, using our recommended method of calculating usage rate, you would not reliably ship customer orders as promised. Just look for these exceptions and make usage rate adjustments as appropriate. See Figure 11.9. Generally speaking, you should trust the usage rate from block 23 to make lot size and order timing decisions.

Blocks 41 and 42—Maintain On-Hand Quantity Accuracy and Determine Auditing Method

Be sure on-hand quantities for components are correct. You must do an annual physical inventory and/or systematic cycle counting. *The point is, to make on-time delivery, your on-hand quantity records must be accurate.* See Figure 11.10.

Blocks 43 and 44—Physical Inventory versus Cycle Counts

From my experience, for both accounting and material control, physical inventorying creates as many on-hand quantity errors as it corrects. I believe systematic cycle counting is more accurate for both functions.

Also, by doing cycle counting your manufacturing operations aren't shut down for the time required to do the annual physical count. Cycle counting improves capital asset utilization and yields a small ROA increase.

The best time to take an inventory count is each time a component reaches its reorder quantity (block 38). One reason this method is best is because you have a chance to delay a new order if the actual quantity is greater than the record. If the actual quantity is less than the record, it gives you a chance to expedite the new order at the earliest possible moment. Another reason is *because the frequency of counting is automatically regulated to count items based on their usage value* calculated in block 31. This

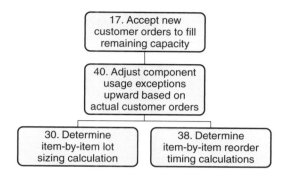

Figure 11.9   Inventory control system.

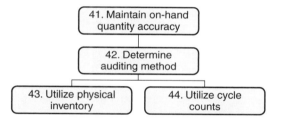

Figure 11.10   Inventory control system.

means *items that impact the inventory investment and customer service the most are counted most often and those items with the least impact are counted less often.*

Be sure to consider paperwork cutoff times when you do cycle counting. The best time to take your cycle counts is at the beginning or end of each day, in concert with when computer transactions are made.

If the above method isn't acceptable to you, you can count in blocks of parts using the classification from block 32 to control frequency. Or *you can count the on-hand quantity each time a new order is received to stock. This is the least expensive way to correct your records but it happens too late to delay or expedite a new order.*

PRODUCTION CONTROL IMPROVEMENT

Use blocks 45 through 66 in these charts as a checklist to document your production control system. Rationalize the things that interest you and identify projects that will yield cost reductions or better customer on-time delivery.

Block 45—Issue Purchase Order Quantity and Due Date

Responsibility for purchased components is relayed from inventory control to purchasing. See Figure 11.11. If supplier lead times are greater than calculated by block 3, *buyers will need to start expediting the order immediately.* If a supplier isn't able to meet the lead time requirement, *communicate this to customers* if no other solution is available.

Block 46—Consider Price Break Quantities

Reorder requirements for a part for which a supplier offers price breaks should trigger two actions. The reason these price breaks exist is because suppliers have large setup costs for some components.

Trigger an improvement project to help a supplier lower setup costs so the lot size can be smaller. Then, determine which price break will give you the lowest total setup cost plus inventory carrying cost. See Chapter 10.

I suggest that your purchasing function list the purchased components that offer price breaks and document what they do when they make a reorder decision. If your buyers have been given goals to reduce unit cost, you may be surprised that they are making decisions to exceed the authorized lot size to the detriment of the lowest-cost buying decision. *Selecting lot sizes is a financial decision that must be governed by lot sizing calculations authorized by top-level managers.*

Block 47—Authorize Blanket Order Releases

If you utilize blanket purchase orders, I recommend you have a clear policy about the release of quantities. *Your policy should dictate that blanket order releases be in authorized lot size quantities.*

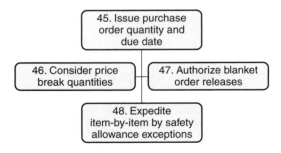

Figure 11.11   Production control system.

Block 48—Expedite Item-by-Item by Safety Allowance Exceptions

When most material control and sales personnel talk about expediting, they're talking about activities performed when a customer delivery date is going to be missed and purchase orders or shop orders for components have missed a due date. Too often actions are taken to run a behind-schedule order in ahead of another. This never solves the problem. It just causes other customer delivery dates to be missed.

I want to help your company get out of the expediting business. Expediting occurs because sales has promised a customer order in less time than is allowed by your company policy and your master plan or because your material control system hasn't performed as I've laid out in these flowcharts.

Most expediting is done too late to fix the problem that caused the delay. Blocks 55 and 57 show how to expedite shop orders by start date. For purchased parts, you must take action as soon as the on-hand quantity reaches 50 percent to 100 percent of the safety allowance quantity.

Block 49—Issue Shop Order Quantity and Due Date

This is when shop orders for manufactured components are relayed by inventory control to production control. See Figure 11.12.

Blocks 50 and 51—Consider Seasonal Load Leveling and Business Cycle Load Leveling

You may need to practice shop load leveling because you have seasonal demand or because you want to purposely invest in inventory just ahead of the business cycle, before you run out of capacity because of processing bottlenecks. You may prove, by using the project evaluation form in Chapter 5, that the annual ROA will be higher if some short-term inventory investment, just ahead of the seasonal demand or just ahead of the business cycle peak, will result in a higher ROA than the investment in capital equipment to meet the peak seasonal capacity demand. To do this you simply add quantities for the necessary components and/or end items to appropriate time periods in your master plan for bottleneck processes.

At one point in each business cycle there's an opportunity to get ahead of competitors by adding some inventory investment in anticipation of significant increases in sales demand. As with seasonal planning, *you have an opportunity to capture sales from your competitors if they're not as*

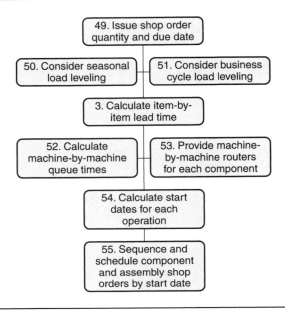

Figure 11.12 Production control system.

well prepared as you are. And, you might meet demand with lower capital investment during the peak of the business cycle from year to year.

Block 52—Calculate Machine-by-Machine Queue Times

Inventory control is item-by-item control and production control is machine-by-machine control. The best way to control shop orders is by start dates for the most heavily loaded machines, as explained in blocks 54 and 55. Continuous operations or manufacturing cells have no queue time between processing operations. *Queue time is the time a batch of components waits between processing operations.* More than one shop order waiting in queue ahead of each machine is a signal that some blocks, up to block 64, are missing or are not being executed properly. *Keep queue times as short as practical because excess queue time causes excess shop order lead time, and excess lead time creates excess investment in in-process inventory.*

Lead time = (Lot size × Run time) + Setup time + Queue time

You work back from the shop order due date to get the start date for each operation.

Block 53—Provide Machine-by-Machine Routers for Each Component

A document is needed to show each process operation in sequence, starting with raw material issue and any setup preparation that can be done prior to the beginning of the next operation. For each operation, the router must show machine number, setup time and run time, operation instructions, and special tooling. *For production control scheduling purposes, you're primarily interested in operation sequence, machine number, and setup and run time.* For queue time, you're interested in minimizing the time that material stands in queue waiting for run time to be applied to the material.

Block 54—Calculate Start Dates for Each Operation

Inventory control, in block 49, issues shop orders with a calculated lot size and a required due date based on the queue time, setup time, and run time for the lot size. The due date is secondary as far as scheduling of component shop orders is concerned. If you don't start each operation at the right time, you know you have no chance of completing the last operation by the shop order due date set by your inventory control system.

Each date set by a material control system serves a dual purpose. The due date for raw material becomes the start date for first operation on shop orders. The due date for a component shop order is the start date for an assembly order. The assembly completion date becomes the customer shipping date.

The simplest way to assign a start date to a shop order is to take the historical lead time for that component from block 3 and subtract it from the shop order due date. You must issue the material and start the first processing operation on that date, no sooner and no later. Then, you move shop orders through all operations with minimum queue time between operations, assuring that you complete all operations by or before the required due date.

When you follow this scheduling method, block 3 lead times shrink and in-process inventory investment will be the lowest it can be until you make additional lead time reductions from projects generated by Chapter 9.

With this method you expedite machine by machine any day you are unable to start initial operations on the required start date. Look for operations with too many shop orders in queue and follow blocks 57 through 60 to add machine-hours. Any other expediting method, such as shuffling orders or splitting lot sizes, is much more expensive than a little overtime to get back to start date.

A slightly more expensive scheduling method may be required if you have equipment that you know, from blocks 61 and 62, has high utilization rates. Generally, these high utilization rates are desirable because it means you are minimizing capital investment. *The advantage to the start date method is that by looking at the start date for every operation, you can know on any day where the bottlenecks are forming and can take expediting action immediately to add hours where required.*

If there is a significant difference between the total lead time for a shop order and its lead time from block 3, you may have discovered a project opportunity. It may tell you that your database for setup time, run time, or queue time isn't accurate. It may be an indicator of how well or how poorly you are executing your overall scheduling. It might tell you that you're still allowing too much lead time and too much inventory investment between operations.

Block 55(A)—Sequence and Schedule Component and Assembly Shop Orders by Start Date

Each day, inventory control releases new shop orders to production control. Supervisors' jobs are much more pleasant if all they need to do is put the new orders in start date sequence with the orders released on previous days. All shop orders are visually displayed so responsible personnel can issue raw material no sooner and no later than needed. If material isn't available you can expedite it. Once material is issued, shop orders are arranged in start date sequence for initial operations. If these same machines are routed for secondary operations for other components, they are placed in the appropriate start date sequence with other operations. This same visual method can be used for all subsequent operations, particularly those that require machines with high utilization rates.

This visual method creates an automatic expediting tool to tell you when to add additional hours to secondary-operation machines. Machines with utilization rates of 50 percent or less will almost never require expediting because their hours can be easily increased simply by moving a machine operator as required. With a few minutes each week, top management personnel and sales staff can know whether a customer delivery problem is developing and whether it's time to take action to expand capacity. Expediters can be assigned to more productive activities such as continuous improvement teams.

Block 55(B)—Sequence and Schedule Assembly Shop Orders by Start Date

The due dates on component shop orders are the start date for an assembly order or a shipping date for a customer order. *The reason most assembly orders can't be started on time is because component shop orders or purchase orders haven't been received into stock or into assembly by their due date.* If you are managing your material control system well, less than five percent of your assembly orders should be started later than their start date. Any percent greater than this means you've got a system problem somewhere upstream in the flow.

Take my flowcharts, customize them to fit your company and customers, and use them as a problem-solving tool to implement projects that will fix your problems. You don't need to wait until you start missing customer delivery dates to know you have a problem.

Block 56—Document Component and Assembly Shop Order Schedules

You likely have a computer screen or computer report that lists the date and quantity requirement and status for all purchase orders, shop orders, assembly orders, and shipping orders. An ideal example would be an assembly schedule that exactly duplicates the master schedule. Another example would be a component schedule that matches with a cycle time chart. Almost everyone likes lists and reports that give them status information. See Figure 11.13. *I suggest you evaluate these reports to see if their expense justifies their existence or if they really tell whether your existing material control system is performing well.* I'll speak more about system evaluation in blocks 68 through 76.

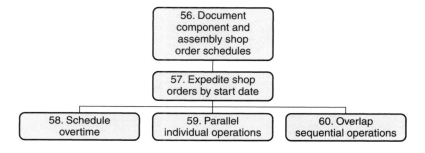

Figure 11.13 Production control system.

Block 57—Expedite Shop Orders by Start Date

The way many companies do expediting it isn't a rational activity, and much unnecessary expense is expended on it. Expediting is a time issue, not a quantity issue. You expedite because you're trying to make up for lost time.

The only effective way to expedite a shop order is to provide machine-hours or worker hours equal to the calendar time you are behind in component and assembly start dates or customer delivery due dates. Expediting is a symptom of a scheduling problem. It's not a cure when one shop order is moved ahead of another that has also passed its start date. Any time you have one work order starting later than its planned start date is a signal that you need to make up schedule time as soon as possible. Either your manufacturing lead times are longer than you planned, from block 3, or you don't have enough manufacturing capacity hours somewhere in the process flow.

There is one way to correct this problem. Expedite by adding processing hours equal to the number of days any process operation is behind its scheduled start date.

For example, you can look at shop orders for any work center and add up the number of processing hours that are behind the current date. That's the number of extra hours, for that work center, you must add to get that work center back on start date schedule. Your basic choices are: work overtime, add or transfer personnel to a parallel setup on similar equipment, overlap operations, or farm out these operations.

Block 58—Schedule Overtime

When you have a behind-schedule condition, *overtime is a less expensive method than calling customers to tell them you must reschedule the delivery date.* Late deliveries are expensive for your customer and your customer's customers. If done too frequently it's going to result in lost sales and lower ROA. Quickly decide to use overtime when no other fast solution is available to meet a shipping due date.

Overtime is a budget expense you want to minimize. But material control is a professional gambling business, and I've already assured you that you're probably going to lose one percent to five percent of the time even if you execute your system perfectly.

Another alternative to overtime is inventory investment for safety allowance. Just think of overtime as an alternative way to temporarily increase capacity.

Block 59—Parallel Individual Operations

This is when you put more than one piece of equipment or more than one person on a given operation to temporarily or permanently increase capacity. Since assembly operations have very low setup costs, adding people or setting up another line may be a good way to get back on schedule or increase capacity. The same applies to component shop orders if the added setup time is less than the overtime expense to get back on start date schedule.

Block 60—Overlap Sequential Operations

When setup costs are high or there is no available equipment or tooling for paralleling, consider overlapping to make up lost time or lead time. *To overlap, you start running the next operation before the current operation is completed.* It's essentially what happens in a manufacturing cell. You simply set up and start running a subsequent operation before the whole lot size is completed on the preceding operation. If a component requires several operations you might gain back one or more days of calendar time. This method requires no additional setup costs. If setup costs are low, you can utilize overlapping in conjunction with paralleling. For assembly operations you might temporarily add some additional subassembly steps.

Since setup plus total run time isn't the same on each operation, you need to do a little advance planning so heavily utilized equipment won't be sitting idle too long.

Planned overlapping is a good way to experiment with how a manufacturing cell (Chapter 10) might work on an individual shop order, or a family of shop orders, for components that are similar and use the same processing sequence.

Block 61—Calculate Machine Utilization Percent

Even if you have a large number of different machines, you should have a good idea about the ones that are most heavily utilized and which ones are usually scheduled for overtime. You may have particular machine numbers that are on your routers with so many hours assigned to them that it's impossible to process all the parts routed to those particular machines during the regular non-overtime hours and the number of shifts you have decided to staff. See Figure 11.14.

Personnel who route and schedule shop orders can start a project to analyze the components routed across the overloaded machines and reroute

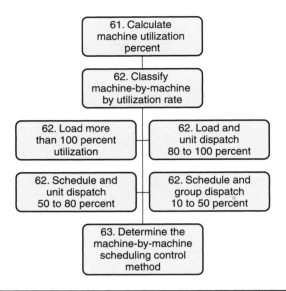

Figure 11.14 Production control system.

them to either get the lowest total setup hours or the lowest total unit cost, or the optimum between the two. Remember, planning is the cheapest kind of material control.

To calculate utilization percent, you total the number of hours each machine is utilized or scheduled in either actual hours or theoretical hours and divide these hours by the non-overtime hours and shifts available to obtain a percent utilization rate. The actual hours will verify what you already know or will reveal to you that your estimate wasn't as good as you thought it was. The calculation of the utilization percent will identify the machines that are excessively overloaded.

To manually gather the actual utilization hours, you can take a random sample of 10 percent of the closed component shop orders for the most recent period of time approximately equal to your cycle time period. Total the setup and run hours for each machine number and you will have enough facts to draw some rational conclusions. If you have some documentation of the actual machine-hours for each machine, this may give even better results.

Blocks 62 and 63—Classify Machine by Machine by Utilization Rate and Determine the Machine-by-Machine Scheduling Control Method

In blocks 31 through 33, I showed you how to classify components that must be kept in inventory so you can focus control on the small percent of them that make up the largest percent of your inventory investment. I suggest the same concept for controlling manufacturing equipment. From block 61, arrange the machine numbers in groups by a percentage range and determine the level of control for each group.

For machines with a rate of 100 percent or more, monitor their load daily and hour to hour. Consider more shifts, offload to another machine, or schedule regular overtime.

You will have multiple shop orders competing for the same start date. Have a specific plan or machine-loading method to resolve these start date conflicts.

For machines with a utilization rate of 80 percent to 100 percent, you can relax only slightly. For these machines, review the start dates each day and increase machine loading control when you see many shop orders with the same start date.

For machines with a rate of 50 percent to 80 percent, control them simply by moving operators to them when the initial operation shows a start date of the current date or when material is standing in queue for a secondary operation.

For machines with a rate of 10 percent to 50 percent, accumulate them in start date groups so you can move an operator to those machines less frequently.

Any time material is in queue for a secondary operation, process it as soon as possible, even if it is sooner than the start date shown for that operation. Running secondary operations sooner than the schedule requires will shorten the recorded lead time for block 3 and will begin shrinking your cycle time and in-process inventory investment.

For machines with a rate of less than 10 percent, consider rerouting to other machines for that operation so the machine can be sold and free up floor space. Or, if this machine has low capital investment remaining on your balance sheet, open a project to determine if it can be permanently set up to eliminate setup time for a significant number of similar components.

If most of your machines, particularly those that are most expensive, are being utilized more than 80 percent, this may be a clue that you may be ready to use the overlapping method to test out the potential for manufacturing cells or order additional equipment.

Taking time to rationalize the material control system will generate projects that decrease material control costs, reduce inventory investment, and increase sales because of on-time customer shipments.

Block 64—Move Completed Components and Assemblies to Assembly, Warehouse, or Shipping

Your goal is to make dramatic decreases in cycle time so more components can be scheduled by customer orders. *When you shrink the cycle time period and reduce your setup costs enough, most shop order quantities can bypass inventory storage and go directly to assembly.* The exceptions will be spare parts orders, which go to the warehouse or shipping. See Figure 11.15.

Be sure the assembly order completion date isn't the same as the shipping date you show for the customer order shipping date unless you consistently do both on the same day. This is particularly important if your product requires significant time for packaging between assembly and shipping.

Blocks 65 and 66—Package Shipments and Ship Customer Orders on Time 95 Percent of the Time

I've included these blocks just to be sure you allow lead time for packaging when you are mapping out your entire process flow. Another reason for including these blocks is in case you use a machine to do packaging

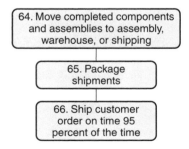

Figure 11.15 Production control system.

that requires significant setup time. If you have this situation, you probably have completed assembled product standing in queue. If assembly orders are consistently completed on time but packaging and shipping operations are causing you to miss customer due date promises, you must consider implementing some of the same scheduling practices you are applying to schedule and expedite component shop orders.

CHARTING MATERIAL CONTROL SYSTEM PERFORMANCE EVALUATION

I suggest that material control personnel use blocks 67 through 76 in Figure 11.16 as a checklist to evaluate the overall performance of the material control system. Identify projects that will result in cost reductions, operate the system more effectively, or improve customer on-time delivery.

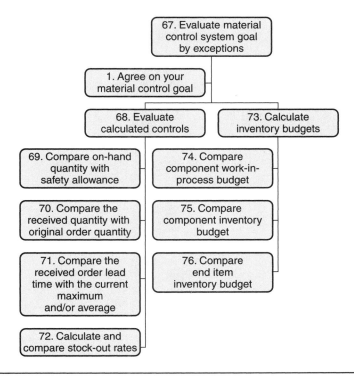

Figure 11.16   System evaluation.

Block 67—Evaluate Material Control System Goal by Exceptions

In block 1, I encouraged you to set a material control goal or mission that says something like, "Better customer service at lower cost." Use the blocks in Figure 11.16 to evaluate system performance so you can initiate projects to make improvements and fine-tune your system where you have variables that can be adjusted. Don't create a voluminous report. *Report the exceptions that are outside your calculated guidelines so you spend more time solving the most serious problems.*

Block 68—Evaluate Calculated Controls

Fortunately you have simple arithmetic and formulas to determine where in the system problems exist. In blocks 67 through 72, I show you how you can evaluate your calculated controls for items that the cycle time chart forces you to keep in inventory before customer orders are received. You evaluate the total system at two different places. One is at the receiving dock for purchased components and the other is at the warehouse when shop orders are completed. Evaluation of these calculated controls is based on actual conditions that exist at the time material is received at the receiving dock or into stock. The factual conditions you find when material is received tell you how well your controls are working.

In blocks 73 through 76, I show how to estimate the minimum size of your inventory investment as determined by your calculated controls. These estimates give you an inventory budget you can use as a target to tell you how well you are managing your inventory budget allowance.

Block 69—Compare On-Hand Quantity with Safety Allowance

This block tells you whether the new material was received at the right time and in the right quantity. To determine whether these two things have happened, you need to make three different comparisons.

First, compare the on-hand quantity at the time of receipt with that component's safety allowance, calculated in block 37. What you're actually evaluating is the formula you used in block 38 to decide at what on-hand quantity to issue a new purchase order or shop order. If the on-hand quantity is 50 percent to 150 percent of the safety allowance, your investment in safety allowance to protect your customer is about as high as it needs to be to minimize the number of times you miss customer delivery promises. Report an exception only when your percentage range is less than 50 percent or more than 150 percent. If you want to increase your risk, just play around with the safety allowance percent you calculated in block 36. Realize that *as your lead times get more consistent and predictable, your safety allowance percent will automatically get smaller and your safety allowance investment will automatically get smaller.*

Block 70—Compare the Received Quantity with Original Order Quantity

If the quantity received is more than plus or minus 10 percent of the order quantity, as calculated by the method you've chosen for block 30, you are exceeding a rational total cost for that component. This excessive cost will eventually show up as lower net profit and a lower ROA than necessary. Just report the exceptions. As you get fewer and fewer exceptions, reduce your evaluation percent so you can measure the average percent variation.

Block 71—Compare the Received Order Lead Time with the Current Maximum and/or Average

In block 3, I recommended that you determine your lead time by averaging the three most recent lead times for each component. If you compare the lead time for the new receipt to the maximum from the three most recent and find that the new lead time is longer than the current maximum, report it as an exception. This may be a signal that your supplier's system isn't providing acceptable control for purchased items or that your shop may not be reducing lead times. If you have implemented projects with a supplier specifically aimed at reducing purchase order lead times, make the comparison with the current average to provide yourself with an ongoing improvement target for you and that supplier. *Using suppliers who continuously shorten their lead time will increase your company's ROA.*

Block 72—Calculate and Compare Stock-Out Rates

You may not be able to maintain a material control system with a consistent stock-out rate less than two percent to five percent unless you have an excessive inventory investment as explained in block 43. *Common sense will tell you that many of your customers will be looking for other suppliers if your stock-out rate exceeds 10 percent.*

Compare the on-hand quantity with your safety allowance from block 69. Sometimes the quantity will be zero. Keep a separate tally of stock-outs for purchase orders and shop orders. Divide the number of stock-outs by the number of opportunities to have a stock-out. The number of opportunities for a stock-out equals the number of purchase order receipts and the number of shop order completions during a specific time period, such as your cycle time period or six months.

For purchase orders, look within the supplier group to discover projects related to specific suppliers that need to improve. For shop orders, look at your own material control system.

You don't actually have a stock-out unless you have a back order for the component that has a zero on-hand quantity. Therefore, if you don't have a good way to exclude these zero-on-hand situations, you can expect your stock-out rate to be overstated.

As an alternative, you could monitor the number of times you ship a customer order a certain number of days late as a system evaluation tool.

Block 73—Calculate Inventory Budgets

Perhaps you aren't aware that there is a way to estimate what your inventory investment should be. This is a critical issue because, for many manufacturers, inventory investment is a significant percent of their total investment.

Your inventory investment hinges on lead time and lot size for each assembled end item and each component or raw material that must be kept in stock. Your inventory budgets, calculated periodically, will document how much progress you are making with projects to reduce lead time and setup cost.

The best way to bring your material control goal into financial focus is through inventory budgeting. An accurately calculated inventory budget will tell you how much inventory investment you should have based on the effective control of each individual inventory item.

If your company financial personnel insist that you arbitrarily reduce inventory levels, they must also tell you how many sales they are willing to lose because of late delivery dates. Keep everyone focused on the fact that reduced inventory only comes from shorter lead times and lower setup costs.

Block 74—Compare Component Work-in-Process Budget

In-process inventory includes component shop orders and assembly shop orders. Lot size quantities only impact in-process inventory if you manufacture custom products. For each component, subassembly, and assembly for which you issue shop orders, calculate a budget based on the following formula and then add them all together to get the total. You can get a good estimate by using a 10 percent sample.

$$\text{In-process budget} =$$
$$(\text{Material cost}/2 + \text{Unit cost}/2) \text{ Lead time} \times \text{Usage}$$

Material cost plus unit cost is divided by two because the component starts as raw material but doesn't reach its total unit cost until all of the labor and overhead have been added. As you reduce setup cost, unit cost gets smaller and your investment goes down a small amount.

The lead time should be the average lead time from block 3. As shop order lead times, including queue times, become shorter, your investment goes down some more. The lead time must be expressed in the same time units as the usage rate. The usage rate is from blocks 23 through 25.

Multiple shifts will shorten the lead time in this formula and, at the same time, more highly utilize your capital equipment investment, resulting in a higher ROA. Some managers who don't like multiple shifts fail to consider the reduced in-process inventory investment when evaluating the costs related to an additional shift.

For subassemblies and assembled end items, material cost is the sum of the unit costs that make up the material list.

Block 75—Compare Component Inventory Budget

A manufactured component, if your cycle time allows, goes directly to assembly and continues to be an in-process inventory investment.

If a component must be held in stock to assure that you meet customer delivery promises, or because the component's setup costs are high, financial personnel need a rational estimate for the component inventory investment. The two quantities that determine the component inventory investment are lot size and safety allowance. Using the following formula, you can calculate the budget allowance for each component and add them to get a total. Or, take a 10 percent sample, add these components together, and multiply by 10 to get the total.

$$(\text{Lot size}/2 + \text{Safety allowance}) \times \text{Unit cost}$$

The lot size comes from block 30. The safety allowance comes from block 37. The unit cost comes from block 26.

Lot size is divided by two to obtain the average quantity in inventory as the lot size is being issued for assembly shop orders or for shipment to a customer or branch.

As you can see, when you reduce setup cost for each item, the lot size decreases. Then when you make lead times shorter and more consistent, the safety allowance becomes smaller. This formula mathematically demonstrates why setup cost reduction and lead time consistency are so powerful in minimizing investment and increasing ROA.

Block 76—Compare End Item Inventory Budget

The end item inventory budget is calculated using the same formula as in block 75. Setup costs for assembled end items may be so small that you make product only to customer or branch orders. However, shipping cost to branches may be such that you can prove that your total costs are lowest if you make larger lot sizes and ship in truckload shipments.

12

Linking Continuous Improvement with ISO 9000

ISO 9000 is another tool project teams can use to discover projects. ISO 9000 is in tune with this book's approach to continuous improvement. I will point out parts of ISO 9000 that provide opportunities to increase your company's ROA. I will name each section of the ISO 9000 standard with a verb/noun or verb/phrase combination so you can name projects that might be missed by other chapters.

I suggest you implement a quality standard, such as ISO 9000, if it is done to increase your ROA. You may see some other suggestions that will help with your quality audits or discover projects that relate to corrective and preventive action projects that will increase your ROA.

For this chapter I use ANSI/ISO/ASQ Q9001-2000, which has been approved as the American National Standard by the American Society for Quality. Look it over for project ideas even if you're registered to another accepted quality standard.

Agree on the Quality Mission. Don't implement a quality standard because a key customer requires it. The best approach is to treat implementation of a quality standard as an investment that results in ROA improvement. If your mission is a strategic decision to identify and prioritize projects that increase sales, hold cost and price increases to a rate lower than inflation, reduce product and process variation, and eliminate quality-related wastes, this approach satisfies both customers and stockholders.

Increase customer satisfaction. Meet customer requirements. Develop, implement, and improve quality management system effectiveness. Identify and manage company activities linked to quality. Continuously improve processes based on measurable objectives.

These are verb/noun combinations directly out of the ISO standard that encourage a process approach to managing the quality system. ISO 9001 focuses on the effectiveness of the quality management system in meeting customer requirements. I will go one step further by using the quality management system to effectively meet stockholder requirements.

Define Quality Management System Requirements. As a manufacturer, you may think of processes as those activities that convert raw material into a finished product. Or you may think of paperwork processes used to control the flow of material through the manufacturing processes. In a quality system, quality standards focus on procedural processes linked in a quality system to meet customer requirements. Therefore, some of the general requirements for your quality management system are:

- Identify processes and applications companywide

- Determine the sequence and interaction of processes

- Determine the criteria and methods necessary to prove they are effective

- Provide resources and information to monitor the processes

- Monitor, measure, and analyze these processes

- Implement projects to continually improve quality processes

Document Your Quality Management System. Record the system's requirements to communicate the requirements to those who must manage the system. The documentation will depend on company size, complexity of the processes, process interactions with each other, and the competence of the personnel who are performers within the documented procedures or script. Some general documentation requirements are:

- Document quality mission, policy, or objectives

- Document a manual to organize procedures

- Document required procedures as a script for the performers

- Identify documents to plan, operate, and control the processes

- Document records required by the standard and for internal auditing

Document the Quality Manual. Your quality manual is the primary device used to communicate your quality system to employees, customers, suppliers, and auditors. You list the top-level procedures that describe the interactions of the quality system processes and how you will control them.

Control the Quality Manual and Procedures. One set of procedures defines how you control copies of your quality manual and how you control top-level procedures listed in the manual. Some of the issues to consider are:

- Approving the manual and procedures
- Reviewing and updating the manual and procedures
- Providing easy access to the latest revisions
- Documenting control of customer drawings

Control the Quality Records. You will experience a quality audit by some of your most important customers, by an internal audit performed by one of your own employees, or by an official registrar to prove you are conforming to a quality standard. It is reasonable that records remain legible and are readily identifiable and retrievable. For good control you must have appropriate procedures to communicate these requirements to employees.

Document Management Commitment. Customers insist on three things: control of prices, meeting the promised delivery date, and quality products. They know from their experience that if top-level managers aren't continuously monitoring the effectiveness of the quality system, they will eventually not experience satisfaction in all three areas. One of your procedures should communicate management's responsibility to communicate to employees the importance of meeting customer and regulatory requirements. To communicate this:

- Focus quality on the customer
- Establish a quality policy or mission
- Establish measurable quality objectives
- Conduct quality system reviews and audits
- Provide resources to keep the quality system effective
- Follow up corrective and preventive actions

Provide Knowledge and Skill Resources. A quality system is only as effective as the performers who come on stage in each quality procedure or script. In Chapter 6, I suggested that you take a knowledge inventory. Look for knowledge and skills required by the quality you've designed for your business. The requirements you place on yourself should include:

- Determine the necessary personnel competence
- Provide the appropriate training
- Evaluate the effectiveness of the training

- Verify that personnel connect training and related activities to the quality system and its objectives

- Maintain education, training, and skills records

Provide and Maintain the Quality Infrastructure and Work Environment. Just as a nation needs an infrastructure for communication of government processes and procedures, you must define the same kinds of elements for the quality system infrastructure. Focus on the communication of the most critical elements of your infrastructure to achieve conformity to product requirements. Some examples are:

- Provide preventive maintenance to minimize equipment dimensional variation

- Require design requirements to match equipment capability

- Provide process routers that match equipment capability with product requirements

- Identify and control processes that are used even if the process lacks the required process capability

- Maintain the health and safety of employee assets

Document Product Realization Procedures. This is used by the ISO 9000 quality standard to define the many procedures required to convert a product from the customer's imagination into a real product that realizes the customer's imagination. It's the processes and procedures in the quality system that make customers' product dreams come true. It's a very broad spectrum and may represent the bulk of your quality procedures and training aids. Product realization requires you to:

- Define customer-related processes and procedures

- Define design and development processes

- Define purchasing processes

- Define production and manufacturing processes

- Define control of monitoring and measuring devices

Determine Initial Customer Product Requirements. When, as an individual, you decide to buy a product, you start with a mental image of its function, size, shape, features, and so forth. You hope an available product won't force you to pay for features you don't need or don't have value to you. As you go through your process of selecting a product, you expect the product supplier to have a user-friendly process to assure you that you are going to get the exact product that meets your needs. Your company's first obligation is to provide each customer with an orderly two-way communication process that helps them articulate their requirements. Your processes should help them:

- Document product requirements, including post-delivery acts
- Clarify requirements not stated by the customer but known by the supplier to be required for intended use
- Communicate statutory and regulatory product requirements
- Recommend requirements that add value for the customer
- Cover prototype or field testing requirements up front

Review Initial Customer Product Requirements. The initial communication with your customers about product requirements is usually conducted by a limited number of people in the organization. If the customer order is a repeat order for exactly the same product, a review process may not be needed. The other extreme is a contract for a new product not yet provided by any supplier. Between these two extremes, your personnel should review the product specifications to minimize the chance that the customer will be dissatisfied with your product. Your processes should help personnel in your organization to:

- Verify that product requirements are completely defined
- Resolve contract or order requirements differing from the initial product definition
- Verify that you have the ability to meet defined requirements
- Document communications with the customer related to the review process
- Confirm customer consensus before accepting the order or revisions

Communicate with Customers. Like any good marriage, marriage to your customer to produce maximum sales should build a relationship of common interests that make both better than you could be otherwise. Advertising and providing catalogs about your products and services are ways to convey the desire for a continuing relationship. Satisfying your customer marriage partner might include:

- Communicating order acceptance and delivery date
- Answering product inquiries promptly

- Communicating unexpected delivery delays

- Communicating quality or performance problems

- Resolving customer complaints to their satisfaction

- Communicating corrective or preventive actions taken in response to complaints

Plan and Control Product Design and Development. Product design and development may range from minor redesigns for an existing product to a contract for development of a major project. For each of these extremes, consider design review checklists that can serve as project plans, schedules, and documentation for record purposes. Consider including customers and suppliers in the design process. A product development plan includes:

- Defining the design and development stages

- Defining review, verification, and validation for each stage

- Defining responsibility and authority for each stage

- Managing the interfaces between different groups involved in the design and approval process

Determine Design and Development Inputs Related to Product Requirements. Design inputs relate to customer product requirements discovered in the communications you had with the customer as you communicated back and forth about the product requirements. Inputs the ISO 9000 standard suggests are:

- Determining and recording functional and performance requirements

- Documenting and communicating applicable statutory and regulatory requirements

- Considering information from previous designs

Determine Design and Development Outputs Related to Product Requirements. Outputs can be prototype testing of a design project or could relate to the routine testing of assembled products shipped to a customer. Outputs can be defined by drawings, bills of material, process routers, and end item test instructions. The ISO 9000 standard requires that the design and development outputs shall:

- Meet input requirements for design and development

- Provide appropriate information for purchasing, manufacturing, and service activities

- Contain or reference product acceptance criteria

- Specify the characteristics of the product that are essential for its safe and proper use

Determine Design and Development Review Related to Product Requirements. In the preceding section you have determined the design stages appropriate for redesign and new design. To be sure product design requirements are met at suitable stages, you perform systematic reviews of the design according to planned arrangements, such as a checklist. Design reviews at each stage will cause you to:

- Evaluate the ability of the design and development process to meet requirements

- Identify problems and propose necessary actions

Determine Design and Development Verification Related to Product Requirements. Perform verification to prove that the output meets design and development inputs. Verification documents for the customer that products meet their specified requirements. Just add this stage to your checklist.

Determine Design and Development Validation Related to Product Requirements. Hopefully, you discussed prototype or field testing in your initial communications with your customer. This is the design stage when you give the product the opportunity to prove it will meet the customer's requirements and your design requirements.

Control Design and Development Changes. After design verification and validation, design or process changes may be needed. You might use an engineering change notice procedure to communicate the recommended or required changes to the product before the change is implemented.

Note: Quality standards related to product design are used to satisfy your customers. There is no better time than the design and development stages to build shorter lead time and lower setup into the product and into the product and development lead time. Consider a parallel checklist, not directly included in your quality system, that includes principles from Chapters 9 and 10 to reduce processing lead time and setup time and cost.

Design reviews should look for ways to design for fewer parts and for more operations to be performed with each holding of a component. Consideration should be given to use of Six Sigma during design and development to limit dimensional variation and match drawing dimensional requirements to capability of the processing equipment. Your quality standard is the minimum you commit to in order to satisfy your customers.

Ensure That Purchased Components and Processes Conform to Design Specs and Purchase Order Requirements. Customers expect both you and your suppliers to be committed to a quality system similar to their own. They know that the product they buy from you is no better than the purchased and manufactured components that go into it. They also realize that you farm out some of your manufacturing processes and expect you to verify that processes performed outside your direct control will meet all product specifications. Therefore, you should:

- Establish selection and evaluation criteria for suppliers

- Maintain records of the results of evaluations and actual performance

- Document corrective actions required for supplier approval

Establish Requirements for Information Communicated to Suppliers About the Product or Process to Be Purchased. The information you communicate to a supplier on a purchase order or other document should:

- Include requirements for approval of product, processes, equipment, and procedures

- Include requirements for personnel qualification

- Include quality system requirements

Verify That Purchased Product Meets Specified Purchase Requirements. You may use inspection to perform product verification. You are the only one who can decide how much inspection is required, whether it will be performed at your facility or the supplier's facility, and which product characteristics are the most critical. State the verification arrangements and method of product release in the purchasing information you communicate. State how the inspection will be performed by you at your facility. To avoid duplicate inspections, require inspection certification to document inspection performed by the supplier.

Ensure That Manufactured Components and/or Services Conform to Product Specifications. This and the next four sections apply to a product manufacturer or a service business that derives its sales from both products and services. What you require of yourself in your quality system for manufactured components is what you would look for in your supplier's facility when you perform supplier evaluation and selection. You would look for how they control the conditions under which manufacturing or service is carried out. Many of these conditions might be included in your process routers, setup instructions, or operations procedures related to equipment maintenance or maintaining the accuracy of measuring instruments. For conformance evaluation or potential improvement projects, you should look for:

- Information that describes characteristics of the product

- Availability of appropriate work instructions

- Use of suitable equipment

- Use of monitoring and measuring devices

- Release, delivery, and postdelivery activities

Validate Processes That Can't Utilize Monitoring and Measuring. Some products and processes are such that the processing output can't be verified by monitoring or measuring. This would include processes where the deficiencies become apparent only after the product is in use or the service has been delivered. Validation is how you demonstrate the ability of these processes to achieve the required specifications. To assure that these processes are under control, you should:

- Define criteria to review and approve the processes

- Approve equipment and qualification of personnel

- Use specific methods and procedures

- Define records requirements

Determine the Appropriate Degree of Identification and Traceability. If your customer or industry doesn't require it, ISO 9000 doesn't require every item to be identified by a part number. During processing and storage, paperwork included in the component container may satisfy your needs. To satisfy the quality standard, you must define the means you will use to identify each component and finished product as well as the way you will provide reliable traceability when you need to recall defective components or finished product. By not having specific traceability by part number and work order number on each component, you may find that you often need to recall more product than you would with an expensive traceability system. Review the economics of what you are now doing to find the least expensive way to satisfy your own and your customers' purchasing information requirements.

Protect Customer-Supplied Property. If your product or service includes customer-supplied materials, you must safeguard them from damage or loss. If damage or loss does occur, you must report the damage or loss to the customer and maintain transaction records. One simple way to satisfy this quality system requirement is to assign one of your part numbers to customer material, treat the customer as a supplier for this material, and allow your purchasing and material control systems and nonconformance systems to control customer material.

Preserve and Protect Components and Finished Product. Use common sense to protect components and finished product during the manufacturing process. For uncontrollable reasons, you may be forced to hold parts and finished products in stock for long periods of time. Or there may be components with sensitive surfaces or with short shelf life that need specific procedures to detail your method of protection or preservation. This type of damage reveals itself in the nonconforming material area. If you have a specific packaging method required by a customer, you may share shipping preservation and protection duties.

Control the Accuracy of Monitoring and Measuring Devices. Your quality system should be the vehicle you use to drive your quality costs down by limiting the dimensional and specification variation in your products. Projects related to measuring instruments can be big profit producers because a very few instruments can impact the dimensional and specification integrity of your components and finished products. Maintenance programs for monitoring and measuring devices can include instruments for measuring component dimensions, instruments for surface measurement, temperature and pressure gages for processes such as heat treating, painting, or mixing, and gages and other devices that may be used in the testing of an assembled product. For project discovery, consider the relationship between measuring instruments and preventive maintenance of manufacturing or processing equipment. If you use preventive maintenance to maintain the capability of a machine to hold close tolerances, you can eliminate inspection operations. To prove conformity of product to required dimensions and specifications, the following quality system requirements should be provided:

- Calibrate instruments at given intervals against measurement standards traceable to national or international standards

- Provide a way to show calibration status

- Safeguard instruments from unauthorized adjustment

- Protect instruments from damage during use and storage

- Maintain records of calibration

- Provide procedures for potential product recall when incorrectly calibrated instruments may cause product performance problems

Accumulate Facts, Analyze Them, and Improve the Quality Management System. Remaining sections of the ISO 9001 standard have improvement projects as their primary goal. The standard encourages you to:

- Demonstrate conformity of your products to requirements

- Ensure conformity of the total quality system

- Continually improve the effectiveness of quality management systems

Measure and Monitor Customer Satisfaction. *Perception* is almost everything in all human relationships. The dictionary says it's an impression received by our mind through the senses. It's like the different eyeglasses our individual minds wear, resulting from past and current experiences. Perception is seldom based on pure facts. Measuring customer satisfaction isn't a pure science because you're measuring customers' perceptions as to whether your organization meets customer requirements. Monitor and measure the perceptions of the 20 percent of your customers that make up 80 percent of your sales to discover projects that help you maintain or increase sales. Get feedback about improvements they suggest for your quality system and analyze them for quality system improvements using a customer survey.

Conduct Periodic Internal Audits of Your Quality System and Monitor and Measure Procedures. An internal audit of the quality system is performed by your personnel. Like a customer satisfaction survey, your purpose is to gather facts and analyze them so you can discover projects that will make your quality system more effective and further improve your ROA. One good way to perform an audit is similar to what an official registrar would do. You go to each section of your quality manual and the related procedures to determine if performers identified in the procedure script are doing the actions described in the procedure and whether your quality manual accomplishes what the quality standard requires. When you find a nonconformance, either prompt the performers immediately to follow the script, work with them to find a better way that still meets the requirements of the standard, or initiate a formal corrective action project to fix the problem. Corrective actions provide a good starting place for future audits.

Measure and Monitor Your Completed Product. If you produce customized products, the contract may require that the product requires acceptance at various stages by a relevant authority, by your customer, or by a customer representative. At the other extreme, your product may be such that you can monitor and measure the product at routine inspection stages such as receiving inspection, component manufacturing, and final end item testing. Every nonconformance, or the accumulation of data from each nonconformance, provides the facts from which good analysis will yield profit-improving improvement.

Control Nonconforming Product. Not only are you using nonconforming product to gather factual data, you should identify nonconforming components and products to prevent their unintended use or shipment. Nonconforming material must be reviewed by authorized personnel to determine its appropriate disposition. You can deal with nonconforming product in one or more of the following ways:

- Take action to eliminate the nonconformity

- Authorize its use by the appropriate authority

- Take action to prevent it being used

- Reevaluate it after being reworked

Analyze Accumulated Data from All Appropriate Sources. From the five preceding sections you will have accumulated considerable factual data that, when analyzed, can be used to demonstrate the suitability and effectiveness of your quality management system and to evaluate where continual improvement can be made. The analysis of the data should provide information to:

- Improve customer satisfaction

- Improve conformity to product requirements

- Improve characteristics and trends of processes and products

- Provide opportunities for preventive actions

- Improve the quality effectiveness of your suppliers

Document a Corrective Action Procedure. This is a way to generate profit-producing projects. Corrective action projects should be focused on eliminating the causes of nonconformities to prevent recurrence. Your documented procedure should define requirements to:

- Review nonconformities and customer complaints

- Determine causes of nonconformities

- Evaluate actions to ensure that nonconformities don't recur

- Determine and implement corrective action

- Record the results of action taken

- Review corrective action taken

Document a Preventive Action Procedure. This is a very important source of projects to preserve the highest level of quality system effectiveness. I want to emphasize, from a continuous improvement point of view, that quality system and continuous improvement program effectiveness must be evaluated and measured on a financial basis.

It's bad business if you don't prove that every quality system project will increase the ROA level over a full business cycle.

As you analyze factual data, such as trends, from your quality system or your company's financial statements, you will see potential problems present themselves for attention.

For example, as you perform preventive maintenance to maintain dimensional integrity of a piece of equipment, it may become obvious that the equipment is no longer capable of holding the dimensional tolerances required by the original customer product design requirements.

Or, from a business point of view, you may see trends that sales of a particular product or in a specific market segment are diminishing, warning you of a potential loss of sales that will negatively affect your ROA.

Improved quality is a financial decision.

13

Projects to Increase Market Share

In Chapters 1 through 4, I hammered away at the fact that "increase market share" and "increase market coverage" are more critical than "increase sales." This chapter supports the fact that permanent sales increases only result from increased market share and specific plans and projects to increase market coverage.

COMPANYWIDE MARKETING PLANNING

Many manufacturing, distribution, and service businesses market products that are commodities in customers' eyes. The importance of the eight sections of this chapter is that marketing plans are a companywide affair. The reason is that plans to improve quality, reduce delivery time, and control price increases can increase sales and market share as well as plans that expand the product line, market segments, and marketing channels.

My approach to continuous improvement is to train all employees to become businessmen and businesswomen so that as you expand products, market segments, or distribution channels, you will have managers and knowledge resources ready to meet the demands of increased sales.

I am greatly oversimplifying the subject of industrial marketing so I can provide you with a checklist of verb/noun combinations to remind you about projects that apply to increasing sales and market share with market coverage.

I will show you some graphics you can use to quickly gather important financial and marketing facts to help discover projects that increase the company's ROA by increasing market share. By using the project evaluation form from Chapter 5, you can allow manufacturing projects to compete head-on with projects to increase market share.

Market Share/Marketing Planning

Many products are commodities in the customer's eyes, such as products in the mature stage of their lifecycle. The importance of this section lies in the fact that increased sales and market share must be achieved by plans and projects that do such things as expand the product line, market segments, and marketing channels, as well as projects found in previous chapters that improve quality, reduce delivery lead time, and control pricing at a growth rate less than inflation.

Your company may not be big enough to have a marketing function separate from your office sales function and your field sales force. My approach to marketing planning will treat marketing planning and the field sales force as two separate functions. My reason for this approach is that your marketing plan to increase market share is the mechanism that links what management wants done within a given time frame with what the sales force must do to increase the market share.

Just selling harder isn't a viable marketing plan.

Your first step in marketing planning is to select the knowledge resources from within your company and your customers' businesses who will, as a team, serve as your marketing function. As a group they will set marketing objectives and design a marketing plan. This could include external knowledge resources such as stockholders, retired personnel, exclusive distributors, consultants, product designers, personnel and functions that are required to demonstrate good customer service, personnel who get customer orders shipped on time, and those charged to see that customer invoices are paid within the contracted time allowed.

MARKET COVERAGE

The graphics in this section are borrowed from The Richmark Group, www.richmark.com. They provide a very comprehensive pattern to help a company identify potential projects to expand market share by analyzing market coverage.

These graphics utilize several verb/noun combinations to demonstrate how a continuous improvement process can be applied to increasing sales and ROA by increasing market share at all stages of each product's lifecycle, for each marketing segment you serve, and for each phase of a company's economic business cycle.

Notice that the first pair of graphics (Figures 13.1 and 13.2) and their lists of verb/noun combinations are very similar to the second pair (Figures

Analytical Assessment of Market Share

- When selling through indirect channels (who carry competing brands), there are five coverage measurements
- When selling through indirect channels (who are exclusive), there are four coverage aspects (that is, brand coverage becomes 100 percent)

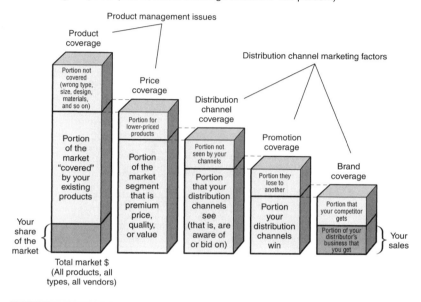

Figure 13.1   Marketing strategy evaluation—selling through distributors and dealers.

Source: The Richmark Group (www.richmark.com). Used with permission.

13.3 and 13.4). The first pair is used when the marketplace requires you to sell through distributors and dealers. The second pair applies when the marketplace, or a group of very large customers, requires you to sell through your direct sales force.

These four figures and verb/noun combinations will save you considerable time when you decide to systematically increase sales by increasing market share with increased market coverage. Following these figures, I will provide you with an organized approach to formulating your marketing objectives, your marketing plan, and actions the sales force and management will take to increase market share.

I suggest that you use your estimate of your current and future coverage for each of the bars in the figures, along with other intelligence you can

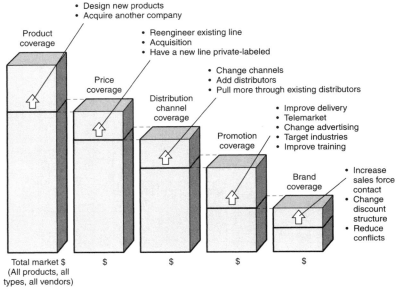

Figure 13.2   Marketing strategy implementation—selling through distributors and dealers.

Source: The Richmark Group (www.richmark.com). Used with permission.

gather, to get a more realistic estimate of your market share before and after you implement your next marketing plan.

Notice: The market share for a specific product line is shown at the bottom of the brand coverage bar in Figure 13.1 and at the bottom of the customer coverage bar in Figure 13.3. The verb/noun combinations suggest how you can set objectives to increase your coverage for each of these bars. The verb/noun combinations will form a considerable part of the marketing plan you will follow to increase your market share. The percent coverage for each bar has an accumulative effect to determine your market share for each product line in each segment you serve. It's this cumulative effect that makes it difficult for any one business to achieve much more than 35 percent to 45 percent of the total market.

One good source of factual data for estimating the annual sales, number of employees, product lines, and market segments for your competitors is a business directory put out annually by CorpTech (www.corptech.com).

Analytical Assessment of Market Share

- When selling through a direct sales force there are four coverage aspects

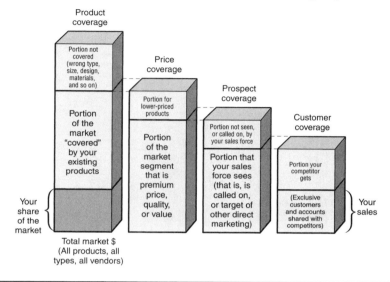

Figure 13.3 Marketing strategy evaluation—selling through the direct sales force.
Source: The Richmark Group (www.richmark.com). Used with permission.

It can be found in the business section of many large public libraries or online. Another source for similar information is the Thomas Register business directory, which can also be accessed online at www.thomasnet.com.

If you sell through distributor or dealer channels, you can design marketing objectives and plans from the following verb/noun combinations:

- Increase product coverage

  - Design new products

  - Acquire another company

- Increase price coverage

  - Reengineer existing product line

  - Acquire an existing product line

  - Have a new line private-labeled

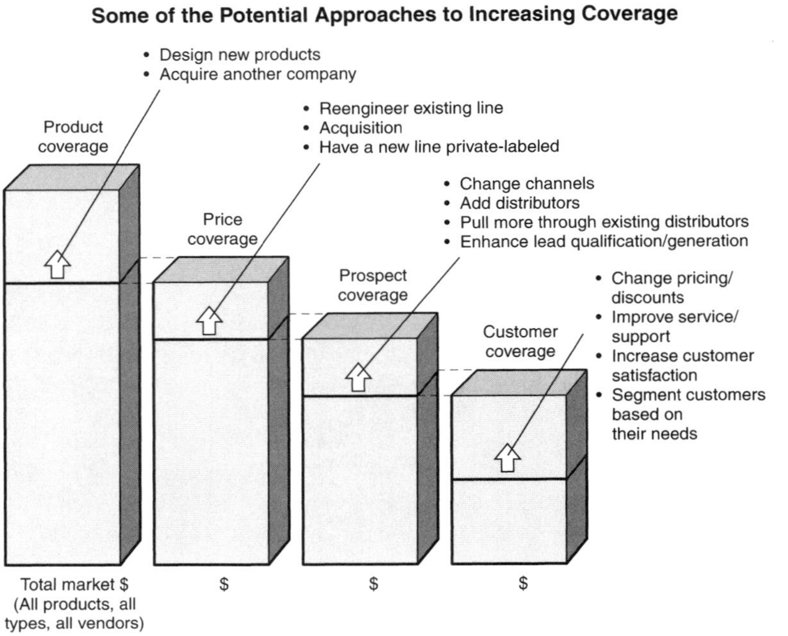

Some of the Potential Approaches to Increasing Coverage

Figure 13.4   Marketing strategy implementation—selling through the direct sales force.

Source: The Richmark Group (www.richmark.com). Used with permission.

- Increase channel coverage

  - Change channels

  - Add distributors

  - Pull more through existing distributors

- Increase promotion coverage

  - Improve delivery

  - Implement telemarketing

  - Change advertising

  - Target specific industries

  - Improve sales force training

- Increase brand coverage

– Increase sales force contact

– Change discount structure

– Reduce conflicts and/or improve distributor relationships

If you reach end users primarily through your own sales force, design marketing objectives and marketing plans from the following verb/noun combinations:

- Increase product coverage

  – Design new products

  – Acquire another company

- Increase price coverage

  – Reengineer existing product line

  – Acquire an existing product line

  – Have a new line private-labeled

- Increase prospect coverage

  – Change channels

  – Add distributors

  – Pull more through existing distributors

  – Enhance lead qualification/generation

- Increase customer coverage

  – Change pricing and discounts

  – Improve service/support

  – Increase customer satisfaction

  – Segment customers based on their needs.

Rationalize Your Coverage and Market Share

This exercise helps you rationalize why you must have a high level of coverage in each of the coverage elements if you expect to achieve and maintain a high market share for each of your product lines.

Figure 13.5 can be used as a guide to help with the arithmetic required to use your estimate of coverage for each coverage element to make an estimate of your market share.

Product		Price		Channel coverage		Prospect/ promotion		Customer or brand		Market share
50%	×	50%	×		×	50%	×	50%	=	6%
50%	×	**50%**	×	**50%**	×	**50%**	×	**50%**	=	**3%**
60%	×	60%	×		×	60%	×	60%	=	13%
60%	×	**60%**	×	**60%**	×	**60%**	×	**60%**	=	**8%**
70%	×	70%	×		×	70%	×	70%	=	24%
70%	×	**70%**	×	**70%**	×	**70%**	×	**70%**	=	**17%**
80%	×	80%	×		×	80%	×	80%	=	41%
80%	×	**80%**	×	**80%**	×	**80%**	×	**80%**	=	**33%**
100%	×	100%	×		×	50%	×	50%	=	25%
100%	×	**100%**	×	**50%**	×	**50%**	×	**50%**	=	**13%**
100%	×	100%	×		×	80%	×	80%	=	64%
100%	×	**100%**	×	**80%**	×	**80%**	×	**80%**	=	**51%**

Figure 13.5   Market share estimator.

The bold lines in the figure apply to the market share you should be receiving for sales you are attempting to capture by selling through distributors and/or dealers. The other lines in the table apply to sales you attempt to capture through your direct sales force.

For example, looking at the first line, if you are selling through your direct sales force and if you estimate you have only 50 percent coverage for the product, price, prospect, and customer elements, you can expect only a six percent market share. If you know you have more than a six percent market share, it probably means you have higher coverage in one of the coverage elements than you realize.

By looking at the 80 percent line for direct selling, you can estimate the increased sales you should receive to be between six percent and 41 percent of the market share. Then you can compare the profit from the increased sales to the investment and increased annual expense to maintain the 80 percent coverage. Then, using the Chapter 5 evaluation form, you can determine whether your ROA will be increased or decreased and whether your marketing objectives in your marketing plan will be achieved.

You can review the lines in bold type, which add the "channel coverage" column, to make the same comparisons for sales you capture by selling through distributors or dealers. Don't conclude that you won't want to use or expand a distribution network because it appears to yield a lower market share than direct selling. You use distribution networks because they allow you to transfer some coverage costs out of your financial statements and into a distributor's financial statements and because you expect the distributor or dealer to operate at lower coverage costs than you can by selling through a direct sales force.

These kinds of trade-offs are the main reason you need to rationalize your coverage and market share as your first step toward setting marketing objectives and toward designing a marketing plan to increase market share. This is where you connect your marketing plan with your business plan. However, I suggest you keep your initial marketing plan separated from your business plan until you have decided on the actions required to increase your market share. It's only after you have proven with a marketing plan that you truly understand your marketplace that you can design the most profitable business plan. The market share plan determines how much your stockholders will invest to capture the increased sales resulting from increased market share. The business plan determines how much you will spend each year to maintain the increased sales and share.

By looking at the last two lines in the figure you can see why few companies can afford to achieve much more than 50 percent of the market. These two lines also demonstrate the influence a full product line has on a high market share. The key to this decision is whether the investment in product development and related coverage expenses will translate into a profitable business decision. These two lines should also signal you that by buying a competitor you might consolidate coverage costs and increase your coverage at a lower cost per sales dollar, which translates to a higher profit. This is one of the reasons companies with a high market share usually operate at a high net profit and a high ROA.

Just keep in mind that your sales and marketing knowledge resources, wherever they exist within company departments, are participants in the continuous improvement process to discover specific projects that will increase ROA a specific amount within a specific time period. Therefore, if you know your coverage is at a high percent and you know that its related expenses are already high for a given coverage element, additional investment and/or expenses will likely lower the ROA. This is true because at some point each incremental increase of coverage expense won't guarantee a profitable increase in sales. On the other hand, if you know your coverage is too low for a given coverage element, that particular element should be a primary target for a market plan project.

MARKETING OBJECTIVES

Make a marketing objectives list to document consensus reached by your group of companywide knowledge resources to get companywide input, as well as key customer input.

Relate Marketing Objectives to Business Objectives

Business objectives should be focused on ROA percent. Marketing objectives must be focused on market share percent. You won't achieve your business objectives for increased sales without a marketing plan. And you can't design a marketing plan without specific documented marketing and market share objectives.

Document Marketing Objectives for All Product Lines

To help simplify marketing objectives for your marketing plan, focus on products that are in the last half of their lifecycle. In the first half of each product's lifecycle, sales may be made primarily by your direct sales force and you may not be considering distributor and dealer strategies. In the second half of each product's lifecycle, the maturity portion, individual product lines are probably sold mostly to end users through distributor and dealer channels.

In these two stages the sales force plays different roles. Marketing objectives and marketing plans must be focused on each product's proper place in its lifecycle so you can correctly communicate the objectives, plans, and actions your sales force uses to increase market share. If you have more than one product line, you may have different marketing objectives for each:

- You may not be able to increase ROA from more investment in market coverage for products that already have a high percentage share.

- Products in a rapidly expanding market may need to grow at a higher rate than other products.

- The product and/or business may not be in the right phase of the economic business cycle to increase ROA the quickest or most profitably.

- Management may have to restrict share growth or coverage growth because of the inability to commit financial or knowledge resources.

- You must allow adequate calendar time for objectives that require new product design or new manufacturing equipment and facilities.

- Clearly identify the key individuals and knowledge resources who set growth objectives so differing viewpoints can be debated and resolved on a nonsubjective basis. This is the best place to start gathering facts. Then let the facts resolve the differing viewpoints.

- Recognize that some parts of your marketing plan may fail. You must free individuals who are most responsible for achieving a given objective from the fear of failure by making all objectives a team requirement companywide.

- Use the project evaluation form to improve the ranking of objectives when trade-offs must be made to achieve the results within the allotted market plan time frame.

Set Growth Objectives Based on Market Share Percent

There are good reasons to express marketing objectives in terms of market share percent:

- Market share percent is immune to sales dollars caused by inflation or the variation of annual sales during the three to five years of an economic business cycle.

- Although an accurate market share percent is difficult to measure, it is still a true measurement of your product's competitive position in the marketplace. You can improve the accuracy of your market share measurement as you more accurately state the percent of coverage for each of the coverage elements in Figures 13.1 through 13.4.

- Manufacturing projects that reduce lead times, reduce setup costs, decrease the ratio of total company salary-related costs divided by sales dollars, provide less quality variance in products, and deliver a very high percentage of customer orders by the promised date dramatically increase sales dollars and market share. On the other hand, marketing projects that increase market share and sales dollars will, by economies of scale, allow the manufacturing operation to be more profitable. This is another reason I encourage you to make market share planning a companywide exercise.

- The financially justifiable cost to increase coverage in any one
  of the coverage elements will tell you when to slow down or stop
  market share growth of your product lines. At some financially
  logical point it will be better to take the excess cash generated by
  continuous improvement projects and invest it in the acquisition of
  a competitor, another business, or a new product line not directly
  associated with your current lines.

- Market share forces the key knowledge resources, those setting
  marketing objectives, to focus new marketing projects on potential
  sales you don't see or don't get.

- For product lines in the maturing phase of their lifecycle,
  increasing market share is the only way to increase sales.

- Exception: If you are a small business in a large market, setting
  marketing objectives based on sales dollars in specific market
  niches is better than measuring and planning on the basis of
  increased market share.

Set Sales Forecasts Based on Marketing Objectives and the Current Economic Business Cycle Phase

Long-range sales forecasts are often based on increased sales dollars every
year of a four- or five-year business plan, without regard for what's going on
in the economy. In these cases, the annual operating budget for each year
of the long-range business planning period may be too high to be prudently
used to make sound manufacturing capacity and other business decisions
during each year. You're admitting with this kind of plan that you don't
have a financially sound marketing plan.

I suggest a more logical approach that helps the sales force meet the
market share growth objectives rather than sales dollar objectives that may
be impossible to achieve because of the economic business cycle.

Documenting Objectives Forces You to Be Specific

Both sales dollars and ROA go up and down significantly during each three-
to five-year business cycle. This same logical approach must be applied to
manufacturing to provide an appropriate level of manufacturing capacity
to ship customer orders on the promised delivery date.

First, start with where your company or each product line is in the
business cycle. When you know that the business is in an economically

depressed phase, you know not to set sales dollar goals that force you to increase manufacturing capacity at an unreasonable pace.

Second, if you have lost market share for specific product models, factor that into your forecast so you won't overstate your business plans and capacity requirements.

Third, increase sales dollars by the amount of inflation you plan to pass on to customers. If continuous improvement is working as it should, consider passing some of the profit improvement on to your customers if such a move will increase your market share. Controlling price increases at a rate lower than inflation is one of your customers' primary satisfiers.

Fourth, look at market share objectives and the marketing plan through specific marketing projects and increase your sales forecast for the next few years accordingly.

Select a Time Frame for Marketing Objectives

Business conditions change so rapidly that marketing objectives that span more than a two-year time frame are unlikely to deliver the desired results. The time frame is most critical when you have ambitious market share growth objectives that may require a separate set of long-range objectives as far as timing is concerned.

If your objectives require introduction of a new product, include these in a longer-range set of marketing objectives. Or you may consider buying or licensing an existing product line or acquiring a competitor. Or you may consider distributing a product from a manufacturer of similar products to yours but in a market segment in which you don't currently participate.

The best marketing projects may require expansion of equipment and facilities that take more than one year to plan and implement. An expansion objective may also cause you to consider acquiring a competitor that sells through existing market segments or distribution channels.

Openly Document Constraints and Limitations Imposed by Management or Stockholders

Force these issues out into the open so they can be discussed and understood by the team that will document marketing objectives and design the marketing plan.

For each marketing objective that can be boiled down to a specific project, use the evaluation form in Chapter 5 to force agreement about investment dollars and knowledge resources required for implementation. The increased ROA from these marketing projects should be compared with your manufacturing projects as a way to allow marketing projects to compete head-on with manufacturing projects.

Document an understanding of the limitations management or stockholders impose on coverage elements, so unacceptable ideas won't be considered until the constraint is lifted.

If you don't have a full-time marketing function, separate those functions or personnel assigned to decide marketing objectives and design the marketing plan from those who have the sales force responsibility. This will help clarify roles played when each group comes on stage to perform its part to increase market share.

THE MARKETING PLAN

Just as new products or new processes must be tested to see if they meet design requirements, marketing objectives must be tested against what your team knows about the marketplace as you generate your marketing plan and the probability that it will deliver the objectives.

The primary goal of a marketing plan is to communicate to management the changes related to policies, constraints, limitations, and investment. Another goal is to inform the sales force about the discipline, structure, and tools they must use to deliver the planned market share growth during the designated time frame defined by the plan.

Consider the Many Marketing Plan Alternatives

As with the manufacturing projects you name and rank using the verb/noun continuous improvement process, there are more marketing alternatives than you will have the financial and knowledge resources to include in a marketing plan for the next one to three years. Therefore, look for those that are:

- *Available* to you to increase market coverage. For example, if you already have a full product line compared to competitors, that alternative isn't available. On the other hand, there may be marketing segments or distribution channels that are available to you.

- *Attainable* within limitations of financial and knowledge resources stockholders are willing to commit, including both one-time investment and ongoing annual expenses. You can accept or reject various alternatives with the help of the project evaluation method in Chapter 5. If a set of projects will increase both market share and ROA, it has the best chance of making it into your marketing plan.

* *Deliverable* within the time frame for which the marketing plan is designed.

Consider Both Numerical Facts and Your Gut Feelings

Those in your company with lengthy experience in your marketplace may have intuitive insight that is equally as valuable as factual information. Just be sure that this insight is put into the best words possible and treat it as a fact until market plan testing proves it right or wrong. If this insight helps your team understand how your marketplace functions, it may be as important as knowing your share of the market.

The point is, to make good marketing decisions, you must understand how and why potential customers make their buying decisions, how they are going to use your product, and why your product does or doesn't fit their application. For example, for a particular product, your key customer contact may be an individual in their purchasing function or a group in their engineering function or a combination of both. At the other extreme, your key contact could be part of the customer's top management.

Apply the 80/20 Rule to Your Marketplace

Another way to gain insight into your marketplace, so that you discover additional marketing objectives, is to remember that 80 percent of marketplace sales come from 20 percent of potential customers and end users. And only 20 percent of the sales come from the other 80 percent of the potential customers and end users. Put another way, 80 percent of marketplace sales are from a few big, well-known customers whose buying habits are also well known and 20 percent come from the 80 percent of the marketplace universe that is too diverse to rationalize into one set of buying habits.

I suggest you consider dividing your customers into at least three groups to sharpen your marketplace insight.

The first group is a small percentage of the largest companies or the biggest buyers in the marketplace, perhaps the five percent that buys 40 percent to 50 percent of the type of product provided by you and your competitors. These well-known big buyers are critical for the design of a marketing plan to increase or maintain market share. Not only do they represent a large percentage of marketplace dollars, they are where emerging technologies, new applications, and changes in product requirements are seen first. They are where you are made aware of each competitor's marketing plan or the lack of one. These are customers and end users with whom you want to maintain direct contact, even if they are being serviced by a distributor or rep. Your marketing plan needs to define the role of your sales force with these customers and the role of marketing and management in providing the appropriate tools. These customers, such as OEMs, may insist on buying direct from you at equal or better than distributor discounts, even though you might prefer that a distributor would serve them.

The second group of well-known medium-sized companies or buyers is probably the next 15 percent that buys 30 percent to 40 percent of the products in your marketplace. They are important because the way the marketplace is structured is well known, even though it is more diverse in its buying habits than the first group. You may need to reach this group through a combination of direct sales and dealer/distributor marketing. If you rely heavily on distributors to capture these sales for you, your marketing plan will need to focus on a marketing program that you design to make it more effective for your distributor and dealer customers to make a buying decision in your favor.

The third group, the 80 percent of buyers who provide only 20 percent of the marketplace sales, shouldn't be ignored even though they buy infrequently in small quantities. If all your competitors are ignoring them, you obviously have an opportunity to increase your market share at a very low cost and with a high return on your project investment. These customers and end users may be too small for your distributors to service economically. You must make it easy for these customers to find you and your distributors or dealers. For these potential sales you may utilize the Internet, or direct mail to those whose names you know. Or you may use targeted advertising and Web site search wording for those whose names you don't know.

Apply Distributor/Dealer Marketing to Increase Share

Distributor marketing may seem complicated because you must sell through another independent business to reach OEMs and other end users to economically maximize your market share. It's important to understand why, under the appropriate conditions, you can capture more share at a lower cost through distributors than with a direct sales force. I learned the following questions about marketing and selling through distributors from Frank Lynn & Associates.

Why Do End Users Buy from Distributors and Why Are They Needed by Manufacturers?

Distributors have a role in the marketplace because they can do more effectively and more economically what a manufacturer and its sales force and reps don't do well or can't do at all. It's these advantages that distributors provide to your customers for which you pay them with a distributor discount.

You pay them for their inventory investment to provide product closer to your customer so delivery can be made more quickly. They invest in inventory that you would be required to maintain at the factory. The only way you can match the distributor's delivery is to locate a branch closer to the customer than the distributor location.

You pay them for taking credit risks, for processing customer orders, for providing customer service, and for absorbing shipping costs for a large number of small-quantity shipments you would handle less economically. You pay them for overhead costs you no longer budget.

You pay them to maintain a sales force, and for advertising and promotion to a much broader audience than you can reach with your own sales force. You pay them because your customers can do one-stop shopping for other products, related to your product lines, that you don't market.

How Does Distribution Evolve in the Marketplace As Products Mature?

New products and new technologies normally require the missionary work that your sales force can do better than a distributor. As more applications or new innovations are identified for a new product, the selling emphasis is on technical selling to communicate directly to the marketplace. Over time, as the product and market matures and servicing of individual customers becomes the most important customer need, distributors replace the direct sales force and the technical specialists. To economically increase share you must recognize and define in which product lifecycle phase each of your products is living so you can provide your new customers with the attention that best fits their individual needs.

What Is the Best Design for a Distributor Discount?

The function of a distributor discount is to transfer cost out of the manufacturer's business and into a distributor's. The distributor makes a profit by performing the transferred activities more economically than the manufacturer. A multi-level distributor discount based on distributor order size is the best way to fairly transfer marketing cost from the manufacturer to the distributor.

It rewards the distributor with a large discount when their purchase orders are combined into one order, paying them for the many transactions the distributor will perform when the actual customer sale is made. If the distributor orders are always very small and frequent, minimal transactions are being transferred and don't deserve a large discount. A multi-level discount penalizes distributors for frequent orders that don't really transfer sufficient cost, and rewards them with a larger discount for large, infrequent orders that maximize the transfer of transactional costs and inventory investment.

What Role Do the Manufacturers Play in Distributor and Dealer Marketing?

The manufacturer is responsible for promoting the product and brand name to end users. The distributor is only paid to supply the product as soon as economically feasible and to service the customer. The demand must be created by the manufacturer, especially if one of your competitors is using the same distributor to transfer out some of their costs.

What Is the Role of the Sales Force in Distributor and Dealer Marketing?

Every distributor services only a specific portion of the marketplace in a given geographic territory. Their coverage is based on their various product lines, their customer base, and their business goals. The share of the market you capture through each individual distributor depends on which of your potential customers come to them for your type of product. In some cases you need to consider more than one distributor in a given geographic area to maximize market share. Therefore, your maximum market coverage in a given territory will depend on how well your sales force and marketing plan have selected the best distributors for each territory that has potential new market share. There may be some customers your sales force will still call on.

What Major Mistakes Do Manufacturers Make When Marketing Through Distributors?

Here are a few:

- Manufacturers think they sell to distributors, not through them.

- Distributors are not your customers. They are a channel through which you reach customers.

- A sale isn't made until your product moves out of a distributor's inventory and into the hands of an OEM or end user.

- Distributors don't develop markets. They service existing markets you and your sales force develop as a specific action in your marketing plan.

- Market acceptance depends on which brands a distributor sells.

- Inventory turnover determines the brands a distributor stocks. If your product doesn't move, they won't stock it.

Connect Your Marketing Plan and Marketing Projects with Your Manufacturing Projects

A business that maintains a competitive advantage in the areas of control of price increases to customers, consistent, predictable quality, and consistent, predictable shipment of products on the day they are promised should promote these advantages to customers. Manufacturing projects, particularly those that claim an incremental increase in sales, should be integrated into the marketing plan. By doing this, the contribution of the manufacturing function to increasing market share can be recognized and encouraged.

For example, if your sales and manufacturing personnel are spending considerable time expediting manufacturing schedules to meet customer delivery date promises, why wouldn't you include in your marketing plan a project to improve your material control system and its performance as a marketing objective to maintain or increase market share?

Focus a Marketing Plan on Its Appropriate Audience

There are primarily three groups of personnel to whom you must clearly communicate your marketing plan and from whom you must get a clear commitment:

- *Management* must commit money and knowledge resources required by the plan. This may include changes in policy and changes in limitations placed on the various coverage elements included in the plan.

- *The sales force* must agree to perform selling tasks the plan requires, to use the selling tools the marketing plan will provide, and agree to specific performance and evaluation measurements.

- *Manufacturing personnel* must agree to the marketing objectives and actions related to delivery date promises, cost control, quality improvement goals, and other issues included in the marketing plan that are under their control and are made an integral part of the market share strategy.

Communicate a Marketplace Perspective and Insight

If you had a picture puzzle of your marketplace that would show the relationship between such things as competitors, marketing channels, segments, geography, the market share pie divided by competitors, the market share pie and your share of the pie divided by segment, and how your marketing plan fits all these picture puzzle pieces together, you would have a picture or perspective of your marketplace.

The key to perspective and insight is understanding the relationships between the puzzle pieces. In your company's marketplace you may see some puzzle pieces I have left out. This is where you generate facts that improve or prove your gut feelings about your perspective of your marketplace. This is the place where you focus your mind's eye on the details of the big picture to help your marketing plan achieve your marketing objectives. Here are details you can add to draw a big picture in a verb/noun format:

- Make a list of company strengths and weaknesses.

- Make a list of your competitors and their strengths and weaknesses.

- Make a list of distributors available to you, and the ones also used by your competitors.

- Prepare a list of end users.

- Estimate the size of the marketplace and the share currently claimed by you and your competitors.

- Identify the coverage areas in which you can most likely take market share away from competitors.

- View the market geographically by competitors, distributors, end users, and marketing segments.

- Make a list of end user applications and the market segments in which they are applied.

- Document in which segments you have a large market share that must be protected or defended because of competitive activities.

- Analyze the market coverage elements that account for a large share of specific segments.

- Determine in which segments you have a small market share and which market coverage elements should be increased that should increase your share the quickest and at the least cost.

- Outline the marketing/selling programs you can use to win more share in each segment in which you want to see an increase.

- Document marketing programs that are out of tune with how your low-share segments function now.

- Reach agreement about where each product is in its lifecycle: a new product with new technology, a mature product, or somewhere in between.

- Relate your constraints and limitations to the real picture you see in your marketplace.

- Identify marketing activities that have minimal impact on achieving your marketing objectives.

- Identify marketing activities that have maximum impact on achieving your marketing objectives.

- Look at the market in terms of the sales and share you don't get as well as in terms of sales you now get.

- Revise the verb/noun combinations in this whole section into vocabulary that fits your company.

- Add verb/noun combinations not included in this section that are unique to your marketplace.

- Look at the big picture again to see more clearly where you fit into it and how your marketing plan must redraw it so you can see yourself in places you didn't appear before.

Prototype-Test Your Marketing Plan, Programs, and Tools

Just as a new product should be tested in the laboratory and/or in the field, test your marketing plan, program, and tools and make appropriate design changes that work better than your original conclusions.

Explain the Key Elements of the Marketing Plan to Its Appropriate Audience

At this point you have gathered, analyzed, and organized facts and perspectives and related them to each other so that they will tell you what things to do, when to do them, and who will be responsible for actions required:

- Explain planned market coverage changes.

- Explain major marketing programs.

- Explain the time frame and schedule to implement the plan, highlighting the few most critical events and decision points for both management and sales force commitments.

- Explain how and why the marketplace has its own way of making buying decisions that is independent of your company's way of selling.

- Explain how the plan takes a specific approach for each specific product line, each specific marketing segment, and each specific group of potential customers.

INCREASING MARKET SHARE THROUGH ACQUISITIONS

One logical answer to the question, "How do I increase market share?" is, "Acquire a competitor." At some point you may want to turn to a consultant to help decide if acquisition is a good option to increase the ROA.

In this section I encourage you to think about acquiring a competitor as you complete your marketing plan to use market coverage to take market share from competitors. In the next section of this chapter I provide a process for you to use to place a value on your own company and your competitor's so you can decide whether it's more profitable to increase market share by investing in greater market coverage or by acquisition. In the section after that I describe the process and the team you might use to complete an acquisition.

Guess What Your Competitors Are Thinking About!

It should come as no surprise that your competitors are trying to take market share from you and may desire to acquire your business. It shouldn't come as a surprise to your competitors that you may plan to use acquisition as a logical strategy to acquire their market share. Therefore, it should come as no surprise to them that both of your financial conditions could be dramatically improved if your two companies were consolidated.

It's not illegal to talk to a competitor about acquisition possibilities, since both may be thinking about it anyway. If both of you have a large market share, ask how you would legally defend your position if the consolidation resulted in a very large share of the market. Logically, if you are applying a continuous improvement process so that you can increase prices at a rate lower than inflation, you could also prove that consolidation would enhance that trend and the wastes that exist in both businesses.

Which Share Strategy: Acquisition or Market Coverage?

In this chapter, I proved that you won't permanently increase sales if you don't increase market coverage. Also in this chapter, I contended that you won't increase share without a marketing plan to increase coverage. Now I say, "It's perfectly logical for you and your competitor to get together so you can prove to yourselves that a consolidation might make both businesses more profitable."

Integrate Acquisition Strategic Thinking with Your Continuous Improvement Projects

If you decide that acquisition of a competitor is the way to increase market coverage and market share, look at your current projects and those of a potential acquisition to see if there is some synergy that makes acquisition more logical and valuable. You may want to acquire similar products you can manufacture in your current facilities and/or sell through your existing distribution channels.

For either acquisition strategy there are some basics about acquisitions you should understand.

Link an acquisition strategy with your current continuous improvement projects. This will show whether there is a big gap between the cultures of the two companies. If they are practicing good continuous improvement principles, you can justify paying a higher price for the acquisition. If the acquisition target is better than you are in most areas and is earning a larger ROA than you are, you might consider paying a premium price.

Link your acquisition strategy with marketing projects. A market analysis for your plan to increase market coverage performs much of the analysis required for the potential purchase of a competitor or for other products that can be sold through existing marketing channels.

As you design a marketing plan, consider acquisition so this same information can be used if or when there is an acquisition opportunity.

If you decide you will never be interested in acquisitions, you've decided that the only strategy you will use is to invest in additional market coverage. However, if a competitor surprised you by asking if you are interested in buying them or selling to them, might you reconsider your acquisition position and what price your stockholders would accept if a premium price were offered?

Simplify the Acquisition Process

Pretend that you are buying a competitor and use the exercise to learn acquisition language, the valuation process, and the information gathering and analysis process. By focusing on acquiring a competitor, the process is easier to understand and apply.

The knowledge required to transact acquisitions is too complicated to describe in these three sections. Authors of a 1000-page merger and acquisition handbook titled *The Art of M&A* state that even their composition is far too small to adequately cover this complicated subject.

Selling a business may be a one-time exercise in your career. Even though you may hire an experienced consultant to help with this infrequent event, you need enough knowledge to understand some vocabulary, and the process, so you can test the advice they are giving you, or test the advice I am giving you. My organization of the process and the arithmetic should help when you decide to explore an acquisition opportunity.

Define Your Acquisition Criteria

I attempt to simplify acquisition so you can quickly accept or reject acquisition opportunities with a minimum of time and expense. I suggest you pretend to buy your competitor because that will be one of the most simple acquisition scenarios. The evaluation of each opportunity may cost up to $30,000 in expenses for your personnel and a consultant. Your up-front investment for an acquisition will be much less if you prepare for it as an integral part of your marketing planning.

You can go to the Web site for a corporation such as Dover Corporation to get ideas about acquisition criteria. In a few words with a seller, Dover can quickly consider or reject an opportunity using the following criteria. Does the company:

- Manufacture high-value-added equipment or machinery products?

- Sell to a broad customer base of industrial or commercial end users?

- Sell through strong national or international distribution?

- Hold a position as a niche-oriented market leader with number one or number two market share position?

- Have strong management teams in place with skill, energy, and ethics?

- Have earnings before interest and taxes (EBIT) above 15 percent and $10,000,000?

- Show expected significant real growth over time?

- Have lower EBIT requirements for "add-on" business that make good sense?

Dover's EBIT expectation gives a clue that they would value acquisitions at five to 10 times the EBIT dollars, depending on how strong or weak they judge it to be in other product, market, or management areas. (See the next section for a valuation process.)

Acquire to Increase Market Share or Product Lines

The same process can also be applied when you have an opportunity to expand with related products that use similar manufacturing processes and/or sell through your distribution channels. This means your initial interests will be related to a business you may have analyzed to some extent during your market planning exercise.

Consider seeking product lines that are in the first half of their product lifecycle, particularly if your products are in the second half of their lifecycle.

One of the things you're looking for with an acquisition strategy is to consolidate with a competitor to reduce overhead costs and minimize investment to maintain the combined market share. The combined sales will be the same as the total before the acquisition but the combined profit dollars will be larger than before the acquisition, and the combined investment should be lower per sales dollar, resulting in a higher combined ROA.

A Summary of Acquisition Steps

Whether you are buying a competitor or company with similar products and channels, there's a logical step-by-step process.

Select an Acquisition Team. This team will include your best knowledge resources to gather and analyze financial information, product design, and manufacturing processes.

Gather Facts About Every Facet of the Potential Acquisition. Pretend that you will duplicate a company that is exactly like your acquisition target, including knowledge resources. Lay this information side-by-side with your company and compare the strengths and weaknesses of both. This exercise will help you decide if the acquisition target has some features for which you might be willing to pay a premium price.

Analyze the Facts to Determine the Fit. Gather facts about products, market segments, distribution channels, market coverage, technical knowledge, organization structure, processes, management, leadership skills, employee empowerment, employee efficiency, inventory control (setup cost and lead time reduction), and financial history (past P&L statements, balance sheets, and annual budgets). You will be looking for similarities and contrasts to see how the two fit together.

Determine a Range of What You're Willing to Pay for the Acquisition. In the next section I show ways to place a value on an acquisition by comparing your financial statements side by side with those of your acquisition target. This exercise will allow you to estimate what your financial statements will look like if costs and knowledge resources are consolidated.

PLACING A VALUE ON A BUSINESS

Perform the Financial Analysis *First*

Most merger and acquisition experts might not agree with my back-door approach. It's like reading the last pages of a mystery novel to see "who done it" before you know the whole story and its characters. The reason I suggest this approach to considering the acquisition of a competitor or a company selling similar products through your distribution channels is that you already know most of the story and most of the characters. Some personnel on your staff may even be former employees of your acquisition target.

Note: When considering an acquisition, you are using past historical facts to predict the *future* funds that will return the buying price within a reasonable number of years. To get the best answers about a consolidation, look critically at predicted future financial numbers related to existing and combined market share.

If, during initial analysis of a potential acquisition, you use your financial statements to place a *future* value on your company, it is relatively easy to place a competitor's factual information or estimates side by side with your company's numbers. Since your marketing plan should have given you an idea about how much you are willing to invest to increase your market coverage to take market share from your competitors, this initial financial exercise will give you a feel for whether acquisition is a better market share strategy than investing to increase coverage.

What Methods Are Used to Value a Business?

To place a *future* value on your business or a competitor's business, there are methods that estimate what a business may be worth in the future. In the final analysis, a business is worth what someone is willing to pay for it. This value varies widely among potential buyers, because the decision is finally made on a subjective gut-feeling basis. If you can imagine you and a competitor openly looking at your two businesses side by side to estimate what both businesses would be worth in the future, separated or consolidated, it is reasonable to imagine that a consensus would eventually be reached that is fair to both sets of stockholders.

Various valuation methods are described in the handbook titled *The Art of M&A.* I briefly describe these before going through the valuation exercise I prefer to use.

- *The replacement value method.* This method helps estimate the cash costs to start from scratch and duplicate your own business or a potential acquisition. For an acquisition that appears to be profitable, but where information about things that produce the profit are lacking, this is a valid method. It includes the investments for facilities, equipment, tooling, and accounts receivable, plus costs for such things as product drawings, recruitment, training, market creation, development of customer and distributor bases, and other costs unique to that particular business. Once replacement cost is estimated, a projected cash flow can be estimated to justify the investment using the internal rate of return method.

- *The average rate of return method.* This method yields a percent rate of return (similar to ROA) by dividing average annual return (profit in dollars) by purchase price. This compares with a company's average ROA over a full economic business cycle of three to five years. Or it compares to the ROA rating of your continuous improvement projects ranked by the form in Chapter 5. Later in this section I will demonstrate this method using the sample company financial statement found in Chapter 5.

- *The payback method.* You may currently use this method to justify purchase of major manufacturing equipment. Normally you would like a new piece of equipment, including freight, installation, tooling, operator training, and process documentation, to pay out in four to five years. You can compare this payback period to your highest-ranked verb/noun projects. Later in this section I demonstrate this method using the sample company represented by the financial statement in Chapter 5.

- *The internal rate of return method.* When you place a value on an acquisition, you guess about what a *future* financial statement will look like. This method, though complicated, gives you a way to assign a present day value to future cash flows. If these more sophisticated approaches are important to your financial management, it will give you one more value on which to arrive at a fair price. I don't provide sample calculations for this method.

- *The market value method.* This method uses the published price/earnings multiples of comparable publicly traded companies to estimate a range of values for a purchase price. If your company or your acquisition target is publicly traded, you may want to consider this method. I don't provide sample calculations for this method.

- *The discounted cash flow method.* The authors of *The Art of M&A* claim that this is the only proper way to value a company. It discounts future cash flows or earnings to estimate their net present value. A reason this is a good method is because it forces buyer and seller to look at *future* annual estimates, based on logical predictions of the future, including opportunities that might not otherwise be uncovered. I don't provide sample calculations for this method.

- *Buying/selling price based on multiples of EBIT, earnings before interest, taxes, depreciation, and amortization (EBITDA), and cash flow.* This is a valuation method often used to place a value on a business. It is similar to the approach of buyers like Dover Corporation who mention the EBIT in their acquisition criteria. See the sample form shown in Figure 13.6.

The idea is to predict the EBIT, EBITDA, or cash flow (earnings before depreciation and amortization [EBDA]) for several *future* years. This prediction for future years is based on financial facts from the most recent years and the market share/business growth plans for future years. Once the past, present, and future financial numbers appear to be realistic, the buyer must multiply the EBIT, EBITDA, or EBDA by some number to determine the highest price that can be justified.

Using EBITDA dollars, the multiplier could range between three and 10. For example, if it appears that much more investment is required to make the acquisition financially sound, a multiplier of three or less might be the maximum offered. Or, for strategic reasons, if the acquisition is a very profitable business that provides big advantages to the buyer, the multiplier could range between seven and 10. Most acquisitions are settled at four to six times the EBITDA.

If the seller is very anxious to sell a business quickly, a price equal to assets for buildings, equipment, inventory, and accounts receivable might be enough to satisfy the seller. The buyer would then need to divide the total assets by the EBITDA to determine if the multiplier is equal to or greater than the business justifies.

If you want to estimate the payout period in years, divide the buying price range you are willing to offer by the average annual future EBDA. Or, make a pro forma financial statement for future years and add together the EBDA, year by year, until it totals the buying price you are willing to pay. This number of years will be larger than the EBITDA multiplier you will consider because the EBDA is smaller than the EBITDA by the cost of interest and taxes. An EBITDA multiplier of four to six might relate to a payout of six to eight years.

Design Your Own Acquisition Valuation Worksheet

Start with your P&L statement. Then add lines for EBIT, EBITDA, and EBDA. See the simplified form in Figure 13.6.

For your acquisition target, compare these lines for the previous three to five years to visualize a full economic business cycle. You may extend each line for seven to 10 future years to cover at least two future economic business cycles. The reason I suggest consideration of business cycle periods is because pro forma financial statements, which show a sales increase every future year, are not likely to be realistic. This variation is because of the ups and downs of annual sales as the economy cycles.

After studying Figure 13.6 for the sample company, make some imaginary financial statements considering a variety of scenarios to see what your future financial statement might look like if no acquisition were made, for the acquisition target if the businesses were not combined, and if the two businesses were joined together.

	Sample company		Your company		Acquisition target	
	$	%	$	%	$	%
Sales	10,000,000	100				
Less direct MLO	7,000,000	70				
Gross profit	3,000,000	30				
Less SG&A	2,000,000	20				
Before-tax profit	1,000,000	10				
Less tax	400,000	4				
After-tax profit	600,000	6				
Plus interest and taxes	500,000	5				
EBIT	**1,100,000**	**11**				
Plus depreciation and amortization	600,000	6				
EBITDA	**1,700,000**	**7**				
Less interest and taxes	500,000	5				
Cash flow (EBDA)	**1,200,000**	**12**				
Sample company assumptions:						
Tax (40% pre-tax profit)	400,000					
Interest	100,000					
Depreciation	560,000					
Interest	40,000					

Figure 13.6   Sample acquisition value worksheet.

Make pro forma financial statements for several scenarios:

- A scenario, separate from your company, if the company retains its market share but makes minimal improvement in its profit performance. This helps establish the minimum price range you would expect to pay.

- A scenario, separate from your business, predicting its market share if your market share plan works to capture some of its share.

- A scenario for your company, separate from the acquisition, if your market share plan works.

- A scenario for your company if consolidated with the acquisition target and including market share you expect to capture from other competitors if your market share plan works.

- A scenario for acquisition looked at separately but consolidated with your company. This might help you establish the maximum price range you would offer.

- A scenario for a consolidated statement showing future years with both companies consolidated into one so you can rationalize whether you will have a higher ROA by using the acquisition to increase your market share. Also use this scenario to decide whether investing in market coverage is a more profitable strategy. This scenario may tell you whether you can justify a premium price to acquire this competitor.

Practice the Acquisition Process by Valuating the Sample Company in This Section

This is the same sample as the manufacturing company sample shown in Figure 5.1, page 43. Look at the sample company as a competitor who is willing to sell. Look at it from the viewpoint of a buyer and a seller, openly deciding on a price that would be fair to both sets of stockholders.

The sample acquisition value worksheet is designed for you to insert some actual numbers for your company to decide what its value might be to a buyer. It also provides places to insert educated guesses about a competitor. If you knew your competitor's actual numbers, you might be surprised how similar your costs compare with each other.

We will evaluate this play-like acquisition of the sample company by asking several questions, assuming the financial statement is a reasonable average for the next seven to 10 years' annual performance:

- *What minimum price will the seller accept?* If a seller is anxious to sell the business, the minimum selling price could be the value of the total operating assets. For the sample company the seller would be willing to settle for $10,000,000.

- *What would be the EBITDA multiplier the buyer would have to accept?* At a selling price of $10,000,000, the multiplier is $10,000,000 \div $1,700,000 = 5.88. With a multiplier this high, the buyer may only be interested in considering this price for strategic reasons to capture the market share or obtain manufacturing capacity. Based on cash flow, the payout period is $10,000,000 \div $1,200,000 = 8.3 years. This equates to

12 percent ROA for the investment. Since this competitor is operating at a low ROA of 10 percent, this acquisition doesn't look like a very exciting investment because it may require additional investment over the next three to five years to double the ROA. As the buyer, you would need to evaluate whether you can obtain the same market share increase by investing in additional market coverage.

- *What maximum price would the seller ask if not in a hurry to sell?* Using the replacement value method, the buyer will want to recover a reasonable value for technical drawings, manufacturing process documentation, and supplier, customer, and marketing channel development, in addition to the $10,000,000 value of assets. For this company, if the seller uses 10 percent of annual purchased material for supplier development replacement cost, 50 percent of annual manufacturing salaries for manufacturing replacement cost, and 100 percent of SE&A salaries and overhead for sales, engineering, and administrative replacement cost, the total replacement cost would be $3,250,000 + $10,000,000 assets = $13,250,000.

- *Will a buyer consider paying $13,250,000?* We've established, at $10,000,000, that this is a questionable purchase for asset value. To pay the maximum asking price, the buyer would settle for an EBITDA multiplier of 7.79 ($13,250,000 ÷ $1,700,000 = 7.79) and a payback period of 11.04 years ($13,250,000 ÷ $1,200,000 = 11.04 or 8.8% ROA).

- *What would the seller need to do to make this business more salable?* I boastfully suggest that the seller (or the buyer if they are willing to pay a 5.88 EBITDA multiplier) must implement improvements to increase the ROA from 10 percent to 24 percent, slightly more than double, as we demonstrated in Figure 5.7, page 58, for this sample company. At 24 percent ROA the EBITDA would increase from $1,700,000 to $3,290,000 for an EBITDA multiplier of 3.18, based on assets increased to $10,440,000 ($440,000 for increased inventory because of 10 percent increased sales). After these improvements have been completed, the seller would claim the replacement cost would be $13,690,000 (because of $440,000 more inventory assets), resulting in an EBITDA multiplier of 4.16. The corresponding payback periods would be 3.8 years (26.3 percent ROA) and 5.0 years (20 percent ROA) respectively. This acquisition, for you as a buyer, makes more sense in this scenario than in the first four, particularly if much of the sample company's increased sales came out of your market share. If the sample company takes some of your market share, it may have a better marketing plan than you do. You can estimate how much more valuable your company will be if you double your ROA percent.

- *What price would the rate of return method place on the sample company?* The rate of return corresponds to the ROA evaluation of projects in Chapter 5. The higher you elevate your company's ROA through continuous improvement projects, the more difficult it will be to justify an acquisition that has a lower ROA percent than the project rating for a project that invests in market coverage to increase market share. In the preceding scenarios we showed the rate of return (ROA percent) in parentheses beside the payback period. (100% ÷ 8.33 years = 12.0% ROA, 100% ÷ 11.04 years = 8.8% ROA, 100% ÷ 3.8 years = 26.3% ROA, and 100% ÷ 5.0 years = 20% ROA). Pay attention to the ROA of a business you might buy and relate it to your current and projected ROA. If buying a company significantly reduces the ROA for current stockholders, you must be prepared to rationalize why the acquisition decision is better than investment in manufacturing and marketing projects over the following years.

THE ACQUISITION TEAM AND PROCESS

Putting together an acquisition team is the first step after preliminary valuation of an acquisition target. The final step will be a revision of the preliminary valuation after these remaining steps reveal facts to set a final offer.

Your acquisition team should perform the valuation of your own company as well as guessing at the value of the acquisition target you are considering.

The most logical acquisition team comprises the personnel who helped design the marketing plan. Also consider personnel who will visit the acquisition target to perform due diligence studies to gather the facts that will help make your decision for you. This could include continuous improvement team leaders who are trained and tuned to the most critical things that affect ROA. If it's an open and friendly acquisition effort, identify employees of the acquisition target who can give you the most in-depth facts.

Pick your most competent knowledge resources who can analyze historical and current financial statements and budgets. This shouldn't be only accounting knowledge resources. Include management, manufacturing, and marketing personnel who understand financial numbers.

Pick product design personnel who can analyze the products of both companies, including material and component suppliers and manufacturing processes. There will be instances when you discontinue some of your products or those of your acquisition. Include someone who has the best imagination about what future product lines and technologies may be required by your market.

Pick knowledge resources who know the marketplace and distribution systems. Include those who design marketing plans and can define how the consolidation will affect the marketplace. This part of the team could include personnel from your acquisition target, if it's an open and friendly effort. Include someone from distributors you trust to give unbiased predictions about the acquisition's impact on the market.

Pick manufacturing process designers, those who can evaluate the condition of capital equipment and facilities, quality system leaders, your best equipment operators, and material control personnel. They are valuable participants in due diligence reviews, particularly if there is going to be a consolidation of manufacturing equipment and facilities.

Start designating some of your knowledge resources for acquisition activities as soon as acquisition is an option in your marketing plan to increase market share.

There's no reason to be overly secretive about the fact that you are open to acquiring a competitor if the price is right, even if they are not the market share leader. The stockholders of your competitors aren't very astute businesspeople if they don't have a marketing plan that considers buying your business as a way to increase their market share. If a competitor doesn't operate in your marketplace, directed at taking share from you, that might be one of the reasons you wouldn't pay a premium price to acquire them, or it could be a good reason to pay a premium price if they have products and market segments that greatly expand your marketing opportunities. If they aren't following continuous improvement principles, that's another reason to reject a premium price. Obviously, the opposite is true. If they are following continuous improvement principles, they're probably experiencing a high ROA and you won't get them if you're not willing to pay a premium.

Gather Facts and Analyze the Acquisition

As you gather and analyze facts about each facet of a potential acquisition, compare it to your own business so you can discover other verb/noun projects to enhance the consolidated business, or to implement in your own business if you can't reach an agreement to complete the acquisition. While gathering and analyzing facts, put a price tag on the acquisition's strengths so you can justify a premium price if required to reach a price agreement.

If your marketing plan is doing its job well, you already have published information about each competitor. Bring this together so it's available to the acquisition team. Include such things as product brochures, Dun & Bradstreet reports, their Internet site, and magazine articles.

Make a checklist of facts you will accumulate. Remember, if you gather enough facts related to any decision you need to make, the facts themselves will tell you what your decision should be. If the decision isn't one you can make with confidence, keep adding questions to your checklist until you feel confident about the decision you will make individually or as a team.

To build a checklist, you might consider going through the verb/noun combinations in all chapters of this book and list those that relate to the acquisition. This exercise will generate more verb/noun combinations and may even discover many other verb/noun project names you haven't yet evaluated and ranked for your present business.

Use your checklist to write a documentary novel to tell the story of the potential acquisition. The prime audience is your stockholders. A secondary audience is the group of people within your own company who must be inspired to believe in the acquisition to help make a successful consolidation. The third audience is the group of people in your acquisition target who must agree to a price and their continued role in the consolidated business. These three groups, as a whole, are the people needed to grow the consolidated market share at the projected ROA.

In addition to checklists you generate, I will provide you with some acquisition process steps to serve as a pattern to write the story. My goal is to save you time by giving you a pattern to follow when you want to consider an acquisition strategy.

Step 1: Document the Target's History. Your business and the target's business have their own individual personalities. Each company's personality has been formed by management leaders and the various stockholders who have provided the investment for the company to perform on the marketplace stage.

Much of the target's personality is documented in your marketing plan. Explain how their products, markets, ownership, strategies, and management leaders evolved. Many businesses publish historical information about themselves that they want their customers to know about. One of the things you must include in this chapter are the important truths in their past and present that they don't want you to know. Your story must talk about strengths and weaknesses in ownership, management leaders, products, and markets, from the beginning up to the present time.

Step 2: Talk About the Organizational Structure and the Key Personnel. You aren't buying only physical assets, product designs, and market share. You are also buying information and knowledge assets that may or may not enter into your valuation for a buying/selling price. Buyers such as Dover only buy businesses with strong management. Knowledge is very valuable.

The personality of a business is heavily influenced by past and present leaders and how effectively they organize their knowledge resources. This is where you describe the key personnel in every function of the business to discover their general attitudes and their specific attitudes about the pros and cons of being acquired and the practice of continuous improvement.

Evaluate the level to which the acquisition has empowered employees. Your company probably has a company culture bias that a high ROA is only achieved by business leaders who empower employees at every level. This is because managers are forced to delegate to employees at every level to make financial decisions hour by hour. The point is, you will be more willing to pay a premium price for a business that has engendered a culture of empowerment. If the target's leaders haven't been successful at employee empowerment, you will want to pay less for the company because you will need to invest money and time to build the culture of empowerment into the acquired personnel.

Look at the compatibility of policies, procedures, and operating systems so you can evaluate the fit and mismatch between the two organizations.

Consider using your continuous improvement culture as a standard to compare your company story to theirs and to dramatize whether the target is a fit or a misfit with its present organization and condition.

Step 3: How Do All Products Fit Your Marketing Plan? Many competitive products are designed to serve the same functions equally. However, products aren't always equal when tested under the same conditions. For example:

- You and the target may provide a product for the same function and market, but one has a lower safety allowance, a shorter life, and a lower cost. The key is, if both can compete head-on in the same market segment, one product may be giving the market more than it is willing to pay for.

- It's possible you or your target are providing more product features than the customers want. This implies that one product may need to be phased out.

- It could be that one product line is specifically designed to serve a distributor market with a need for a broad range of product configurations and applications while the other is designed for more standard requirements of one or more OEMs.

- Perhaps your target is brand-labeling a product to keep you from capturing that market share.

- It could be that your target has a product line that has captured a big market share in a segment you haven't been able to penetrate with your product line. This product might also use marketing channels that don't fit any of your products.

My point is that this chapter of your story, as well as chapters you include about distribution, market segments, and market coverage, must include your company, your target, and other competitors as characters in the story.

The reason I suggest you do a financial analysis first is that as you gather and analyze facts in each chapter, you find logical financial reasons why you should or should not offer a premium price to capture more market share.

Step 4: How Well Do the Target's Market Segments and Distribution Channels Fit Your Market Share Plan? This is where you look at your marketing plan to see how much the acquisition would impact each market coverage element. Your checklist and story should consider:

- How much does the acquisition increase each coverage percent? Remember, the only way to increase market share is through the cumulative effect of increasing the percent coverage in each of the market coverage elements.

- How comparable is the economic business cycle of the target's product lines to your own? For your target to have a business cycle that is out of sync with your own may be a positive aspect that justifies a premium price. Having out-of-sync business cycles might offer more consistent utilization of capital equipment after the consolidation is completed.

- Has the target raised selling prices at a rate lower than inflation? If they can do this and you can't, obviously you have something to learn from them that may justify a premium price. Determine if they are a price leader or follower. Find out if they have a documented pricing policy and compare it to yours, if you have one.

- How critical is product service and the quick supply of spare parts? How does their service compare to yours? Do your dealers and their dealers perform customer service?

- Is their adherence to industry quality standards the same as yours? Is their measurable level of quality higher or lower than yours?

- Are they ahead of you or behind you in successful new product development? Do they have patents that can be exploited?

Step 5: Compare Each Manufacturing Facility. See if this review gives you any reason to justify a premium price. Some questions to ask are:

- How many days does it require for them to convert a customer order to a purchase order or shop order? This will give you a clue to determine how many days of inventory investment you might remove from their component inventory if you can shorten this lead time.

- What percent of their direct labor cost is for setup? This will help you calculate how much you can reduce their component inventory if you initiate projects to invest in setup cost reduction.

- How does their purchasing and manufacturing lead time compare to yours? How does the ratio of in-process inventory assets divided by sales compare to yours? Answers to these questions will tell which of your businesses has the better lead time controls and material control.

- How does their ratio of total company salary and wage costs divided by sales compare to yours? Measure this ratio, not only in total, but for direct labor, total manufacturing labor, indirect labor, and SE&A labor. Compare their ratio to yours to determine which of you is most efficient in various areas. You can make the same comparison for nonlabor cost categories to determine opportunities for increased profit from the consolidation.

Step 6: Finalize Pro Forma Financial Statements. Now we're back to where we started in our valuation process when I suggested you perform a financial analysis first. I provided you with a simplified P&L statement so you could calculate the EBIT, EBITDA, and EBDA for seven to 10 future years. The reason for at least seven to 10 years is to cover at least two economic business cycles and force both buyer and seller to be more realistic about their forecasts of future years.

For the finalized pro forma financial statements, buyer and seller can make adjustments to more accurately state what can be expected from a consolidation and what facts can justify a premium price.

IMPROVING CUSTOMER SERVICE

A company's products are often viewed as commodities. State-of-the-art customer service is one thing companies can do to stand out from the crowd. Customer service concepts in this section are taken from www.gilbreaths.com training manuals to provide customer service that differentiates a company from rivals. Utilize Gilbreath's "I CARE" attitude (see pages 253–54) so every member of your company, particularly those who have direct customer contact, can get a feel for things they might do differently to make customers feel at home.

Why Implement Customer Service Projects?

This section has a profit motive designed to discover customer service projects that will increase your stockholders' ROA. You owe it to both your stockholders and customers to consistently demonstrate an "I CARE" attitude at a level competitors will find it hard to match.

How Does a Company Gain Superior Customer Service?

Start with a project named "Implement Customer Service Training." Or, as an umbrella for all customer projects, consider "Implement Customer Service Attitudes."

Ask the question, "If our company became a customer service superstar, by what percent should sales increase?" Using the evaluation form in Chapter 5, estimate how much attitude and behavior changes might increase ROA. Using the sample company from Chapter 5, we can calculate that a one percent sales increase would increase ROA from 10 percent to 10.47 percent. A percentage sales increase from improved customer service may be subjective and difficult to prove but the training investment will be very low. Therefore, subjectively we can agree that sales and profit will increase as customer loyalty increases.

Who Needs Customer Service Training?

Three groups of company personnel play unique roles to provide championship customer service that increases customer loyalty, market share, sales, and profit.

- *Company leaders,* owners, and managers must make a commitment to customers by promising superior customer service as a business way of life.

- Good coaching from *managers and supervisors* helps even the best customer service performers do a better job of taking care of the details as they communicate with customers. Managers and supervisors too often overlook the coaching job.

- The *performers,* those on the customer service stage, the 20 percent of employees with 80 percent of the direct contact with customers, must be well led and coached because they deliver 80 percent of your customer-committed service.

How Do Customer Service Principles Help These Three Groups?

Customer service principles provide a solid foundation for mastering the art of developing customer-oriented employees:

- For company leaders they are a blueprint to reveal day-to-day operations of companies known for great customer service.

- For manager/supervisor/coaches they contain step-by-step approaches for giving ongoing coaching to service employees. They provide tools and techniques to coach employees to high levels of customer service.

- For the employee performers, who directly deliver 80 percent of the customer service, they provide guidelines for the skills and attitudes needed to score high with customers.

Define and Communicate Customer Service Objectives

There are some broad, subjective objectives that need to be stressed, such as "keep the customer happy" or "treat every customer like a guest in your own home." Here are some specific objectives that can be measured:

- Model behavior that delights your customer.

- Communicate and practice techniques that deliver good customer service.

- Learn ways to avoid problems for your customers.

- Learn how to handle difficult customers.

- Learn how to handle service breakdowns.

- Distinguish your performance against competitors'.

- Promote your customer service commitment.

- Increase sales and profit with great customer service.

Understand the Importance of Customers

A Wal-Mart quote by Sam Walton says, "There is only one boss. The customer. And he can fire everybody in the company, from the chairman on down, simply by spending his money somewhere else." A logical question is, "How do I communicate this understanding through my day-to-day customer contacts?"

Demonstrate Customer-Committed Behavior

Communicate to your customers that you and they are on the same team. A way to communicate this understanding is to demonstrate and communicate to customers that you and your company are obsessed with looking after their needs and wants:

- Cultivate lasting relations based on trust, respect, and understanding.

- Deliver unequaled solutions to customer problems.

- Listen to customers' wants and needs, so well that you can repeat them back to their satisfaction.

- Complete the details of every transaction.

- Help customers immediately to solve each problem.

- Keep customers informed frequently as a problem is being resolved.

- Be consistent and predictable about the service customers can expect from you.

- Become addictive when you question your customer about their needs and wants.

Show an "I CARE" Attitude

Committed behavior flows from a caring attitude. You become what your mind thinks most about. A caring attitude approach summarizes attitudes that owners and leaders, coaches, and performers must internalize to be the customer service champions in the marketplace:

- *I* for *information understood.* Be sure to understand everything customers tell you they want or need and verify that you really understand.

- *C* for *courtesy.* Treat everyone like a guest. Use your best manners. When with a customer, act professional, gracious, refined, polite, and respectful until it comes natural to you.

- *A* for *attention to details.* It's the special touches or extra things you do that set you apart. Understand *every* aspect of a customer's needs and wants. Assure that every detail of those needs is delivered in a timely and accurate manner.

- *R* for *responsibility.* Show customers they are valued. Be available and ready as customers present themselves. Respond quickly. Keep customers informed about the status of transactions.

- *E* for *every time.* Every time, in every way, every day, practice these attitudes from your mind-set. Your customers will be extremely satisfied and impressed with you and the company.

Ask Questions to Get *Information*

To get and understand the right information when helping a customer, ask the right questions so you can give the right answer:

- Ask background questions such as name, company, phone, order number, and so on.

- Ask open-ended questions that begin with *how, why, what, when, which,* and *where* to get all the information.

- Ask closed-ended questions that are answered "yes" and "no." These begin with *is, are, do, does, have, has, can, will,* or *would.*

- Ask illustrative questions to get the customer to describe a problem or situation.

- Ask clarification questions to be sure you understand.

- Ask consequence questions to find how the situation, or your suggested fix, will affect them.

- Make sure you know, and can express back to them, what they need or want.

- Close with a thank-you question. "Thank you. Is there anything else I can help you with today?"

Build Customer Service on a Foundation of *Courtesy*

There are several ways you can demonstrate courtesy, good manners, and being a gracious host to a guest.

- Show your best manners by saying, "How can I help?" "Please!" and "Thank you!"

- Show friendship with a smile. Show a personal interest in them by listening. You can hear a smile over the telephone or read a smile in an e-mail.

- Prove that their needs and wants come first with you.

- Put the person ahead of the paperwork.

- Talk the customer's language and vocabulary. Avoid jargon, abbreviations, and terms unfamiliar to them.

- Don't rush a transaction. Make them feel important.

- "Make their day" by turning their contact with you into a memory they will turn into a story to tell to others.

- Use their name and yours and "invite them back."

Design a System to *Pay Attention to Details*

A star performer on the customer service stage isn't finished when the customer audience leaves. A star immediately prepares for the next performance with each customer. To do this you need to design a system that fits you and your customers:

- Organize your work area into a system of reminders and checklists for transactions that require follow-up.

- Arrange easy access to up-to-date, reliable information.

- Keep notes that are up to date and specific.

- Manage your time and actions with day planner "to do" lists so you can be more *responsive.*

Measure Your *Responsiveness* with a Stopwatch

How quickly do you appreciate or expect a response from others to whom you ask a question, ask for help, leave a phone message, or send an e-mail or letter? Perhaps a stopwatch isn't always the most appropriate measuring instrument, but it makes the point.

- Be available. Respond quickly.

- Keep customers informed on an ongoing basis.

- Return phone calls and e-mails quickly.

- Answer mail promptly and prove it by acknowledging your receipt date.

- Share your time plan with a customer if a response will require hours, days, or weeks to meet their needs.

- Give the customer truthful and reliable delivery dates.

- Notify customers at once about delayed delivery dates.

Measure Your *Every Time* Performance

When you spend money or time to watch or listen to a star performer, you expect a star performance *every time*. That should be what you expect your customers to expect from you. The key to major-league performance for you as a customer service professional is to practice caring behavior every time, in every way, every day!

Mimic Your Best Suppliers, Companywide

Ask your purchasing function to provide a list of your own suppliers with whom they are highly satisfied. These are suppliers who seldom come up in company conversation because they seldom create problems for you and your customers. They probably provide superior customer service, reliable quality, and on-time delivery.

I remind you that manufacturing and material control personnel can be unsung heroes in your company's commitment to heroic customer service. Also, consider your personnel who design and implement your marketing plan, and its continuous improvement projects, to increase your market share.

Train company leaders, customer service coaches, and customer service performers. Company leaders are shown the important attitudes that must be a company culture element for your business. Training ideas for leaders and coaches are customized to speak directly to their individual roles. Training ideas for customer service performers, those who have 80 percent of the direct contact with customers, include many additional details required for them to effectively deliver your customer-committed service.

14

Plotting Your Economic Business Cycle

All through this book I've encouraged you to plot and use your economic business cycle to make business decisions and to determine the best time to implement continuous improvement projects. With minimal effort you can use your three- to five-year business cycle to know more precisely when to implement major and minor projects or make major business decisions.

Your sales will cycle about every three to five years in concert with the national economic business cycle and various economic indicators such as bond prices, stock prices, housing starts, and the *Business Week* index.

It helps you make confident business decisions six months to one year sooner than your competitors. It also helps you understand why net profit and ROA cycle up and down as your business experiences the national economic cycle.

A BUSINESS CYCLE PICTURED AS THE PERCENT RATE OF CHANGE

Take a few minutes each month to plot a picture of your company's business cycle. To calculate the percent rate of change (ROC) you divide your total sales for the last 12 months by the same 12 month total for the same month one year earlier. The percent will be either greater than or less than 100 percent. A perfectly smooth ROC curve would look like Figure 14.1 as it cycles above and below the 100 percent line.

An actual ROC curve would look like the picture of a real manufacturing business for a period from 1973 to 1997 shown in Figure 14.2.

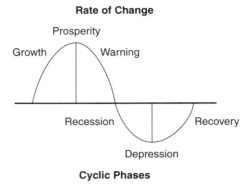

Figure 14.1 The generic business cycle.

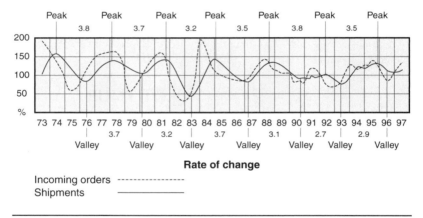

Figure 14.2 Rate of change cycle for a manufacturing business from 1973 to 1997.

REASONS TO PLOT YOUR BUSINESS CYCLE EACH MONTH

There are three reasons to plot a business cycle monthly.

First, as you gather a large inventory of potential projects, there are certain phases of the business cycle when each project can be implemented best. Large capital investments or introduction of new products will pay back the investment in the least calendar time if implemented at the beginning of the growth phase. During the recession and depression phases, you may be reluctant to invest cash in projects. You can save smaller projects that will pay back in less than a year for implementation during these phases. Your net profit will be greater with the implementation of these projects even if you treat the investment as an expense. I make this point to show you that there's never a time during a business cycle to not implement projects.

Second, your business cycle helps you to confidently make business decisions sooner than you would without it. It allows you to stay one move ahead of competitors. Later in this chapter I provide a list of other decisions you can make with great confidence six months to one year earlier than your competitors.

Third, profit measurements usually go up and down as a business cycle goes through its phases. It's important to realize that the return on assets improvement must be viewed over a period of time approximately equal to your most normal company business cycle time period. If you don't want to calculate and plot your company business cycle, you should use your average financial performance over a three- to five-year period to be more confident that projects are yielding improved overall results.

CALCULATE AND PLOT YOUR COMPANY'S BUSINESS CYCLE

Your company business cycle can be calculated and plotted to look something like the preceding figures. Each month calculate and plot a percent value to represent the rate at which sales are changing. When the percentage is more than 100 percent you know the rate at which annual sales are growing. When the percentage is less than 100 percent you know the rate at which sales are shrinking. Historically, for many companies and industries, each cycle covers a period of about four years. It's actually a picture of the peaks and valleys of a nation's economy reflected in the sales peaks and valleys of your business. Presidents of nations or individual businesses have almost no control over it. It will take about thirty minutes each month to calculate and plot it. If you have the information, you can plot both shipments and incoming customer orders. Plotting both expands how many months you can get the jump on your competitors.

We learned the ROC concepts from William L. Schubert. The basic concepts and calculations were conceived by Chapin Hoskins, a Harvard MBA and managing editor of *Forbes* magazine in the late 1930s. See Related Web Searches in the Bibliography for up-to-date contributors about this tool.

INTERPRETATION OF A BUSINESS CYCLE PICTURE

Referring to the preceding ROC chart (Figure 14.2) for a manufacturing business in the oil well drilling and construction equipment segments, you can visualize why this business was more profitable than its competitors during the period from 1977 through 1984. The business cycle signaled in mid-1976 that the depth of the valley had been reached. Based on the peak in 1974, it could make a good guess about the timing of the next peak and could make business decisions much sooner than its competitors.

When the curve is initially above the 100 percent line and is trending upward, it means new orders and shipments are increasing at an increasing rate. As this sample curve turns downward at the peak in 1978, it means sales were continuing to increase but at a decreasing rate. Notice that the next valley occurred in early 1980, above the 100 percent line. This simply means that sales continued to increase during 1980 and 1981.

Usually, business cycles are significantly influenced by national inventory levels. As you can imagine, businesses in the industry segment represented by our sample curve were adding capacity and were building raw material inventory to match the new capacity requirements. In the latter part of 1981, the managers of this business were alerted by the downward trend that the warning phase had arrived. They were also warned because distributors had already cut back on new orders six months earlier in mid-1981.

Early in 1982, end users, dealers, and distributors began to cancel existing new orders. There was no merit for this company to force its customers to accept shipment for their purchase orders and contracts because their cash was also tied up in inventory. In this particular business cycle, it wasn't until after the peak in 1985 that inventory was reduced enough that competing businesses could have a decent ROA again.

As you can see from this real-world example, there are times, such as the period 1990 through 1995, when the peaks and valleys aren't as pronounced as other periods. However, that doesn't invalidate the fact that your company will have business cycles that, if monitored, will allow you to make better business decisions sooner than your competitors.

COMPANY DECISIONS DURING EACH BUSINESS CYCLE PHASE

We could have titled this section "Management Decisions During Each Business Cycle Phase." As you look at the verb/noun combinations shown in *italics* in the next few pages, you will realize that many of these decisions can be made at various levels of responsibility as soon as company management declares in which business cycle you are currently operating. Look at these verb/noun combinations to generate your own list that allows you to quickly delegate actions that fit your business cycle. I will suggest some of the major categories of decisions to help you get started.

For example, some time during the warning phase, you and your distributors can start taking actions to minimize your inventory and capital equipment capacity. Then, at the beginning of the growth phase, you and your distributors can slowly increase inventory, ahead of actual demand, to provide faster delivery before your competitors realize it is time to start increasing their capacity.

Manufacturers Should Link Shop Order Start Dates with Business Cycle Transition Points. One of the places reduced or increased incoming orders will first be revealed is when shop orders begin to reveal whether more or less manufacturing capacity is needed to meet shop order start date demands. Watch this carefully when you get an indication that the business cycle curve is about to cross the 100 percent line. The key is to monitor the shop order start date/capacity demands in concert with the business cycle curve as it moves up or down toward the 100 percent line.

Control Inventory Levels. In Chapter 10, I covered ways to control inventory levels by utilizing a financially sound lot sizing formula based on existing setup costs and inventory carrying cost percent. You can prudently manipulate your lot sizes as your business cycle curve prepares to cross the 100 percent line to make the transition from one phase to another.

- *Reduce inventory levels* in the warning and recession phases. Consider distributor inventories to maximize distributor loyalty by helping them minimize their inventory as well as your own. To minimize inventory during the ending of the warning phase and the beginning of the recession phase, the best way is to *reduce lot sizes* by *increasing the inventory carrying cost percent* in your lot sizing formula for a reasonable period of time. This action temporarily reduces inventory investment while your material control system automatically reduces usage rates.

- *Increase inventory levels* during recovery and growth phases. With this action you improve distributor relations and their ROA by helping them increase their sales. Here you *reduce the inventory carrying cost percent* so it will slightly *increase lot sizes* across the board. Temporary adjustment to the inventory carrying cost percent is a simple method to manage inventory levels. It yields a temporary, balanced automatic adjustment to items you must carry in inventory.

- *Maintain inventory levels* during the prosperity peak and depression valley by using the true inventory carrying cost percent. These two periods of time account for 80 percent of the months included in each business cycle. Be sure to use the project evaluation in Chapter 5 to decide if each specific action will increase the ROA over a full business cycle.

Adjust Employment Levels. Business cycle peaks and valleys are often too extreme to only *consider attrition* as the only way to adjust employee levels. That's why layoffs are often necessary after a business cycle downturn. On the other hand, you want to be sure you *maintain your key knowledge resources* during the recession and recovery phases. You also want to *look at projects that will pay back in less than one year* and be sure to *maintain a number of project teams.* Remember, these teams, if your project evaluations are accurate, are never an expense and should always result in increased profit and increased market share, even in the valley of your business cycle.

- *Increase project team levels* during all phases at a level to which stockholders will commit funds.

- *Control manufacturing employment levels* during growth, prosperity, and warning phases to meet capacity demands signaled by shop order start dates.

- *Minimize addition of new employees* during all phases to *reduce salaries and wages per sales dollar* as you *implement increased employee efficiency.*

- *Consider more overtime* during the later portion of the warning phase, as dictated by shop order start dates, to avoid hiring and training employees that may need to be laid off.

Use your own imagination to time projects to increase sales and market share:

- Introduce new products

- Enter new market segments

- Add new distributors

- Implement new discount structures

- Implement new marketing programs

- Eliminate low gross profit product lines

- Add or subtract capital equipment investment

- Dispose of excess or underutilized equipment

- Order new equipment or facilities to increase or maintain capacity

THE CALCULATION AND PLOTTING PROCESS

In a very few minutes each month you can perform the simple arithmetic to calculate and plot the rate of change for your total sales or for sales of each product line if you decide you want that much detail. You can perform manual calculations and plot on graph paper or design a computer spreadsheet that will perform the calculations and plot a computer-generated curve (see Figure 14.3).

Sales/Shipments 12 Months Running Total (12MRT) Rate of Change (ROC) %												
	1996 Monthly	1996	1996	1997 Monthly	1997	1997	1998 Monthly	1998	1998	1999 Monthly	1999	1999
Month	Sales	12MRT	ROC	Sales	12MRT	ROC	Sales	12MRT	ROC	Sales	12MRT	ROC
JAN	417,700			457,500	5,226,000		589,600	6,259,000	120	580,800	7,441,700	119
FEB	379,200			441,800	5,288,600		707,100	6,524,300	123	613,400	7,398,000	113
MAR	426,500			483,400	5,345,500		676,700	6,717,600	126	584,900	7,256,200	108
APR	381,800			506,600	5,470,300		602,500	6,813,500	125	530,900	7,184,600	105
MAY	408,100			538,600	5,600,800		629,300	6,904,200	123	482,900	7,038,200	102
JUN	375,500			519,000	5,744,300		534,700	6,919,900	120	469,500	6,973,000	101
JUL	501,900			538,800	5,781,200		678,700	7,059,800	122	533,900	6,828,200	97
AUG	437,200			536,900	5,880,900		660,600	7,183,500	122	441,800	6,609,400	92
SEP	446,800			530,300	5,964,400		611,700	7,264,900	122	484,100	6,481,800	89
OCT	501,300			569,200	6,032,300		698,300	7,394,000	123	521,000	6,304,500	85
NOV	434,700			545,000	6,142,600		538,200	7,387,200	120	525,700	6,292,000	85
DEC	477,000	5,186,200		459,800	6,126,900	118	523,100	7,450,500	122	366,500	6,135,400	82

Incoming Orders 12 Months Running Total (12MRT) Rate of Change (ROC) %												
	Incoming			Incoming			Incoming			Incoming		
Month	orders	12MRT	ROC	orders	12MRT	ROC	orders	12MRT	ROC	orders	12MRT	ROC
JAN	458,100			779,200	5,900,600		550,200	7,190,400	122	500,600	6,829,100	95
FEB	394,400			727,300	6,233,000		652,200	7,115,300	114	567,200	6,744,100	95
MAR	434,300			532,700	6,331,400		957,200	7,539,800	119	503,400	6,290,300	83
APR	480,700			582,200	6,432,900		500,800	7,458,400	116	697,200	6,486,700	87
MAY	472,700			638,200	6,598,400		668,700	7,488,900	113	488,200	6,306,200	84
JUN	544,700			432,900	6,486,600		599,400	7,655,400	118	437,600	6,144,400	80
JUL	399,100			396,600	6,484,100		706,600	7,965,400	123	344,100	5,781,900	73
AUG	426,500			553,600	6,611,200		436,500	7,848,300	119	365,400	5,710,800	73
SEP	525,400			781,100	6,866,900		604,300	7,671,500	112	338,500	5,445,000	71
OCT	511,700			746,900	7,102,100		216,600	7,141,200	101	397,700	5,626,100	79
NOV	289,400			599,500	7,412,200		417,300	6,959,000	94	544,800	5,753,600	83
DEC	642,000	5,579,500		649,200	7,419,400	133	568,900	6,878,700	93	344,600	5,529,300	80

Figure 14.3 Spreadsheet showing rate of change calculations for sales and incoming orders.

The spreadsheet in Figure 14.3 will serve as a pattern and example of the calculation process:

- Create a spreadsheet for sales/shipments and incoming orders. Plot these two curves on the same graph so you can see them move in concert.

- Initially plot as much history as you have available. The year-to-year curves will tell you whether or when the curve will become usable for predicting future transitions from one phase to another.

- Divide the 12-month running total (12MRT) for each month by the 12-month running total for the same month one year earlier to obtain a percent rate of change (ROC). (Example: DEC 1996, $6,126,900 ÷ $5,186,200 = 118%)

- For the first historical year you decide to use, you will list the monthly sales or monthly incoming orders in their appropriate columns. (Example: JAN 1996, $417,700)

- For the first historical year, record the annual sales or annual incoming orders in the 12MRT column on the DEC line. (Example: DEC 1996, $5,186,200)

- For each month of the second historical year list the monthly value in the sales and incoming order columns.

- Each month of the second year, calculate a 12-month running total in the 12MRT column, beginning with JAN 1997. To make the 12MRT calculation for the latest month, subtract the monthly value for the same month of the previous year from the 12MRT for the previous month and add the results to the monthly value for the new month, and record the results in the 12MRT column for the new month. (Example JAN 1997, $5,186,200 – $417,700 + $457,500 = $5,226,000).

- Beginning with DEC of the second historical year, DEC 1997, calculate the monthly ROC percent. This is obtained by dividing DEC 1997 12MRT ($6,126,900) by the 12MRT for the same month of the preceding year ($5,186,200 for DEC 1999) to obtain 118 percent.

- Starting with JAN 1998, and for future months, values are recorded in the monthly sales or monthly incoming orders columns and calculations are made for the 12MRT and ROC columns. (Example: For JAN 1998, the 12MRT is obtained by subtracting the JAN 1997 sales value [$457,500] from the DEC 1997 12MRT [$6,126,900] and adding the JAN 1998 monthly sales value [$589,600] to obtain the JAN 1998 12MRT [$6,259,000].) This same recording and calculating is repeated for each following month.

The ROC percents are recorded on the spreadsheet and the calculations are recorded on the graph in Figure 14.4. Since I knew the actual ROC values for the years before 1998 (for Figure 14.2) and after 1999, I included them to give a better picture of what the business cycle looked like for this manufacturing business.

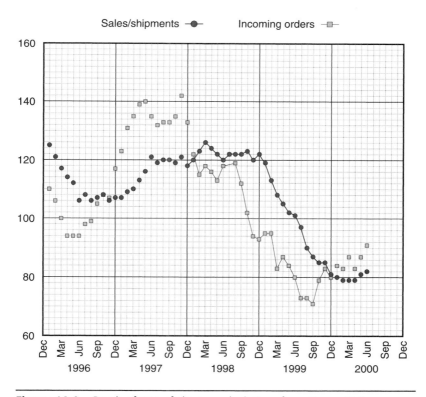

Figure 14.4 Graph of rate of change calculations from Figure 14.3.

This curve clearly shows that you can gain an advantage over your competitors by realizing that your curve for incoming orders is going to lead your shipment curve. These curves should also give you a tool to time the implementation of projects to increase your ROA during both the peaks and the valleys. The peaks and valleys will also explain why your ROA should be evaluated over an entire business cycle because the lower sales and lower net profit during the valleys also force a lower ROA in the valleys. This is another reason why you want to time your inventory and capital equipment investment changes so you can minimize their impact on ROA during the valley. I encourage you to take this long-range view so you will reserve much of your excess cash for continuous project investment at the peaks, including investment for project team personnel.

LEADING AND FOLLOWING ECONOMIC INDICATORS

The chart in Figure 14.5 shows another way to use the ROC as a planning and management tool. There are several economic indicators whose ROC cycles in a predicable fashion. The ROC of your business will cycle in a similar pattern and timing to one of these economic indicators.

These indicators are status indicators on your company's dashboard just like light indicators and gages on your car's dashboard. They serve to inform you that the economy is going well and sometimes they warn you that it's time for you to pull over to the curb and check some things before you continue on your financial business journey.

Some of these indicators cycle ahead of the *Business Week* index and some cycle behind it. It happens that the ROC for the sample business I've used as an example cycles very similarly to the *Business Week* index. The dotted line on the chart in Figure 14.5 shows the ROC of the sample company from Figure 14.2. It's not a perfect match, but close enough that our sample company should pay attention to bond prices, stock prices, and housing starts to get an early indication of what to expect in the next one to two years.

When these economic indicators are watched, you will greatly build your ability to make risky business decisions with much greater confidence.

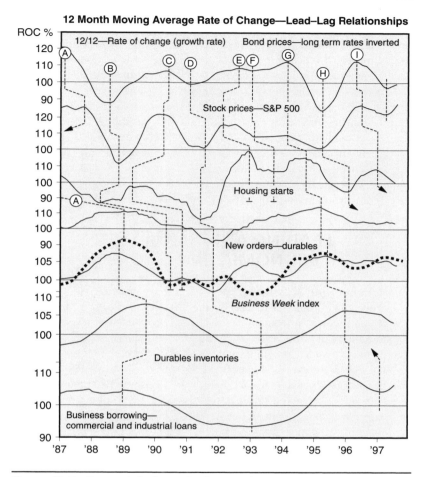

Figure 14.5 Economic indicator business cycle sequence.

15

Continuous Improvement versus Creativity

Many businesses that have implemented companywide improvement programs such as Six Sigma, ISO 9000, total quality management, lean, or something like the innovative version of continuous improvement using verb/noun combinations from the seven critical business elements presented in this book, have had the debate that these programs hamper creativity. This issue is particularly pronounced for businesses whose sales depend on the invention of new products.

I happen to come down on the side of creativity. It is my conclusion that not all functions of some businesses must participate in the companywide activities for efficiency in operational functions that are the focus of these various improvement programs.

Every business must have creative personnel whose creativity can be successfully applied to all seven of the business elements from an operational point of view. However, there are a very small percentage of knowledge workers who must be allowed to exercise their imaginations to dream up new products or applications of new technologies.

If you can factually prove to yourself that a high percent of your annual sales, from year to year and over several recent business cycles, are consistently made up of new products, you have a basis to identify and make allowances for these few specific knowledge workers.

Some businesses, whose sales and market share depend on these kinds of new products or applications of new technologies, should purposefully excuse these few people from the obvious restrictions that are clearly required to double your ROA over a period of three to five years. It doesn't mean they shouldn't be exposed to and trained in these practices, which they may consider to restrict their creativity and inventiveness. They need to know what other employees are doing to generate cash so they can be allowed to create new products to feed the operational functions.

I don't know a good short-term way to measure the ROA for true inventors and their trial-and-error process of imagining new possibilities. Any business will be blessed to have one or more individuals who possess this magical thinking process, if that's what the business requires.

If you want to allow this kind of individual the freedom to experiment with new products or new applications of ideas, you may have to almost completely remove them from the restrictions imposed on the operational employees to implement a successful year-in-and-year-out continuous improvement program that demands relatively short-term financial payback for improvement projects.

However, this doesn't mean you don't measure the long-term performance of these inventive activities. It's obvious that your stockholders, and even key customers you consult with, won't want you to keep investing endlessly if new sales or market share don't pay back the investment by increasing the ROA above what it would have been without it. You don't have to let these creative people see your measurement process because, for them, measuring is just another restriction they don't need to be concerned with.

I encourage your management to accept the reality of the tension that results from your most creative people, even those in the operational functions, bowing to the restrictive financial arithmetic required to greatly increase your ROA. I believe that your creative operational knowledge resources will always respond positively when they are recognized by both management and peers as helping elevate the business to new financial heights.

16

Seven Sources
of Entrepreneurial
Innovation

Much of the knowledge in this chapter was learned from the following books: *Managing for Results* by Peter Drucker, *Innovation and Entrepreneurship: Practices and Principles* by Peter Drucker, and *The Definitive Drucker* by Elizabeth Haas Edersheim.

There are three goals for this chapter:

- To convince managers of any business that they can become successful entrepreneurial innovators.

- To get you to read, study, and apply the knowledge found in these books, and any other Drucker books.

- To show you what I've learned from Drucker about what an entrepreneurial innovator looks like.

This chapter is directed to the managers in your business, who should desire to apply an entrepreneurial style of management to discover opportunities to and expand the current business through what Drucker calls the "seven sources of innovative opportunity," in concert with continuous improvement projects from the seven critical business elements, to double your ROA. Now I will make it clear that the reason to generate cash assets from projects to double your ROA is to have investment funds to perform entrepreneurial innovation.

One of Drucker's goals in his 39 published books on management is to show that entrepreneurship and innovation are things any hard-working manager can do by using a systematic thinking process.

THE THREE GROUPS OF KNOWLEDGE RESOURCES

In Chapter 1, I introduced the concept that there are three separate but integrated knowledge resource groups that each requires its own policies, practices, and measures of performance. The first two groups are focused on the seven critical business elements. The third group focuses on the seven sources of entrepreneurial innovation.

In very large businesses, these may be distinct groups that infrequently share the same knowledge resources. Small- to medium-sized businesses will find it necessary to include a few individual knowledge resources in all three of the groups.

Each group requires its own unique systematic process to effectively manage its allotment of the company's knowledge resources. Each group causes major change in the culture of the business. Because of this change, each group requires top-level managers, those who hire and allocate the major knowledge resources, to be the champions of change.

The operations group uses the principles contained in the seven business elements to assure on-time delivery of high-quality products at the lowest cost in all phases of each business cycle. The bottom-line measure is maintenance of the ROA, established over several business cycles.

To move the company culture to the point of delivering on-time, lowest-cost, high-quality products and services 95 percent of the time requires top-level management to commit to and champion this mission so all the right knowledge resources are allocated.

This group may resist the belief that consistent quality, consistent low cost, and on-time delivery of products and services 95 percent of the time is actually achievable until a management champion trains them and shows them that it can be done.

The continuous improvement group also utilizes the seven business elements to discover and implement continuous improvement projects, with a goal to double the ROA over a three- to five-year business cycle. One purpose of the dramatic ROA increase is to continually provide the cash to support both continuous improvement and entrepreneurial innovation.

To change the company culture to accept and implement company-wide continuous improvement to double ROA requires top-level management to champion this mission and to make the investment and allocation of knowledge resources necessary to discover and implement a massive number of continuous improvement projects during every phase of every business cycle.

This group may resist the idea that the ROA can be doubled over a three- to five-year period unless a manager proves to them that it can be done and proves to them that the necessary investment in money and people resources will be made.

The entrepreneurial innovation group uses the seven sources of innovation to assure long-term survival of the business by replacing products, market segments, or distribution channels that no longer fit, and by looking for opportunities to start new businesses that fit with or extend the existing business.

To change the culture of top managers to the point that they become managers of entrepreneurial innovation requires top manager commitment and participation to manage this group of knowledge resources so they will set a course to extend the life of the business many business cycles into the future.

As surprising as it may seem, this group of professional managers can be expected to resist becoming innovative entrepreneurs on the basis that entrepreneurs are "born that way" and can't use a systematic process to do the job. Or it could be that they don't yet realize that ensuring long-term survival and growth of a business is a basic requirement of professional managers, each and every year of business cycles into the future. Perhaps they haven't been given the tools and training to identify the changes that occur every year in the lifecycle of a product, service, market segment, or distribution channel.

MANAGING ENTREPRENEURIAL INNOVATION

The pure definition of innovation is, "The introduction of a new idea, a new material, or a new device." I suggest that this book is an innovation because it presents the seven critical business elements as the only source of projects to double the ROA with continuous improvement projects. I know of no other source for this particular approach.

The pure definition of an entrepreneur is simply someone who organizes, manages, and assumes the risk that a business will produce an acceptable profit. This definition could easily apply to any employee at any level who systematically makes financial decisions every day or hour.

In this chapter I expose you to a more elevated definition that Peter Drucker explains in his book *Innovation and Entrepreneurship*. He harnesses these two words together to go beyond what I covered in the preceding chapters of this book. Just as I contend that employees at every level can use this systematic approach to double the ROA of a business, Drucker contends that managers at every level can use a systematic approach to become top-notch innovators and entrepreneurs.

A September 2007 *Tulsa World* newspaper article reported that Procter & Gamble's annual sales "earnings per share grew 15 percent and operating cash flow improved 18 percent." They claimed that growing market share and innovation was a result of a "deep" understanding of consumer demand, cost savings, and the integration of acquisitions such as Gillette, Duracell, and Braun. Investors in Procter & Gamble (P&G) have experienced an increase in dividends for the 52nd year in a row.

What explains P&G's superior economic behavior? The answer—"innovation and entrepreneurship"—from Drucker's book by the same name.

By applying systematic processes to managing a business for the long term, small- to medium-sized enterprises can demonstrate a record similar to that of P&G. The key is to use a systematic approach to discover and implement projects to exploit new opportunities that satisfy the needs and wants of current and potential customers.

Just as good continuous improvement change agents and champions accept change as a normal and healthy way to increase ROA, good innovative entrepreneurs accept changes in the marketplace as fertile ground in which to plant the seeds of innovation. Innovation is the seed that entrepreneurs plant to harvest year-to-year financial growth.

Entrepreneurial farmers manage risk by shifting their best knowledge and financial resources from a less fertile field to one that will yield a bigger and more profitable harvest.

Just as planning is the lowest-cost method of control in a material control system for a manufacturing business, systematic entrepreneurial innovation is the lowest-risk system to grow a business from year to year and from business cycle to business cycle.

And just as I have provided a way to financially judge continuous improvement projects in Chapter 5, I point to a way in this chapter for you to develop your own means to decide between innovation projects. Drucker can show you how to discover business opportunities, evaluate their chance of success, measure the risk of failure, and combine existing resources into a new configuration that continues to satisfy customers and stockholders.

So, how do managers go about a systematic search for changes? How do you systematically analyze opportunities the changes offer for innovation? Drucker suggests two analytic exercises:

- A "business X-ray"

- Seven sources of innovation

THE BUSINESS X-RAY

Once your company has overcome managers' resistance to see themselves as entrepreneurial innovators, a logical step is to apply what Drucker calls a "business X-ray." This is simply a systematic way to segregate products, market segments, and distribution channels into groups or categories by documenting:

- Which ones are growing old, are near death, and will soon need to be abandoned or repaired

- Which ones are just wasting valuable knowledge and money resources

- Which ones are young and need extra resources to grow through various stages of development

In Chapter 8, I suggested a similar way to segregate and annually monitor the sales and gross profit for product lines, market segments, and distribution channels as a way to discover continuous improvement projects. Gross profit trends can help your teams discover problems and opportunities.

Drucker's book gives a very comprehensive way to make this analysis, which you can redesign to meet your own needs. His categories are:

- Today's and yesterday's breadwinners

- Investment in managerial ego

- Repair jobs and failures

- Productive, unnecessary, and unjustified specialties

- Development products, segments, or channels

My point is this: each year, entrepreneurs systematically analyze data to know where to allocate knowledge and money resources to identify and exploit opportunities to extend the life of the business. Study Drucker's and Haas Edersheim's books to make this an integral part of your entrepreneurial thinking.

THE SEVEN SOURCES OF INNOVATION

Drucker recommends you monitor seven sources that offer entrepreneurial opportunity. He calls these "symptoms" that are "reliable indicators of changes that have already happened, or can be made to happen with little effort."

First is the unexpected success, unexpected failure, or unexpected outside event:

- *An unexpected success* may be hard for managers to accept because it may be something for which they can't honestly take credit. Therefore, they fail to exploit it. Normal quantitative financial reporting may not flag these successes nor recognize the qualitative aspects. To exploit this marketplace symptom requires you to analyze the symptom until you discover an innovative opportunity. It should be apparent that a manager should quickly shift knowledge and financial resources by assigning specific individuals to analyze, innovate, and implement entrepreneurial change.

- *An unexpected failure* can't be ignored. It's not usually viewed as a symptom that provides innovative opportunity. If the original design and marketing strategy for a product or service was well thought out, there's a probability that something in the product's use or value has changed. Therefore, go talk to the marketplace and let it tell you what has changed. Then, accept the change and assign resources to purposefully define the opportunity.

- *An unexpected outside event* may be a market change that opens an opportunity to apply existing products or distribution channels to some new use or application where a reconfiguration or alteration will make it fit the marketplace.

The second source is an incongruity in reality as it is assumed to be or as it ought to be. An incongruity exists when you have a dramatic increase or decrease in weight and your clothes no longer fit. Incongruity is recognizable when the musical notes of a choir or orchestra no longer harmonize with each other. These are obvious symptoms that something is out of balance. Incongruities signal change and reveal opportunities for improvements where a minor innovation can yield big results. Lack of harmony or better-fitting clothes can be qualitative as well as quantitative changes. They are clearly visible, yet are often overlooked because we have slowly become accustomed to the bad fit or the disharmony:

- *Financial performance* of products or services that is dramatically better or worse than expected during the various phases of a business cycle would be a signal to analyze good performance so you can duplicate it or look at bad performance and correct it. An opportunity or symptom might be signaled if a product performs better than other products during the valley of the business cycle.

If exploited, it and similar products might dampen the extreme peaks and valleys of each business cycle and greatly improve your capital asset utilization.

- *Look for things that don't harmonize* in new products, new services, or new processes. Look for an abnormal business cycle phase because of war, major natural disasters, or major energy shortages. Be aware of innovations that require unusually high capital investment to meet current demand, which may not grow as rapidly as the capital investment required for the current demand.

- *Look for opportunities where there are long lead times, combined with or separate from large capital equipment investment.* A Drucker example is the long lead time consumed to load and unload cargo ships, a very expensive capital investment, before the innovation of large cargo containers. Processing equipment manufacturers executed a similar change when they provided machines with large magazines of cutting tools combined with multiple indexing tables and holding fixtures. This allowed many individual parts to be processed with a minimum of setup time and lead time on a very expensive piece of equipment. As a result, the inventory investment for those parts was essentially eliminated, allowing delivery to assembly once each shift or each hour.

- *Search for the mismatch between your customers' and your beliefs about their needs and wants.* The difference between the two is a symptom and an opportunity for an innovative alteration to make a better fit. If you hear yourself saying that customers are irrational and unwilling to pay for certain features or services, you may be blocking out the voice of reality, which is trying to tell you that this mismatch is an opportunity for a simple innovation. Just ask each major customer what they need or don't need in your product and service. Stop being so arrogant in thinking that you know what is best for them.

The third source is innovation based on process need. Processes and procedures exist in both your and your customers' businesses. Visualize one of your company procedures to see a picture of Drucker's five criteria and two constraints to discover and formulate innovations for a process need.

The five criteria are:

- A self-contained process

- A weak missing link or step in the process

- A clear definition of the purpose for the process

- A solution that can be clearly defined

- A consensus from the process users that there ought to be a better way

The two constraints are:

- Some of the process users may not yet understand or accept that there is a mismatch or that something is out of harmony with its purpose

- Even if you understand the need for a change in the process or procedure, you may not possess knowledge to make the alterations so it will fit, or to change the notes to bring it back into harmony

The fourth source is "Changes in industry and market structure that catch everyone unawares." Wal-Mart stores in small towns brought a dramatic change to many main street businesses. Many business owners and some employees see Wal-Mart as a threat that will ruin their way of life and the life of the town. Therefore, they ignore the opportunity. The innovators see this change as an opportunity. They see it as a reality that can't be ignored, based on the fact that a Wal-Mart store creates many jobs in each small town outside its walls. How can innovators be so sure of themselves? They are businesswomen and businessmen who accept change and watch for the indicators of change that will specifically affect their business.

Systematic innovators in the smallest business can easily spot rapid growth in an industry that might affect them. All businesspersons and political leaders in small towns were signaled many years in advance that Wal-Mart might change the structure of their town. They didn't conclude that innovative opportunities were the best solution to their problem. At the same time they watched Wal-Mart's rapid expansion, they could have looked at other industries that were growing faster than the economy or population and, in advance, brought in those industries that could have systematically and innovatively reconfigured the knowledge and assets on their main street into something that fit the changed market structure.

Another change to look for is that as some industries grow rapidly, they might become complacent and not realize that what originally satisfied their customers is in the process of changing. Innovative opportunities may be found in the way the market segments itself, requiring innovative changes in its products, services, or marketing channels to reach a changing customer base.

Rapidly changing industry structure also opens a door for innovative opportunity when two technologies meet each other at just the right time.

It's like the rapid structural change that occurs in two people's love lives when they meet each other at just the right time. The wedding of telephone and computer technologies has produced a huge family of products and services, including support products such as cell towers and satellites. Watch for new kinds of technology and their applications. Be ready to introduce two of them to each other when the time is right.

An innovative opportunity may be waiting around the edge of an industry that is dominated by one or two large companies. As structural changes begin to occur, the companies with big market share may be neglecting the fastest-growing market segment or distribution channel. An alert and systematic entrepreneur can design simple innovations that can gain market share and a foothold in that industry at a relatively low investment.

The fifth source is demographics. These are population changes in areas such as geographic location, area size, age, employment, income, and education. It's an obvious place business managers should watch. Demographics are always in a very slow state of change. However, that's the reason they provide so many opportunities for the systematic entrepreneur. The very slow rate of change is the reason many business decision makers ignore it. Consider the irreversible national structural changes in the United States created by illegal Hispanic immigration that has happened over a very long period of time. Those who look for innovative opportunities that meet the needs and wants of this demographic group may find significant markets they can have all to themselves. Look for demographics that are changing more quickly than the norm to find entrepreneurial opportunities.

The sixth source is "Changes in perception, mood, and meaning." Both individuals and industries have a perception. It is the way a person or industry sees things. It's a pattern of thinking. Sometimes as people get older they have a broad range of experiences that change their pattern of thinking and the way they see things. We sometimes say people or industries experience a paradigm shift. Changing perception is just another opportunity for entrepreneurial innovation.

When a person has a change in their thinking, past facts haven't changed. Only the meaning or interpretation of the facts has changed. The same concept is true of industry. The person or industry may not understand it, but it's a fact that significant change has occurred. For these kinds of opportunities, timing is critical. To exploit changes in perception, the opportunist must be the first one there with a relatively small initial idea to offer.

The seventh source is "New scientific and nonscientific knowledge." I won't use a lot of space talking about innovations from new knowledge. It's a complicated source because it takes a very long time between discovery and the application of any new knowledge to technology. Then it's another long time before products and a marketplace are developed. If you need to learn more about opportunities to be had from this change, refer to the books mentioned at the beginning of this chapter.

MEASURING ENTREPRENEURIAL ACTIVITIES

The entrepreneur must also have a way to measure entrepreneurial and innovative activities. A critical truth to remember is that financial measurements, such as ROA, aren't appropriate because business development is often a long, slow process that may take years to grow products, market segments, and distribution channels. One way to minimize this truth is to not wander far from the base and structure of your current business.

Drucker points out that these activities must be separated from normal financial measurement until they have had time to develop, just as you don't expect a growing child, in whom you make a big investment over several years, to become productive. Drucker points out that manager meetings and business reports need to be broken into two separate parts, one for normal profitable operations and one that primarily measures progress on creative activities that have been agreed upon to keep the business moving in the right direction.

Here's my final point: the reason you use continuous improvement projects to double the ROA is to have the money and knowledge resources to invest in continuous improvement *and* new entrepreneurial business enterprises.

Bibliography

Chapter 1 of this book listed the sources of knowledge I was exposed to during my long career, which was used to describe an innovative approach to continuous improvement. Few direct quotes are used because much of the knowledge related to the innovative approach of the book came from seminars, being exposed to consultants in the course of being a manager in various functions of a manufacturing business for many years, and experimenting and testing simplified business concepts suggested in this work.

Other sources and acknowledgments are included in the same chapter as the learned information. Every effort has been made to avoid infringing on copyrights and to provide specifics about how the reader can access a broader scope of related reading.

BOOKS AND STANDARDS

American Society for Quality. *ANSI/ISO/ASQ Q9001-2000 Standard.* Milwaukee: ASQ, 2000.

Drucker, Peter. *Managing for Results.* New York: Harper & Row, 1954.

———. *Innovation and Entrepreneurship: Practices and Principles.* New York: Harper & Row, 1985

Edersheim, Elizabeth Haas. *The Definitive Drucker.* New York: McGraw-Hill, 2007.

Reed, Stanley Foster, and Alexandra Reed Lajoux. *The Art of M&A: A Merger Acquisition Buyout Guide.* New York: McGraw-Hill, 1998

U.S. Department of Commerce, National Institute of Standards and Technology. *Manufacturing Enterprise Partnership.* Washington, D.C.: NIST, 2003.

VanDeMark, Robert L. *Inventory Control Techniques.* Dallas, TX: VanDeMark, 1972.

————. *New Ideas in Materials Management.* Dallas, TX: VanDeMark, 1967.

————. *Production Control Techniques.* Dallas, TX: VanDeMark, 1970.

WEB SITES

www.gilbreaths.com, customer service and quality standards

www.richmark.com, market coverage and marketing strategy

www.huntpatton.com, buying, selling, and merging businesses

www.franklynn.com, marketing planning

RELATED WEB SEARCHES

The Economic Business Cycle, www.quickmba.com

Business Cycles by Christina D. Romer

Rates of Change: A Slippery Slope

Value Analysis, VEVA Seminars

Dover Corporation, Acquisition Criteria

PACCAR, Inc. and PACCAR Winch Division, the best business school the author ever attended

Index